A POLITICAL DIARY, 1828-1830 (VOLUME 2)

A POLITICAL DIARY, 1828-1830 (VOLUME 2)

Ellenborough, Edward Law, Earl Of, 1790-1871 and colchester, Reginald Charles Edward Abbot, Baron, 1842-1919

www.General-Books.net

Publication Data:

Title: A Political Diary, 1828-1830
Volume: 2
Author: Ellenborough, Edward Law, Earl Of, 1790-1871 and colchester, Reginald Charles Edward Abbot, Baron, 1842-1919
Publisher: London : R. Bentley
Publication date: 1881
Subjects: Great Britain – Politics and government 1820-1830

1

A POLITICAL DIARY, 1828-1830 (VOLUME 2)

1. DIARY.

April 1, 1829.

THE Duke of Wellington wrote to the King to ask if he had any objection to raising the galleries. He had none. So we sent for Sir T. Tyrwhit, and had him at the Cabinet dinner to ask him whether he could fix the galleries by four to-morrow. He said No. So we must do as we can.

Forty foreigners applied for seats to-day after four o'clock.

In the House I made the second reading of the Bills an order of the day at the desire of Lord Malmes-bury and Lord Grey. It is more formal so, but the second reading might have been equally well moved without it.

Lord Grey said a few words on presenting a petition expressing a hope to be convinced on the subject of the Franchise Bill, but laying ground for voting against it. Lord Malmesbury likewise expressed himself against it. We shall be hard pushed on this Bill. The Duke says we have 122 sure votes and no more upon it.

The Bishop of Chester read prayers, his wife having died about ten days ago. Really some one of the other Bishops might have relieved him.

VOL. II. B

A Political Diary, 1828-1830 (Volume 2). Ellenborough, Edward Law, Earl Of, 1790-1871 and colchester, Reginald Charles Edward Abbot, Baron, 1842-1919

1

Lord Shaftesbury, in the absence of the Chancellor, sat as Speaker. I moved the bills pro formâ for him.

At the Cabinet dinner at Peel's, Peel said the Bishop of Oxford was ready to speak at any time, and wished to follow a violent bishop. He may easily find one.

We had much talk about our approaching debates. Peel, after the Duke was gone, regretted his having taken the line of expressing his anxiety to relieve himself from the obloquy cast upon him, and his having put that desire forward as his reason for pressing the second reading of the Bill on Thursday. The Duke having said so, we could not back him out. We might avoid taking the same ground, but we could not alter it.

Aberdeen mentioned the case of the Candian blockade. I am sorry to see he does not communicate beforehand now with the Duke. He never looks forward to the ultimate consequences of his measures. Now he talks of convoying English ships to Candia, and telling them they may go there safely, and if stopped shall be indemnified. But if the English ship finds a Eussian off Candia, and is warned off, yet persists, under the expectation of indemnity, we should be obliged to pay the indemnity. The Eussians, having given warning, would be justified in taking the vessel.

So if we give convoy, and the convoy ship persists, we should come to blows. All these things should be foreseen. Aberdeen thinks Lieven is ignorant of Hey-den's having had any orders. He excuses him as having acted in the spirit of the treaty, to avoid the effusion of blood!

One thing is clear; we cannot permit Russia, as a belligerent, to defeat the objects of the Treaty of London, and yet act with her under that treaty.

April 2.

Second reading Catholic Relief Bill. The Duke made a very bad speech. The Archbishop of Canterbury drivelled. The Primate of-Ireland made a strong speech, his manner admirable. Both these against. The Bishop of Oxford had placed himself at our disposal to be used when wanted. We put him into the debate here, wanting him very much. The first part of his speech was very indifferent, the latter excellent. Lord Lansdowne spoke better than he has done for some time, indeed for two years. The Bishop of London against us; but he made a speech more useful than ten votes, in admirable taste, looking to the measure as one to be certainly accomplished, c. The Duke of Richmond spoke very shortly, but better than he has ever done, in reply. We adjourned at 1.

229 members in the House. Eoom for thirty more; the House not oppressively hot; numbers of women. The tone of the debate temperate.

April 3.

A speech from the Bishop of Durham, full of fallacies and extravagant, but having its effect.

The Chancellor spoke admirably, endeavouring to bring up Eldon, but the old man would not move. He wanted more time to consider his answer, by which he will not improve it.

A speech from Goderich, very animated in his way, and very heavy. The House did not cheer him once. He pressed himself upon it with bad taste. He spoke upon all the collateral and unimportant points. He swung his arm about like a boy throwing a stone from a sling.

Lord Mansfield spoke, sleepily and ill-naturedly. I was exhausted, and could not have answered him, had he said anything worth answering.

We adjourned at two till one to-morrow.

April 4.

House at 1. A long absurd speech from Lord Guildford, which must have given much pain to Lady Øh. Lindsay, who sat under the throne, and who must have been much annoyed at seeing to what her family had fallen. We had then Lord Lilford, who rested too much on his notes, but who has a good manner. He drew his points well, and spoke like a man, not like a boy.

Lord Tenterden was not powerful. Lord Grey spoke better than he has done since 1827. He made a speech too long, and indeed the last half-hour was of no use. He beat the brains out of the Coronation Oath, as an obstacle to Catholic Concession, and read a curious letter of Lord Yestor to Lord Tweddale, dated April, 1689, before William III. took the Coronation Oath, in which Lord Yestor mentions that it was understood that the king had in council declared his understanding of the sense of the Coronation Oath that it bound him in his executive capacity, not in his legislative. Lord Westmoreland made an odd, entertaining from its manner, and really very good speech. He supported the Bill.

Lord Eldon, who, after an ineffectual attempt on the part of Lord Redesdale to speak, followed Lord Grey, made a very weak, inefficient, powerless speech. He seemed beaten, and in some respects his memory had failed him.

Lord Plunket drew, with great power, a picture of the state of society in Ireland as affected by the laws. The whole of his speech was powerful.

His speech and Lord Grey's were excellent.

After a few sentences from Lord Farnham we divided.

Present for 149

Against.79

Majority.68 Proxies for.70 Against.33

Total Content.217 Not Content.112

Majority.105

This will quiet Windsor. The King was to have received a number of petitions to be presented by peers to-day. The Primate of Ireland was to have gone, and the Irish Bishops. The latter went. If they had not gone, the King would have made some excuse for not receiving them.

The majority must put an end to all agitation in England, and tranquillise Ireland. Indeed as regards this question Ireland is tranquil. The conduct of the Catholics has been as excellent as that of the Protestants. Hitherto the announcement of the measure has produced effects beyond what was anticipated from its adoption.

The Duke of Rutland, who was not expected, and indeed every doubtful vote was with us.

The Protestants are subdued.

Lord Grey's speech, but still more Lord Plunket's, will have a greater effect upon the public mind, than any which have yet been delivered.

Eeally it seems like a dream! That I should, if I lived, live to see this I did expect; but that I should see it so soon, and that I should happen to be a member of the Government that carried it, I did not expect. I must say with what delight I view the prospect of having Catholics in Parliament. I am sure it will do more for the happiness of Ireland, and for the strength of the Empire, than any measure that could have been adopted.

April 5.

Dined with Lady Sandwich and met the Arbuthnots, with whom I had a long talk. She told me the Duke wanted to bring in Lord Chandos, by way of conciliating the Tories. She thought Lord Eosslyn ought to have the Privy Seal, and that, considering their late conduct, the Whigs should be preferred to the Tories, whom we should have at any rate. That it was enough not to punish them by depriving them of their offices.

In all this I agree. I think if the Duke should go to the Tories and turn his back upon the Whigs after what has taken place, he will make Opposition very acrimonious, and our debates very disagreeable.

I told her if the Privy Seal was to be a Tory, I thought the Duke of Eichmond the best. He is the most popular man in the House of Lords, and a good debater. The Duke and Lord Bathurst say he is cunning; but as far as I can judge he acts fairly.

April 6.

House. Second reading Franchise Bill, Opposed by the Duke of Eichmond, Lord Malmesbury, Winchelsea, and Clanricarde. Lord Holland spoke in favour of the Bill as connected with the Eelief Bill. The Whigs voted with us. Dudley spoke in favour, just to separate himself from the Canningites, for whom Haddington spoke, more reluctant than the "Whigs.

Lord Winchelsea was very mad, wished to expel the bishops, to prevent translations, equalise their sees, c. We had 139 to 19. The minority were Dukes: Cumberland, Gloucester, Brandon, Eichmond, Newcastle; Marquises Salisbury, Clanrickarde; Earls Winchelsea Malmesbury, O'IsTeil; Lords Falmouth, Penrhyn, Boston, Grantley, Glenlyon; Earl Digby, Earl Romney.

The Duke goes to Windsor on Saturday to get the King to consent to give the Eoyal assent on Thursday, the day before Good Friday. The Duke of Cumberland has been mischievous at Windsor. The King fancies he is in the situation of Louis XVI. That he shall run down by Liberalism. The Duke of Cumberland swears he will turn us out, let who will be Ministers.

April 7.

Lord Eldon and others opened afresh the question as to the principle of the Bill on the first clause. We divided with more than 2 to 1.

The Bishops and Lord Eldon got into a theological discussion.

The Chancellor made a strong attack upon Lord Eldon, who really spoke very childishly.

We had as many women as ever, but a new set, and some of the prettiest girls in London Miss Bagot, Miss Sheridan, and others.

At Windsor, last Sunday, the Duke of Cumberland spoke very warmly indeed to Aberdeen about the Duke of Wellington. He said he had sat by us as our friend, till the King's Ministers joined in the hoot against him. (This was particularly Lord Bathurst, who shook his head at him and cheered offensively.) He seems in speaking of the Duke of Wellington to have used terms hardly to be expected.

He told the Chancellor to-day that he should, before the Bill passed, declare he never could again feel confidence in His Majesty's Ministers; that the country was ruined; and that he should leave it and never return.

The Chancellor told him he advised him not to ma e the last promise. I hope he will make it and keep it.

I observed him afterwards address the Chancellor very warmly, after he had attacked Eldon.

A man of the name of Halcomb has advertised for a meeting on Friday, on the road to Windsor, to carry petitions to the King.

April 8.

Committee on Eelief Bill. No division. Several amendments. Those of Lord Tenterden very silly. I said a very few words twice. The third reading is fixed for Friday. When the

Duke of Cumberland heard the third reading fixed he left the House like a disappointed fiend. He did not take his hat off till he had got half-way down. Lord Eldon seems quite beaten.

April 9.

Lord Eldon went to Windsor to-day with petitions. Yesterday Lord Howe and three others went. I believe these peers have been: Duke of Newcastle, Kenyon, Eolle, Howe, O'Neil, Bexley, Winchelsea, Farnham, and six bishops.

Cabinet at 2. A meeting is advertised for to-morrow, to take place at Apsley House. Then to proceed to Slough or Salt Hill, or to Eton, to deliver there a petition to the Duke of Cumberland, who is then to present it to the King, and the people are to wait for an answer.

The Duke has written to the King, acquainting him with the plan, and advising His Majesty to refuse to receive the petition except through the hands of Mr. Peel.

Peel is going down to Windsor himself. The Duke writes to-night to tell the King he is going, and to repeat his advice of this morning as coining from the Cabinet.

If the King will not take Peel's advice we go out.

The Duke thinks the King will yield, and that the meeting will be a failure. So have I thought from the first. There is no agitation in London. No feeling, no excitement. The King will know Peel is coming in time to be able to inform the Duke of Cumberland, and prevent his setting out.

In the House about nine the Duke received a letter from Sir W. Knighton, informing liim that he had no doubt the King would take his advice respecting the petitions. Eldon was there, and probably saw the letter.

House. Got through the report of the Franchise Bill. Third reading fixed for to-morrow. I had to say a few words.

April 11, 1829.

House. A long speech from Lord Eldon, containing no argument, and both flat and bad.

Then a speech from Lord Harrowby, long and sensible; but heavily delivered and not wanted. A long speech from Lord Lansdowne, still less wanted, and very dull.

The Duke was obliged to say something civil to the "Whigs, but he did it sparingly, and contre cceur.

We had a majority of 104. The Franchise Bill was likewise read a third time.

The mutual congratulations were cordial. The House is in good humour again. All are glad to get rid of the question. The Duke of Cumberland, Fal-mouth, and Winchelsea, perhaps Kenyon, are lost to the Government, but no others.

Lord Middleton voted with us, having been against on the second reading. The Duke of Eutland against, having been with us before.

The Duke of Clarence was absent, being ill. He had fourteen leeches on his temples.

The House was full of ladies. Mrs. Fox, Lady Jersey, Lady Pitt and her daughters, Lady A. Brudenell, Lady Harrowby, Lady G. Wortley, Lord Eldon's daughters, Lady Glengall, Mrs. and Miss Sheridan, the old Duchess of Eichmond, Lady Manners, Lady Eolle, Lady Haddington, and many others.

The intended row failed altogether. Only four carriages went down to Windsor. Halcomb and his two friends saw an equerry. They were told their petition must be presented through the Secretary of State, and went away quietly.

The Duke of Cumberland said he must withdraw his support from the Government; but he was temperate. In fact he was beaten.

The Duke of Norfolk was in the House, as happy as man could be.

April 11.

Dr. Clarke and H. Fane both spoke of the Chancellor's speech in attack upon Eldon, as in bad taste and offensive. I shall endeavour to ascertain whether this is the general opinion. Not having heard Eldon, they cannot know how very mischievous and disingenuous he was.

April 12.

Met the Lievens, Lyndhursts, Sir J. Murray, and others at dinner, at the Esterhazy's. The King has not yet sent back the commission to pass the Catholic Bill.

The Lievens are more shy of me than ever.

Lord Bathurst seemed to be much pleased with my idea of carrying on the Government of India in the King's name. He said it should be under a Secretary of State for India.

The Chancellor approved highly of my notion of suggesting Herries for the Government of Bombay, if the directors will not have Courtney. He is useless to us, and a discredit. Besides, we want his place.

Had some talk with Vernon at Lady Jersey's. He has the Canning venom about him still, and said we should still regret having lost Huskisson, c.

I said NEVER. He was an able man, but he would never do as a member of a Cabinet in which he was not chief. The Government would not have lived if he had continued in. I told him I had become satisfied from my short experience that a coalition Government could not conduct the affairs of the country with advantage especially where the difference was

The Duke of Cumberland is gone to Windsor. If the commission should not arrive to-night I dare say the Duke of Wellington will go to Windsor early to-morrow.

Lady Jersey was very loud in her dispraise of the Duke of Richmond. Every one who knows him says he is very cunning. There is a mixture of good and bad taste about him. He is popular, and he would make a good man of business.

April 13, 1829, Monday.

Chairs at 11. Informed them of Sir Sidney Beck-with's appointment to the command at Bombay.

Told them my general idea was that it was necessary to fix a Lieutenant-Governor at Agra. I showed them it could be done without expense. Sir Charles Metcalfe should be the person appointed, with precise instructions obliging him to a system of non-interference in the internal concerns of the Malwa and Rajpoot States. Sir J. Malcolm would have interposed.

The treaties with the Rajpoot States generally secure their internal independence. Those with the States of Malwa give us the right, and impose upon us the duty of supervision. It requires, therefore, a most delicate hand to bring the whole into one system animated by one spirit.

I said incidentally to-day, ' I will not sit here to sacrifice India to England," a sentiment which escaped me, but which I feel to be correct, not only socially but politically.

Ashley came and bored me about a petition of some Hindoos and Mahometans in Calcutta, who wish to be grand jurors. I told him I could not proceed hastily in any matter of legislation, and that this was one of much delicacy. I should speak to Fergusson.

A Cabinet had been fixed for 3. I concluded it was on account of a delay on the King's part in giving the Royal assent to the Relief Bill. The Cabinet was counter-ordered, the Commission having arrived at two.

The Chancellor had sent a note to the King with the Bills, calling his attention to them. The King, on sending them back with the Commission signed, thanked the Chancellor for having called his attention to the Bills, and said he gave his assent reluctantly.

The Chancellor had sent a note last night to Watson, the Equerry, desiring him to remind the King of the Commission.

So at a few minutes before four to-day the Chancellor, Lord Bathurst, and I sat as Commissioners to give the Royal assent to the Eelief Bill, and about thirty-nine others. So many had been kept back to force an early decision. The Indemnity Bill was one of the Bills, and the Militia Lists Bill another. There were thirteen peers in the House, and seven or eight more about. Lord Savoy, his son, young Lambton, Lady Petres, and her daughters, Mrs. Fox, and some other ladies were there Lady Stanhope. The old Duchess of Richmond came too late.

I observed that in passing each other very close the Duke of "Wellington and the Duke of Cumberland took no notice of each other.

Lord Durham said to me, ' Now the King will turn you all out in revenge as soon as he can," to which I assented. He certainly will when he dares.

The Duke of Norfolk and Mr. Petres were in the House, giving and receiving congratulations. All parties congratulate the Duke. Falmouth alone still looks sad and sombre. The Duke of "Wellington has a bad cold. He was very hoarse, and wrapped himself in his cloak as soon as he had done speaking.

April 14.

Saw Mr. Fergusson respecting a petition from Hindoos and Mahometans at Calcutta, praying to be allowed to sit on grand juries. He thinks they should as they are allowed to sit on petty juries. If the matter had been well considered, the privilege they now ask should have been granted before that they have obtained.

Mr. Fergusson is, however, rather afraid of allowing them to sit on the trial of Christians.

By the newspapers I see that there has been a quarrel at Teheran, between some of the Russian Ambassador's suite and the populace, which led to an attack upon the Russian palace, and to the death of the Ambassador and all his people except two. This is an unfortunate event, as it will give the Russians a new claim to indemnity, which they will exercise inexorably. Probably they will insist on the junction of Persia in the attack on Turkey, as the only satisfaction they can accept.

It is just possible that the example once given, and the people despairing of pardon, a rising against the Eussians may take place, and something of a national feeling arise in Persia. But I fear this will not be the case. I suppose our Minister was at Tabriz.

April 15.

The Duke was at Windsor to-day to ask the King's permission to restore the resigners. The King said he thought the Duke could not do better. He just mentioned Wetherell's name as if he thought he was to be excepted from the restoration, but desired to be certior-factus.

The King was cold. The Duke had to wait twenty minutes, the Duke of Cumberland being with the King. However, I believe this delay may only have originated in a necessary change of dress on His Majesty's part, as lie was sitting for his picture in a Highland dress. The Duke saw a large plaid bonnet in the room, and he believes the King had still on plaid stockings. The business of the restoration was finished in ten minutes, when the conversation flagged, and the Duke was rising to go away.

However, something more was then said, and the interview in all lasted twenty minutes. The King said he was delighted with Lord Winchelsea. He was so gentlemanlike, and spoke in so low a tone of voice He likewise thought Lord Farnham very gentlemanlike, and Lord Rolle more violent than any.

The Duke had to wait twenty minutes before he could see Lady Conyngham. They seemed to wish him not to see her. However, he did. She said all would have been quiet if the Duke of Cumberland had not come over, and all would be quiet when he went away. The King seemed relieved since the Bill was passed.

On his return the Duke sent for George Bankes and offered him his place again. Bankes asked two or three days to consider. The Duke gave him till to-morrow.

It seems he has now a notion that he owed his place not to the Duke but to some other influence. I think this has been insinuated to him since his resignation. The fact is otherwise. The King had mentioned Bankes for other situations, but not for the one he holds. On my return home I found Bankes had called upon me.

After dinner we considered whether the prosecution of Lawless for his conduct at Ballybeg should be persevered in.

Goulbourn, Peel, Lord Bathurst, Sir G. Murray, and I were for dropping it. I think the Chancellor inclined the same way. The Duke and the rest, Aberdeen being absent, were for going on.

I thought no benefit would be derived from success.

Even success would revive feelings and recollections which are dying away, and which we wish to be forgotten. If we decline proceeding we can say we did so from the fear of exciting dormant passions. If we proceed, we shall have no excuse should we revive the memory of bad times.

Keference is to be made to Ireland to ascertain the feeling about it there.

Bankes came at twelve o'clock. He told me he had been with the Duke, and had received from him the ofier of his old office. He had asked permission to consult one person, whose name he did not mention to the Duke, it was the Duke of Cumberland. He had called at the Palace and found the Duke of Cumberland was at Windsor. He wanted to write to him to ask if he had any objection to his taking the office again.

Bankes said he had attended none of the meetings at Lord Chandos's. He had avoided as much as he could all communication with the Duke of Cumberland. He had fully determined not to take a part with any new Government which might be formed, unless it should clearly appear the King had been unfairly dealt by, or unless there should be an attempt to make peers to carry the Bill. The Duke of Cumberland had always said that he made him his first object, and he had reason to think that he had mentioned him to the King, and had been instrumental in his appointment. The Duke of Cumberland had desired him to come to him (during the Bill), and had apparently intended to name some particular office for him, but seeing his coldness 7 VOL. ii. C had only sounded him, and had received the answer I have mentioned above.

The Duke of Cumberland had told him it was an understood thing that all were to be restored, and that he saw no reason why he should not take his office again.

This was ten days ago.

I told him I advised, if he thought it necessary to write to the Duke of Cumberland at all, that he should merely state his intention to take his office back again, refer to his conversation with the Duke himself upon the point, and add distinctly that, taking office, he could no longer have any communication on political matters with a person who had declared his hostility to the Government.

I advised him to send off his own servant on a post-horse at six o'clock to-morrow morning, with a letter to the effect I have stated to the Duke of Cumberland, and whether he received an answer or not, to go to the Duke of Wellington and accept at 12.

I advised him to tell the Duke the whole state of the case, and all he had done.

The Duke of Wellington did not seem by any means well to-day. He was blooded yesterday.

April 16.

Cabinet at 3. It seems Bankes called on the Duke this morning, but he was engaged. I told him all thai passed between Bankes and me last night. If Bankes should go out the Duke means to offer his place to SirJ. Graham.

We met upon foreign affairs. Aberdeen read his instructions to Gordon, who goes to Constantinople. They are unobjectionable.

We then considered what was to be done in consequence of this second violation of their word on the part of the Eussians in blockading Candia.

Count Heyden has written two letters to Sir Pulteney Malcolm. In the first he justifies the blockade of Candia on the ground of its being necessary to protect the Morea from the Pacha of Egypt; in the second he rests it on the necessity of blockading the two extremities of Candia for the purpose of watching Constantinople.

We cannot permit the Eussians to make fools of us in this way to promise one thing as parties to the Treaty of London, and to do another as belligerents.

After the Cabinet I asked the Duke whether he still wished me to press Courtney upon the Directors. He said, Yes, he very much wanted his place. I said it had occurred to me that Herries might take the Governorship of Bombay. It did not seem to have occurred to him. He said he thought Herries would not go; but he evidently thought it would be a very good thing if he would.

The Duke said he wanted to have the places of Courtney and Sir G. Hill, and to bring in Lord Chandos and M. Fitzgerald. We mentioned Ashley. I suggested Ashley's going to the Treasury, and Sir J. Graham I taking his place. This would, I dare say, be done, if we could get the place at the Treasury.

I have not as yet heard a surmise as to the new Lord Privy Seal.

Lord O'Neil has signed the Duke of Bichmond's protest against the Franchise Bill. It is very hostile to the Government, and Lord O'Neil will probably be put out.

The Duke of Eichmond has been very imprudent. Had he taken a moderate line he probably might have been Privy Seal. His time is now gone by.

April 17.

Went by appointment to see Lady Jersey. Found there Duncannon and Lord Sefton. Duncannon talked big about O'Connell's power, and in the same sense in which he talked to Fitzgerald, wishing to induce the Government to let him take his seat. I said we could not. It depended not on us, but upon the law.

Lady Sefton came in afterwards for a few minutes, and Lord Eosslyn. Lady Jersey talked a great deal about the restoration, and feared the Whigs w r ould imagine they were never to come in, and would form a violent opposition. She mentioned Mr. Stanley as being much annoyed, he having made a laudatory speech in favour of Peel.

I told her it would have been very harsh to have eliminated those who had taken office under the idea that the Government was rather against than for the Catholics, certainly neutral, and that it was a little unreasonable to expect others to be turned out to make way for new friends.

April 18.

The Duke thinks he could not offer the Privy Seal to Lord Grey, but he would be conciliated by having friend that is, Rosslyn in. If we could get Lord Beresford out, Lord Rosslyn would go to the Ordnance.

The Duke says the King would make it a point of honour to resist the introduction of Lord Grey, though in reality he was in communication with Lord Grey in 1820-21, after the Queen's trial, and then intended to bring him in and to turn out the then Ministers for the Milan Commission, he having been himself at the bottom of that Commission. The Duke, the only member of the Cabinet who was not mixed up with the Milan Commission, induced the King to give up his idea of making a change.

Bankes received a letter from the Duke of Cumberland, very long, and against his acceptance of office; but he begged Bankes to go down to see him and talk it over. He did so. Bankes told him he would not accept if he on consideration objected, but he was determined not to join any other Government. The Duke of Cumberland spoke of himself as having been ill-used by the Duke of Wellington. This was explained. The conference ended by the Duke of Cumberland's acquiescing entirely in Bankes's acceptance of office. Bankes saw the Duke of Wellington and detailed the whole to him.

April 2L.2 1

Called on Sir H. Hardinge at Eichmond. He told

E5 the Duke had at first great reluctance to have ything to do with the Whigs. By his account he ist have principally contributed to lead the Duke to adopt that view which he has now of admitting Rosslyn, c.

April 22.

The Duke of Norfolk called, and, not finding me, left a note begging me to ascertain privately from the Duke of Wellington whether the King would be pleased if the English Catholics presented an address to him thanking him for the Belief Bill.

Received a letter from the Duke of Wellington expressing a decided opinion against any address from the Eoman Catholics. He says," Everything has been done that is possible to efface all distinctions between the King's subjects on the score of religion, and this with a view to the general benefit, and riot to that of a particular body. I confess I shall think that this measure has failed in attaining its object if there should be any general act of a particular body.

' In respect to the King himself I am certain that the most agreeable thing to him would be that all should remain quiet.

' We must have no distinct body of Eoman Catholics except in the churches and in affairs of religion. The less we act inconsistently with the principle the better."

I so entirely agree in opinion with the Duke of Wellington that, having for my own amusement written an address for the Eoman Catholics in the event of their making any to the King, the first sentence I imagined was this: ' The Roman Catholics of England approach your Majesty for the last time as a body distinct from the rest of your Majesty's subjects."

April 25.

I had a good deal of conversation as to the next Director. There are three city men candidates, but none are good Lyall, Ellice, and Douglas.

Of Ellice no one knows anything. He is brother to the Ellice who married Lord Grey's sister. Lyall is, or was, Chairman of the Committee of Shipowners. Douglas is brother to Lord Queensbury. They say his is not a very good house.

April 28.

Eead the correspondence between the Duke and Lord Anglesey. Then read a memorandum of the Duke's in reply to one of Hardinge's on the subject of the discipline of the British army. Hardinge wished introduce the Prussian[1] discipline into ours. The Like shows that with our discipline we have more ten fit for duty in proportion to our numbers than the Russians in the proportion of two to one. That in Russia the army is everything. There is no other profession. All are soldiers the officer lives much with his men they are always in masses, always in fertile countries.

In our service the worst men in the community enter the army. The officers are gentlemen. They cannot mix with the men. Without discipline our army would be inferior to others. It is not even now the favourite profession. There is much jealousy of it.

[1 Which did not include capital punishment. See Wellington Correspondence, vol. v. p. 932.]

It is not popular with the common people. It is difficult to find recruits even in times of distress.

I was in an army, the Duke concludes, which cannot be governed on the Prussian principle. You cannot treat the English soldier as a man of honour.

The Duke had been with the King, who was in very good humour. He had not, however, got to close quarters with him as to the changes.

April 29.

Cabinet at 12. A letter has been received from Lord Heytesbury, from which it is clear that Russia will very soon resume altogether the exercise of her belligerent rights in the Mediterranean.

Nesselrode communicated to him the blockade of Candia. Lord Heytesbury only observed that ' it was a resumption of belligerent rights." This Count Nesselrode did not deny, and he said they could not long remain in the false position in which they now were in the Mediterranean.

Count Heyden at the end of January blockaded Candia on pretexts arising out of the state of Greece. In three weeks from that time he rested his interception of the Egyptian vessels near Candia on the necessary exercise of his rights as a belligerent. Lieven, when first spoken to, disavowed Heyden. He now changes his tone, and it is evident that Russia now for the second time breaks her word. The French do not behave much better. They have 6,000 men in the Morea, and mean to keep them there notwithstanding their engagement to withdraw their troops as soon as the Egyptians were embarked. To be sure, they say if we insist upon it they will withdraw them.

I have always been for getting out of the treaty. We have been dragged along very unwillingly we have been subjected to much humiliation. We seem to me to have gained nothing by all our compliances. We have been led on from the violation of one principle to that of another. Our position has discouraged Turkey. We have been made the tools of Russia, and have been duped with our eyes open. I think the sooner we get out of this false position the better, and there is no time so favourable for us to hold strong language as this, when by the settlement of the Oath oh c question we are really strengthened, and when all foreign Powers believe we are yet more strengthened than we are. The Duke is certainly for getting out. He has long wished it.

A paper of Peel's was read suggesting the difficulties in which we should still be placed by our moral obligation towards the Greeks, and by our reasonable fear that on the principles of the Greek Treaty, to which we have unfortunately given our adhesion, Russia and France may combine and make a partition treaty. My expectation is that Russia and France would soon quarrel, and I think I could before now have made them jealous of each other, but we have done nothing.

After much conversation, V. Fitzgerald agreeing with me and the others saying nothing, it was determined to insist upon the freedom of communication with Candia under the protocol, to insist upon the
Greeks withdrawing from their advanced position near Prevesa under the protocol, and to insist likewise upon the withdrawing of the French troops from the Morea, according to the engagement.

I am not satisfied with this. Every part of our diplomacy has been unfortunate. We have succeeded in nothing. I predicted if we became engaged in the war, it would be ultimately on a little point and not upon a great one. Our diplomacy cannot be defended. It is our weak point.

House. All the Catholics there. Every good old name in England.

The Duke of Norfolk is much pleased with the Duke of Wellington's answer to his enquiry as to the propriety of addressing the King. I am going to send him the Duke's original letter as a record.

The King certainly received the Protestant peers, and particularly those who had been at Windsor, with great favour, and so the Bishop of Durham. The Duke of Cumberland stood at the King's left hand, and quizzed the people as they passed. He seemed rayonnant.

After dinner I had some conversation with Loch, the Chairman, as to governing India in the King's name. He does not positively object. I think I shall be able to carry that point. I consider it to be of the most essential importance.

April 30.

Cabinet at 12. Determined to fund eight millions of Exchequer Bills. No taxes to be taken off or imposed.

We had some conversation as to the East Retford question. V. Fitzgerald communicated a proposal from Littleton to propose the adjournment of all discussion upon the subject till next year, as it is evident nothing can be done this year. Littleton proposed this because he wished to disappoint the mischievous designs of some people. (Palmerston particularly.) It was determined to adhere to the line taken by the Government last year namely, to that of throwing East Retford into the hundred. The Duke was decidedly of opinion that whatever we did we should do from ourselves, and certainly not act in concert with an enemy. The Tories look to our conduct upon this question as the touchstone.

Drawing-room. The King, as yesterday, very civil to the Brunswickers and' taking no notice of our friends. He took particular notice of the Brazilians. Madame de Lieven is endeavouring to form a Government with the Duke of Cumberland, the Ultra-Tories, the Canningites, and some Whigs.

The King is very Russian. I believe all this will end in nothing. The Chancellor thinks they may try to make a change when Parliament is up, and so have six months before them. They may think of it; but the only object of such a Government would be revenge. They cannot repeal the Relief Bill, nor do they wish to pursue a different line of policy either at home or abroad.

The foreigners think that having settled the Catholic uestion we are ready to draw the sword, and find a field of battle wherever we can. This the Russians are afraid of, and hence arises in some degree their wish to overthrow the Duke's Government; but the real foundation of all the Eussian intrigues is Madame de Lieven's hatred for the Duke, and her rage at feeling she has overreached herself.

Sir Thomas Tyrwhitt was with the King for two hours to-day, the Duke of Cumberland being in the room and the King in bed. The King is very much out of humour, and abused everything and everybody. He is very angry at ladies being admitted to the House of Lords, and particularly at their going in such numbers the day the Duke of Norfolk took his seat. The Duke of Cumberland has sworn he will not leave England till he has turned out the present Ministers. He is the only colonel of the Horse Guards who ever does duty Lord Cathcart being absent and Lord Harrington incapable. When he last got the gold stick from Lord Harrington he swore he would never let it out of his hands. As gold stick he ordered the gates of the Horse Guards to be closed the day of the Drawing-room, and thus obliged all the Ministers who dressed in Downing Street to go all round.

He told Clanwilliam to-day with great satisfaction that the King never could again be on good terms with his Ministers.

No arrangement is yet made with the Master of the Rolls. Everything waits for the legal promotions. The King will be delighted with Scarlett [1 as Attorney-General, [1 Sir James Scarlett, afterwards Lord Abinger,]

and the Chancellor tells me Bickersteth is to be Solicitor. I recollect hearing of him at Cambridge. He is a very clever man and a good speaker. Tindal is of course to be Master of the Rolls. I am most anxious to give up the Privy Seal to Rosslyn.

Cabinet at 2. Decided the Government was to take the same line exactly this year as to East Eetford (that is, as to giving the two members to the Hundred) that it took last year. However, as it is impossible to get any Bill through the Lords this year, Peel will be very willing to accede to any proposition for postponing the whole question till next session.

On the question of Irish Education and on that of the grant to Maynooth, the vote will be as before it being said that the state of the session and the circumstances of the present period make it advisable that the question of any change should be deferred. Indeed, Ministers have not had time to consider it.

Many of Lord Anglesey's letters to Peel and of Peel's answers were read. We have a very strong case against him on his letter to Dr. Curtis, which by a letter from Dr. Curtis to the Duke we know Lord Anglesey directed Dr. Murray to publish if it could be done with Curtis's consent, and which Dr. Murray did publish without obtaining such consent.

Curtis's letter is dated January 2.

Lord Anglesey wrote to Curtis for the Duke's letter ind his answer, and had them two days before December 23, the date of his letter to Curtis.

Peel thinks the East Indian Committee should not be refused. It is better for the East Indian Company that it should be granted than refused. I entirely coincide with him.

Coal Committee at 12. Met Lord Bathhurst, with whom I had some conversation as to the Duke's reading letters in answer to Lord Anglesey. He begged nie to go to the Duke, and try to induce him not to do so. I found the Duke agreeing with me entirely as to the danger of the president, and disposed to read only what might be absolutely necessary.

Lord Anglesey brought forward his motion for ' the letter of recall."

The Duke answered him, and so well that even Lord Holland could not say one word. So the thing ended.

The Duke had been assured by the King, and within the last fortnight the King had given the same assurance to Aberdeen, that Lord Anglesey had not permission to read confidential letters.

Lord Anglesey stated that he had the King's permission.

The Duke certainly seemed to contradict him.

Lord Londonderry threw a note over to me suggesting that the contradiction was so direct there might be an awkward explanation out of doors unless the thing were softened down.

I mentioned this to Lord Bathurst. He thought not.

However, when he replied, Lord Anglesey treated the contradiction as absolute, and Lord Bathurst told the Duke he must give some explanation, which the Duke did, saying he did not mean to accuse Lord Anglesey of declaring he had the King's permission when he had not, but only that he had reason to think he had not. In fact, the King, as we always thought, told the Duke one thing and Lord Anglesey another; and the only result of the debate is that the King is proved to have told a lie.

Lord Wharncliffe, who overtook me as I was riding home, considered Lord Anglesey to be blown out of water.

At Lady Brownlow's ball I talked with Lord Farn-borough, Longford, and Beresford. All thought the reading of the letters should have been stopped, and that the Duke did wrong to read anything. We could not stop the reading of the letters when the King's permission to read them was stated distinctly by Lord Anglesey. The misery is that we have a lying master.

I called at the Treasury and saw the Duke. On the ibject of what took place yesterday he said, that taving received the King's commands to declare Lord Anglesey had not his permission to read the letters, he xmld not do otherwise than make the observations he lid. The gravamen of the charge against Lord Anglesey as arising out of those letters is that in the last he declares his intention of using them as public documents; and this being the ground upon which the had acquiesced in his being relieved, for the King have afterwards permitted the reading of those letters would have been a withdrawal of confidence from his Ministers.

I met Lord Ravensworth and talked to him upon the subject. He seemed to be in a sort of alarm as to what took place yesterday. This is superfluous. The Duke's explanation that he did not mean to say Lord Anglesey had reason to think he was permitted to read those letters was quite sufficient. The Duke added that he had understood the contrary.

Lord Eavensworth seemed to think his Eoyal master came the worst off which is true.

He told me the Duke of Cumberland had been abusing every one at Lady Brownlow's last night, and had declared, as he has before, that he would not go away till he had us out.

Lord Anglesey is reported to be very ill to-day.

May 6 Cabinet dinner at Sir G. Murray's. The Duke saw the King to-day. He was in good humour, and said the Duke was quite right in declaring Lord Anglesey had not his permission to read the letters. It seems the King said the same thing in the Duke of Cumberland's presence on Monday at dinner, and this made the Duke so very angry that evening.

We had a very good division last night on the Ret-ford question. Almost all the Brunswickers voted with us none against us.

In fact the Government is very strong.

There are disturbances at Manchester, which look rather serious.

33 May 7 Nothing in the House.

The meeting respecting the statue to the Duke of Wellington seems to have finished in detestable taste. Hunt proposing a vote of thanks to Lord Anglesey and O'Connell, and Lord Darnley speaking for it. Both iese said the Catholic Bill arose out of Lord Anglesey's rovernment. Lord Darnley repeated the same thing me to-day in the House. I told him the contrary r'as the fact. That Lord Anglesey had placed the carrying of the question in peril that without his; all it could hardly have been carried. There have been serious disturbances at Manchester, 'he bakers' shops have been broken open and robbed, id money extorted by fear. This arises out of real distress; but it seems, as might be expected, that notorious thieves lead on the mobs.

May 8 The disturbances at Manchester have more the chaster of robbery than of riot. Baker's shops have broken open and pillaged, and money has been extorted.

At Rochdale an attack was made on the military, tey behaved with extreme forbearance; but at last fired, and killed and wounded many.

May 9 Dined at the Trinity House. Hardinge, whom I met there, told me Wood had been asked by Lord msfield to go to the Pitt dinner on the 28th. Wood VOL. II. D said he did not know whether the Ministers would go or not. Lord Mansfield said, ' Why, you must know, it is understood that as soon as Parliament is up the Government will be changed. At this dinner we shall make such a display of Protestant force as will enable the King to take us as his Ministers."

It is surprising to me that any able man as Lord Mansfield is should be so deluded by the lies of the Duke of Cumberland. The country is not agitated, it is not dissatisfied. It would repudiate, as an act of the basest treachery, such conduct towards a Government which had been permitted to carry a great measure, and which was displaced solely on grounds of personal pique.

Manchester and its neighbourhood more quiet.

Had some conversation with Peel about the next member for the direction. He inclines to Marryatt. Hardinge reported a communication from E. Ellice, who canvasses for his brother, Eussell Ellice. E. Ellice offers some votes in the House of Commons if we will support his brother.

I believe E. Ellice would be a good man, but the brother is a nonentity. I said we must strike at the mass and not at individuals. We must gain the city by assisting a fit man on public grounds. Peel agreed in this sentiment. I am sure it is the only wise course for any Government to pursue.

Monday l, May 11.

The King has got the habit of taking large doses of laudanum. He sent for the Chancellor yesterday, as usual, at two o'clock. When he got to the palace the King had taken a large dose of laudanum and was asleep. The Chancellor was told he would not wake for two or three hours, and would then be in a state of excessive irritation, so that he might just as well not see him.

The East Retford question was last night deferred till next session, so we may, I think, finish all our business by about June 10; that is really allowing full time.

O'Connell published yesterday an argument on his right to sit in the House of Commons in the shape of a letter to the members. At first Lord Grey thought it unanswerable (as founded on the provisions of the Eelief Bill); but at night he told me he had looked into the Bill and found it certainly excluded him. A large portion of the letter is quite absurd, that in which he assumes a right to have his claim decided in a court of law. Parliament alone is by common law the court in which the privileges of its own members can be decided.

House. Lord Lansdowne put a pompously worded estion as to our intentions with respect to the course of proceeding on Indian affairs.

I answered simply that we were as sensible as he of the extreme importance of the question. That for my own part my mind was never absent from it, and that I had not been many days in office before I took measures for procuring the most extensive information, which would be laid before the House at the proper time. That the Government was desirous of forming its own opinion on the fullest information and with the greatest consideration; and that we wished the House to have the same opportunities. That I was not then prepared to inform him in what precise form we should propose that the enquiry should be made. The Chancellor introduced the Bill for appointing a new Equity Judge, and separating the Equity Jurisdiction from the Court of Exchequer. The latter object, by-the-bye, is not to be accomplished immediately, but it is part of the plan opened. He soothed Lord Eldon by high compliments to his judicial administration and to the correctness of his judgments. The wonder of the day is that Lord Eldon should have lived to hear a Chancellor so expose the errors of the Court of Chancery as they were exposed by Lord Lyndhurst to-day.

Recorder's report. The King not well. He has a slight stricture, of which he makes a great deal, and a bad cold. He seemed somnolent; but I have seen him worse.

Before the Council there was a chapter of the Garter. The Duke of Eichmond was elected. The knights wore their ordinary dress under the robe, which was short, and had no hats. The procession was formed by Garter. The Chancellor and Prelate of the Order and the Dean were present. It looked rathei like a splendid funeral. The Duke of Cumberlan took a great deal upon him.

Cabinet dinner at Vesey Fitzgerald's at Somerset House.

Much talk about Indian matters. Both Peel and Fitzgerald seem to be for Free Trade, and unreasonable towards the Company.

In the House of Commons yesterday the motion for Committee on East Indian affairs was negatived with-mt a division, but promised for early next session, and ipers promised immediately.

May 16 Chairs at 11. We spoke of the Charter. They ither dislike the notion of using the King's name, and fear Mr. Elphinstone and all the Indians will give their evidence against the change. I may be outvoted, but I shall not be convinced. [1]

May 17 Nothing political, except a grand dinner at the lake of Norfolk's, given to the Duke of Wellington, which was very fine and very dull.

The Duke told me he had read the Persian papers. The Eussians had brought it on themselves.

May 19 In the House of Commons last night O'Connell was heard at the bar. The debate seems to have been temperate. It was decided on a discussion, 190 to 16, that he must take the Oath of Supremacy.

[1 This change was effected in 1858.]

At the office had some conversation with Mr. Leach as to the plan of governing India in the King's name the Directors being made ex officio Commissioners for the affairs of India. He seems to have some prejudices against the plan, but he adduced no real objections. I have begged him to put on paper all the objections which occurred to him.

Wrote a long letter to Lord W. Bentinck on all subjects connected with the renewal of the Charter, and the general government of India.

Dined at the Freemasons' Hall with' the Society for Promoting Christian Knowledge. There were present 200 persons. I thought they would be very hostile to a Minister. However, when my name was mentioned by the Bishop of Durham, as a steward, there was much cheering. The Bishop of London, who was in the chair, begged me to return thanks for the stewards, which I did. I spoke of course of the wish entertained by the Ministers that a Society might prosper the interests of which were so much connected with those of the Established Church of their determination in their several departments to further its objects. It was the duty of us all as Christians, but more peculiarly that of the Ministers, to advance objects intimately connected with the individual happiness of the people and with the stability of the State. I said something too of the intrinsic strength of the Protestant Church of its rising in proportion to the difficulties which might surround it, to the dangers if dangers there were (the Primate had spoken of them) of its security in the zeal and ability of its ministers, arid in the purity of its doctrines.

On the whole I did well. I was loudly cheered indeed, so much interrupted as to be enabled to think what I should say next.

Indian business in the morning Coal Committee.

May 20 Dined at the London Tavern with the Directors, at what is called a family dinner, to meet Mr. Elphinstone, the late Governor of Bombay. He has been thirty-three years absent from England, having left it at fifteen. He is one of the most distinguished servants the Company has ever had. He seems to be a quiet, mild, temperate man. I had some conversation with him, and have fixed that he should come to the Indian Board on Tuesday. I wish to have his opinion as to the expediency of governing India in the King's name.

The Duke told Lord Bathurst and me the King had been very angry with him for going to the Duke of Norfolk's dinner, and now openly expressed his wish to get rid of his Ministers. The Duke wrote to the King and told him it really was not a subject he thought it necessary to speak to him about, that he dined with everybody and asked everybody to dinner, that had he known beforehand who were to dine with the Duke of Norfolk, which he did not, he could not have objected to any one of them. That the King himself had dined with the Duke of Norfolk. That most of the persons invited were either in his Majesty's service, or had been.

40   It seems the king desired it might be intimated to the Duke that he was much displeased at the dinner, and that he and Cumberland damned us all.

I told the Duke and Lord Bathurst what occurred at the dinner yesterday, with which they were much gratified.

May 21 Went to the Cabinet room at 2. Eead papers, by which it seems that the Eussian army is very little stronger than at the commencement of the last campaign, and that its materials are not so good. It has as yet no medical staff. The resources of the principalities are exhausted; the cattle of the peasants have been put in requisition; the ordinary cultivation of the land has been neglected. The river is worse than last year. There are reports of the successes of the Turks near Varna, and of that place being in danger.

The recruiting of the Turkish army goes on well. House of Lords. The Chancellor's Bill, which creates a new Chancery judge. Opposition from Lord Eldon, Lord Eedesdale, and Lord Holland, all saying they wished to see the whole plan before they agree to a part. Lord Tenterden approved of the making of the new judge, but wished his functions had been better defined.

The Duke of Cumberland said the Non-contents had it; but he said it too late, and his people did not wish to divide.

Lord Londonderry would have voted against us. I fear he is half mad. The House seems to treat him so.

41   The Chancellor told me the King did many things personally uncivil to the Duke. He did not ask him to dinner to meet the Duke of Orleans. He wishes to force the Duke to offer his resignation. This he is much too prudent to do upon a mere personal pique.

The King, our master, is the weakest man in England. He hates the Duke of Cumberland. He wishes his death. He is relieved when he is away; but he is afraid of him, and crouches to him.

In reality the King never was better satisfied than dth his present Ministers. He knows they will not flinch that he is safe in their hands.

May 22 In the House Lord Melville presented the petition)f the City of London praying, if the House persisted ordering the production of their accounts of pro-erty other than of a public nature, to be heard at the ar by counsel. He moved that this petition should considered on Tuesday. It being expected that on onday these very accounts would be produced in the mmittee, and thus the order of the House rendered innecessary. In this we were beaten too. Indeed, ur management under Lord Melville as Admiral does lot answer.

We shall certainly lose the London Bridge Ap-roaches Bill.

Dined at Lord Hill's. A party chiefly military.

42   Cabinet at Peel's at 11 P. M.

May 24

The arrangements determined upon. Lord E. Somerset to have Sir W. Clinton's office, and Trench Mr. Singleton's. Lord Eosslyn the Privy Seal. Lord Chandos was proposed, I should rather say suggested, but rejected immediately, as not of sufficient calibre for the Cabinet. Besides, his elevation for the purpose of holding the Privy Seal would offend the peerage, and be an insult to his father. It would not gain us the Brunswickers, and we should have the Whigs hostile. It would be saying to them, ' You shall never come in."

Eosslyn's appointment will be most useful. He will be of value in the Cabinet and invaluable in the House. His accession will break the Whigs, he is so popular with everybody.

This is to be proposed to the King to-morrow. It is thought he will take no step without asking the Duke of Cumberland. He may refuse altogether. Then we go out. The legal arrangements cannot proceed, because Best [1] communicated with the Duke of Cumberland and refused a peerage as the condition of resignation. Alexander would go if he could have his peerage and a pension. Leach will not go unless he is to have a peerage and a pension of 7,000. a year, a thing impossible.

Cabinet at 3. Waited a long time for the Duke. He came smiling and victorious. The King said he [1 Afterwards Lord Wynford] would manage Best. To Eosslyn he made some objection, and suggested Lord Dudley or Melbourne. This was referred to and rejected by such of the Cabinet as could be on a sudden collected at the Foreign Office. I was not there. I should certainly have rejected both, although very willing to have Dudley. The other would never have done. With Lord E. Somerset and Trench the King was well pleased. As the Duke left the room the King said,; Come, you must acknowledge I have behaved well to you." This he said frankly and good-humouredly. The Duke said, C I assure your Majesty I am very sensible of it, and I feel very grateful to you."

Having thus established ourselves as a Government we were going to break our necks by attempting to pass the Chancellor's Bill, which the House of Commons does not like. However, after a talk, it was solved to give it up.

It seems the Tories have deserted us again. We much in want of winter quarters. In the House we had the City of London petition, took a more active part than usual in the conversation. Lord Eosslyn, having just lost his son, is gone to 'unbridge Wells, and the offer of the Privy Seal will postponed till after to-morrow, when the King is to 3 Best at two, and it is hoped the Duke may be able tell Eosslyn that Scarlett is to be Attorney-General.

The King sent Knighton for Chief Justice Best, and desired him not to tell the Duke of Cumberland; Best was sent for. So Best went, and accepted the terms offered. Thus we shall get Scarlett, and the King and the Duke be separated a little.

Yesterday the Duke of Wellington did his business with the King while the Duke of Cumberland was hearing a clause in the House of Lords. The Chancellor, knowing how the Duke of Wellington was occupied, kept the Duke of Cumberland as long as he could.

Committee on London Bridge. Lord Londonderry, who came from the review in his uniform just covered by a frock coat, spoke against time on a collateral point for an hour and a half, and disgusted the Committee.

May 28 London Bridge Committee. Lord Londonderry a little better than before, but not much. He is running down his character altogether. He has now formed an alliance with the Duke of Cumberland, and through him made his peace with the King. The Duke of Cumberland wishes to be reconciled to the Duke of Wellington. In the House of Commons there is a small Ultra-Tory party, not fifty. In our House I doubt whether there are twenty.

May 30 Chairs. Lord W. Bentinck seems to be so ill as to make it doubtful whether he can remain in India should he recover. The letter is dated January 27. He was then in danger. The vessel did not leave

45 Calcutta till the 30th. The news then was that he was better, and had sat up for six hours. It was a coup de soldi. Soleil.

London Bridge Committee.

The Duke showed me a letter from Lord Eosslyn, accepting most cordially the Privy Seal.

I suppose we shall have a Council on Monday, or on une early day next week, for me to give it up.

June 1.

To the Cabinet room.

There is a report that Varna 1 is cernée by 40,000 men, Bazardjik taken, the Eussians running from Karasan, and from 6,000 to 8,000 Eussians, who had been thrown over the Danube at Hirsova, driven into it at Czernavoda by the garrison of Silistria. [2] Clan-william wrote me he thought the Duke attached some credit to this last rumour.

News from Calcutta of February 1 states that Lord William Bentinck was then out of danger. Lady William, who was going to set off to join him, had determined to expect him at Calcutta.

Lord Eosslyn's appointment is in the newspapers lay. The ' Times' highly delighted.

June 2.

London Bridge Approaches Committee. Lord Londonderry very anxious to have an adjournment over the Derby; however, he must attend to ' the last concern. [1 Varna was in the hands of the Russians, having been taken in the previous campaign.

2 These reports seem to have been unfounded. Soon after this date the decisive battle of Kouleftcha opened to the Russians the road to A drianople.]

46 House. Anatomy Bill put off till Friday. The Bishops, Lord Malmesbury, and many others very hostile to it.

It seems certain that the Eussians have recrossed the Danube. I am inclined to think they have been beaten.

June 3.

The Bishop of Oxford is dead; a great Grecian is to succeed him.

The King is in excellent humour. The Duke of Cumberland rather going down.

We had some talk about the Anatomy Bill. The Duke is afraid of passing it. Indeed, it is not a Government measure. Probably it will be withdrawn for the year. The Bishops are very hostile to it.

June 4.

London Bridge Committee from eleven till four. We made great progress in our evidence, and, indeed, nearly proved our case.

From four to five we had a very painful discussion in consequence of some words which passed between Lord Durham and Lord Beresford. We succeeded at last in settling the difference.

Lord Beresford, having no good word at his disposal, said he did not second the evil deeds or improprieties of noble lords. He really meant irregularities, and irregularities only as a member of the Committee. Lord Grey was present and much distressed. The Duke of Wellington's authority induced both to become amenable to the wish of the Committee.

June 5.

"1." "2"

Anatomy Bill. Some talk; but a general agreement suggested by the Archbishop of Canterbury, that the Bill should be read a second time, and not proceeded with this session. The Duke of Wellington expressed his general approbation of the principle, but thought postponement desirable. He pledged himself to cooperate in bringing in a Bill on the same principle, and having the same objects, next year; but did not pledge himself to brin it in himself.

June 7.

Cabinet at half-past three. First question: whether we should extend the time for putting an end altogether the Brazilian slave trade from March 13 to September 13, 1830, for the equivalent of obtaining for ever the right to seize ships fitted up for the slave trade, whether they had slaves on board or not. The Brazilians have been encouraged by their Government to interpret the treaty as permitting the return of any vessels quitting the Brazils on slave expeditions before March 13.

Dr. Lushington, who was consulted by Aberdeen, seemed to think it was worth while to obtain the concession, but still seemed to think that by extending the time, we should permit the transportation of a very large number of slaves, of whom many might be destroyed by ill-treatment, and that it was hardly justifiable, with a view to a distant advantage, to sacrifice immediately and certainly a great number of persons.

This prevailed, the real fact being that Peel does not like awkward questions in the House of Commons.

So the treaty remains as it is, and both parties will interpret it as they please. There will be many disputes, for the interpretation is very different.

June 8.

Eeceived a private letter from Colonel Macdonald at Tabriz, with copies of letters received by him from a gentleman he had sent to Teheran on hearing of the massacre of the Eussian mission; and from another gentleman, travelling unofficially, who first heard the report between Tabriz and Kamsin.

These accounts only confirm what we had already heard of the arrogance and violence of the Eussians. They deserved their fate.

Colonel Macdonald says that General Paskewitz cannot dispose of more than 25,000, or, at most, 30,000 men, although he has a nominal force of 110,000 men under his command.

Colonel Macdonald says there has been no serious resistance on the part of the Turks, except at Ak-halsik.

He has done what he can to dissuade them from war with the Eussians; but I think the universal feeling of the people will propel them.

The insurrection at Teheran appears to have been instigated by the Mollahs and the women, but it was evidently national, or it must have failed.

June 10.

Council. Lord Winford kissed hands. He walked in with great difficulty on two crutches, which he placed behind him and so leant back upon. The King had a chair brought for him, and had him wheeled out. The man who pushed his chair very nearly shipwrecked him at the door.

The Attorney-General (Scarlett), [1] the Chief Justice of the Common Pleas (Tindal), and the Solicitor-General (Sugden), [2] all kissed hands. The Chief Justice of the Common Pleas was sworn in as Privy Councillor. Lord Eosslyn was sworn in as Privy Councillor and Privy Seal. The King did not address a word to me, who gave up the seal, or to Eosslyn, who received it. House. Nothing of moment.

Dinner at Lord Bathurst's. Lord Eosslyn dined here.

Aberdeen read a paper lately received from the Eussians, in which they concede all we ask about blockades, c., except as to the Gulf of Enos. The Duke says he shall bring Lieven to the point about this, and generally about their views. He feels the Government is stronger now than it was that the country is stronger, and we may insist more. He says the question is," Shall we permit the ruin' of the Turkish Empire? ' I have long felt that to be the case, and to that I answer No

We had some conversation as to the charter. The Duke seems rather inclined to continue the name of the Company. I am for the name of the King.

1 Afterwards Lord Abinger.

2 Afterwards Lord St. Leonards. Lord Chancellor 1852.

VOL. II. E

June 11.

The world has had imposed upon it a story of the Chancellor's selling his Church preferment. The ' Age' is to bring forward its charges on Sunday next. This is an arrow from the Cumberland quiver.

I mentioned Lord Clare's wish to look forward to the Government of Bombay or Madras to the Duke last night, and he did not by any means receive the proposition unfavourably. I told Clare so to-day.

June 13.

Gaisford has refused the Bishopric of Oxford wisely, for he was only a Grecian and had good preferment. He is a rough man too. I am glad he has refused it. I do not think mere Grecians good bishops.

Lord Clare told me Glengall was to be the new Irish peer.

June 15.

Committee as usual. Lord Londonderry more insane than ever. The Duke said he had never seen anything more painful.

We made hardly any progress. The victory will belong to the survivors, and I do not think Lord Durham will be one of them.

House. Lord Londonderry made a foolish speech, and the Duke an excellent one, very severe upon him, and defending the City. If we do not get the City by this Committee the City is impregnable.

Hardinge told me Lord Grey seemed out of humour. I do not think he is in good humour.

June 16.

At last some hope of a compromise respecting London Bridge.

June 17.

The eternal Committee is, I trust, at an end. The agents have come to a compromise, and if the Common Council should confirm the terms, as I conclude they will, the thing will be at an end. We shall then have Parliament up by Monday or Tuesday next.

Cabinet dinner at Lord Melville's. The Duke was astonished at Lord W. Bentinck's strong and sudden step of transferring the Supreme Government pro tern-pore to Meerut. He said he always expected some wild measure from Lord W. Meerut was in too exposed a situation.

Twenty thousand Afghan horse might ride in upon the seat of government if placed in the north-west provinces. It is astonishing how much the Duke is prejudiced by his old Indian feelings. Whatever is he thinks best. Meerut is ill and absurdly chosen, but Calcutta is certainly the worst chosen seat of government.

We are to have a Cabinet on Saturday for the King's speech. On Monday or Tuesday Parliament will be up. On Wednesday we dine at the India House, and on the Monday following, the 29th, will be the fish dinner.

June 18.

Called to compliment the Duke on the anniversary of Waterloo. Left with him Lord W. Bentinck's minute and despatch on transferring the Supreme Government Departments and all pro tempore to Meerut, and a proposed letter, censuring the Governor for having done this without previous sanction, and directing the members of Council and the Departments to return. The Duke objects to any removal of the seat of government to the upper provinces. It would there be exposed to the sudden inroads of cavalry. In India a cloud of cavalry rises like a squall in the Mediterranean. At Calcutta the Government, protected by the rivers, is safe, and always accessible from England.

June 19.

Eode to town. Met Eosslyn. He told me Lord Clanrickarde[1] intended to make some observations on foreign policy this evening.

Had some conversation with the Duke. He doubted whether the Supreme Government could leave Calcutta and preserve its powers. I told him of the newspaper report of to-day that leases for sixty years were to be given to indigo planters, and this without any authority from home. He seems to have suspected from the first that Lord W. would do some monstrous thing, and certainly he does seem to be emancipating himself.

House. Lord Clanrickarde made his little speech. Aberdeen his. Then Lord Holland, and then the Duke. Afterwards Goderich. Lord Holland talked as usual very vaguely. No notice had been given, and few people knew there was anything to be done. So ends the House for this year.

[1 Lord Clanrickarde was son-in-law of Mr. Canning.]

June 20, 1829.

Cabinet. King's speech. Some time occupied in wording it, but no material alterations. Aberdeen's the worst part. The King is made to auspicate and to pray, but not to trust that the Franchise Bill and the Eelief Bill will be productive of good.

The Chancellor has prosecuted the 'Morning Journal' for a libel accusing him of having taken money for Sugden's appointment as Solicitor-General. I heard him tell Lord Bathurst, with reference to another calumny against him, that he had fortunately preserved through his secretary the grounds on which he had given every living he had disposed of.

June 21.

Had a visit from Loch. He wishes the despatch to Lord William to be worded more gently, as he thinks Lord William meant well. This shall be done.

June 22.

Wrote draft paragraphs to the effect above stated to Lord W. Bentinck, and added a paragraph giving the Duke's reasoning against the removal of the Government from Calcutta to the north-west provinces.

I had some conversation in the House with Lord Lauderdale on China trade, c. He seems friendly to the Company and to the Government.

Went to the House at 4. Found a good many peers there. By mere mistake a Bill, slightly and necessarily amended by the Lords, was not sent down to the Commons, although directions to that effect were given, and it by accident was placed amongst the Bills ready for the Eoyal assent. So it received the Eoyal assent. It became necessary to pass a Bill to make this Bill valid in law. Lord Shaftesbury thought our House ought to inform the Commons we had discovered the error; but the Speaker, [1] to make a flourish, insisted on announcing it first to the House of Commons. All the steps to be taken were settled between the Speaker, Lord Shaftesbury, and Courtenay. When I went down I found it had not been settled that anything should be done first by us. I suggested that Lord Shaftesbury should acquaint the House with the circumstance, and that we should appoint a Committee to inquire before the message from the Commons came up. This was done.

"We ordered a message to be sent, but before our messengers left the House we heard the Commons would not receive a message, so I moved that the order we had just made should be rescinded, and we had a second conference. The Commons were well satisfied with our reply. The last sentence had been, ' The Lords hope the Commons will be satisfied with this explanation." As we in the first paragraph expressed our desire to preserve a good understanding between the two Houses, and in the second one regret that this mistake had taken place, I thought it was going too far to express a hope only that our explanation would be satisfactory.

[1 C. Manners Sutton, afterwards Lord Canterbury.]

We inserted; the Lords doubt not' instead of 'the Lords hope.'

At night received a letter from the Duke of Wellington, saying he thought we might get Courtenay to resign at once and get in Lord Chandos. I am to see him at ten to-morrow on the subject.

June 23, 1829,

Wrote early to the Chairs and begged them to come to me immediately. Sent Loch the Duke's note and told him why Lord Chandos's being brought in was of so much importance. Saw the Duke at 10. The King was very much out of humour yesterday. He wanted to make Nash a baronet. The Duke refused. The King then went upon his Speech, which he did not like and had altered. He left out the specific mention of the Eelief and Franchise Bill, and there he was right, and he converted the prayer that the measure might tranquillise Ireland, c., into a hope that it would thus making it a little stronger, but that he did not know.

The Duke of Cumberland, on hearing of Castlereagh's appointment, said, ' Whoever ratted he would not alluding to Lord Londonderry, who has been nibbling at the Cumberland faction. However, Lord Londonderry is much annoyed at Castlereagh's taking office. He neither likes the expense of an election for Down-shire, nor losing a vote he thought he could dispose of.

Hardinge will not sit again for Durham. Without Hardinge Lord Londonderry will have trouble enough there.

The King was much out of humour during the
Chapter of the Garter, and said everything was done wrong.

Saw the Chairs. They had just got a letter from Sir John Malcolm, resigning from December 1, 1830. This would have been in any case a long time for Cour-tenay to wait out of office; but they said the idea of his being proposed had got wind, and several of the Directors were very adverse. Neither of the Chairs likes him, and if they supported him they would do it very reluctantly. As Loch goes out of office in April, and we cannot tell who will be deputy, and six new Directors come in, there really are not the means of saying to Courtenay, 'You are sure of your election," and without this he could not be asked to resign.

I took the Chairs to the Duke. He received them very cordially, told them I had stated the circumstances to him, and he gave up the point.

We then talked of the legality of the removal of the Supreme Government from Calcutta. On looking into the acts it seems very doubtful whether any act done by the Governor-General in Council away from Calcutta would be valid unless it were one of the acts the Governor-General might do of his own authority. For instance, c a regulation ' issued by the Governor-General in Council at Meerut would not be valid, because the Governor-General alone could not issue one.

The Duke said Lord William did everything with the best intentions; but he was a wrong-headed man, and if he went wrong he would continue in the wrong line. Other men might go wrong and find it out, and go back; but if he went wrong he would either not find it out, or, if he did, he would not go back.

June 24.

Sat as Commissioner to prorogue Parliament. The King's alteration in the Speech certainly made it better and stronger. He now expresses his sincere hope the measures of the session will produce tranquillity, c. People thought the Speech rather short and jejune.

Dined at the ' Albion' with the Directors. The dinner was given to Lord Dalhousie. There were there the Duke, the Chancellor, Peel, Sir J. Murray, Lord Eosslyn and Goulburn, the Speaker, the Attorney General, Courtenay, Ashley, and Bankes; Duke of Buccleuch, Lord Camden, Lord Montagu, Lord Hill, Sir Herbert Taylor, Sir Byam Martin, Sir A. Dickson, Colonel Houston, Lord Dalhousie, and Sir Sidney Beckwith, and their aides-de-camp; a great many Directors, and in all rather more than 100 people.

The Duke, in returning thanks, spoke of the cor-iality and good understanding existing between the Directors and the Government, which was never more necessary to the Company than now.

I said the good understanding would always exist while such men as Loch were in the chair, and while I I was at the Board of Control. I paid a high compliment to Loch, and then congratulated them on the appointments of the two Generals. Their mildness of manner, their benevolence of character, and the goodness of their natures would obtain for them the affectionate devotion of a grateful soldiery, and, edu_ cated in a school of continued victories, they were the fittest leaders of an army which had never met an enemy it had not subdued. I ended by saying I was sure they would devote themselves to the maintenance under all circumstances, not only of the efficiency, but of an object which they would pursue with equal interest of the happiness and well-being of the native army of India. I spoke rather well, was attentively heard, and well received. I sat by the Duke of Buc-cleuch. We had a good deal of conversation. He seems a fine young man. Lord Eosslyn complained he could never see a draft till it was a month old, and that there had been no new despatches placed in the boxes since he came into office. I told him no one complained more of the same thing than Aberdeen did when Dudley was in office, and I believe all Foreign Secretaries had a shyness about showing their drafts till they were sent off and unalterable.

June 25.

At the office found a letter with enclosures from Colonel Macdonald, dated Tabriz April 20. What he has been doing in Persia I do not know.

I have written to him to call upon me on Saturday.

Called on the Duke to tell him the substance which is, that the Turks have already 30,000 men and sixty pieces of cannon at Erzeroum. That a dispossessed Pacha is in arms at Akiska. That the Eussians have reinforced the garrisons of Natshiran and Abbas-abad, and have withdrawn all their troops to the left bank of the Araxes, with the exception of those who_ garrison Bayazid. The plague seems rife at Erivan. The Eussians about Count Paskewitz abuse the English very much.

June 27.

The Chairs told me Lord W. Bentinck had extended to all persons the benefit of the regulation as to coffee planters, omitting *, however, all the restrictive clauses. They think very seriously of this, and very justly. The Calcutta newspapers consider the principle of colonisation to be conceded.

We must abrogate this *'Regulation' without loss of time. I went to the Duke to tell him of it. He said Lord W. Bentinck was not to be trusted, and we should be obliged to recall him. He is gone down in a steamboat to Penang.

No news of much importance at the Cabinet room, except that Lord Heytesbury's despatches confirm the. account of the sickness of the Eussian army.

The Turks seem to have given the Eussians a great smash at Eski Arnaut.

June 30.

A battle near Schumla between the Eussians and Turks. The Turks were besieging Pravadi. Diebitsch marched from Silistria and moved upon their communications with Schumla. The Turks seem to have been surprised. They fought gallantly, however, and seem to have caused the Eussians great loss.

Saw Arbuthnot. He came to the India Board to speak about his friend, Russell Ellice, whom he wishes to make a Director. We afterwards talked of the House and the Government. I think all will turn out well. We have six months before us, but certainly at present we are weak in the House of Commons, though I believe gathering strength in the country, and already very strong there. If we play the great game, striking at the mass, we must succeed. It would never do to go picking up individuals. We must do our best for the country, and we shall have it with us. The worst of it is, the King is the most faithless of men, and Cumberland is at work.

The Duke asked Hardinge the other day what he thought of the Government. He said he thought that by losing Canningites and Brunswickers it was fifty weaker than Lord Liverpool's, and these fifty go the other way, making a difference of one hundred on a division. Lord Camden thought if the Brunswickers would not come in we must get a few Whigs Aber-cromby, Sir James Graham, the Althorpe people. Stanley would come for anything good, and Brougham too.

Arbuthnot asked me if I thought Lord Eosslyn would be cordial with us. I said Yes. His letter of acceptance was most cordial, and with the Lords he was on excellent terms. The only danger would be if Peel and the Commoners were shy.

Lord Grey, I said, I did not think in very good humour, but he would differ on foreign politics rather than on questions of a domestic nature. The Duke will not be coquetting with him, because he says very honestly he should be exciting expectations in Lord

Grey which, while the King lives, he does not think he can gratify.

Saw Mr. Elphinstone by appointment. I wished to have his opinion with regard to the new settlement of Indian Government, which may take place on the expiration of the present Charter. He seemed to think that the Administration of the Government in the King's name would be agreeable to the Civil and Military Services, and to people in England. He doubted whether, as regarded the princes of India, it would signify much, as they now pretty well understood us. He doubted whether the orders of Government here would be better obeyed. He thought there might be an advantage in keeping the King's authority in reserve, to be used only on grand occasions. He confessed, however, that ' having been educated, and having lived under the existing system, he was not best qualified to propose to another. He had his prejudices." He thought the best mode of arriving at the truth would be by taking the opinions of practical Indians as to reforms and alterations suggested by theoretical men.

I asked him to consider the expediency of dividing the territory as now into three unequal Presidencies, of giving to the Governor-General the labour of superintending the Administration in detail of the Bengal Presidency of having Members of Council. I told him there were many minor points of detail discoverable only by those employed at home, which required and must receive amendment. Such, for instance, is the interpretation given to the Act of Parliament, by which a regulation must be sanctioned

62 or rejected in extenso, there being no power to alter a word, or to reject part and take the rest.

Mr. Elphinstone seems to dread a long peace in India. We hold everything together by the Native Army, and we cannot retain that unless we retain the affections of the European officers. In the present state of our finances this is difficult.

July 1.

At half-past five received a letter from the Chairman, and the draft relative to the removal of the Governor from Calcutta. The Court wished to have it back to-day. That was impossible; but they have omitted words I inserted in the precis, and must restore, declaring that had the removal been legal, still the Members of Council would have been ordered back. I have now been obliged to give reasons for this addition, and the reasons will be so much worse, as matters of record, that I have suggested to the Chairman he had better substitute a draft containing the words.

I think we must detain the Pallas that it may take out both letters this and the one relating to the leases which is not yet prepared, or we must have an overland dispatch.

Delay is one of the inconveniences attending the present system of Indian Government. I told the Chairman in my private note that if we allowed Lord W. Bentinck to emancipate himself in this manner we should really be abandoning all real control over the Government of India. I see clearly there is a Bentinck party in the Court.

.?--,.' rbft.:-"frv i J. ri ';, ivtf" t i i yv 2 . 'Kf 1i 'f MKJ!

63 July 2.

Saw Hardinge. We had some conversation upon the subject of the Government. He seems more alarmed than I am. I trust to the King's fears and the Duke's fortune; besides, we have the country.

Hardinge told me the King was very much out of humour. The admission of Lord Eosslyn had not answered. None followed. Lord Durham, Calthorpe, and others left Lord Lansdowne to coalesce with Lord Grey. Hardinge wished me to try Herries again with the view of opening the Mint by making him Chancellor of the Exchequer in India; but I told him Herries said his domestic circumstances made it impossible, and the Duke did not seem to like it at all.

Herries thinks Lord Durham would be glad to be Minister at Naples; for my part I am sure nothing will win Lord Grey but a place for Lord Grey himself, and that, in the present state of the King's mind, the Duke is not in a condition to offer.

July 4.

Cabinet at half-past three.

The Duke read a list of the several points to be considered before the next Session. I cannot recollect half of them. East India Charter; Bank Charter; Usury Laws; East Eetford; Duties on Sugar; Duties on Tobacco; Canada; West Indies; Education in Ireland; Irish and English Churches; Poor in Ireland; Public Works; Commission on Ecclesiastical Courts; Reform of Iglish Courts; Reform of Welsh Judicature; Eeform *64* of Courts of Equity; Scotch Law of Entail; Salaries of Scotch Judges increase; Salaries of English Judges reduction; Grand Juries, Ireland; Militia Laws; Stamp Duties, c., c.

The only talk we had was about Irish Poor, and Public Works in Ireland. The feeling seemed against anything like Poor Laws, and against Public Works too. This is mine. The first productive of mischief, the second useless.

Undoubtedly it is a great hardship that the English parish should have the burden of Irish poor, but on the other hand in many cases the payers of poor's rates in these parishes have derived advantage from Irish labour.

Fitzgerald, Peel, and Goulburn are to look into this subject, and all connected with Ireland.

Fitzgerald, Peel, Lord Eosslyn, and, I think, either Herries or Goulburn seemed to think the opposition to the continuance of the China monopoly would be much greater than we expected. Fitzgerald seemed desirous the question of commerce should be reserved, and that of Government decided. I told him the two were inseparably connected.

July 6.

Wrote to Lord W. Bentinck telling him I much regretted the having been obliged to send the two letters, relative to the removal of the Government, and the leases told him the Duke coincided in opinion with the Court.

I then expressed my surprise that the Local Government did not obey better. Said they seemed to forget the orders of the Directors were the King's orders transmitted through the channel of the Court and the Board. I added I should endeavour to introduce into every branch of Indian Government the subordination and the improvements now established in the King's service depended on his co-operation, c. I sent the letter to the Duke to ask him if I should send it.

July 7.

At quarter to six a messenger arrived from the Duke, to whom I sent yesterday my letter to Lord W. asking if I should send it? The Duke desires to see the despatches to which it refers. I have accordingly begged Jones to send them to him. I shall however be in town early myself to-morrow.

I told the Duke in my note I should stay in town till late to-morrow to sign the letter as to the six regiments if they passed it. I am glad to have an excuse for not going to Windsor to the Eecorder's Eeport.

July 8.

Office at 2. Wilson absent, so I could not transact any military business. Carried the letters relative to the leases and the six regiments to the Duke. He said mine about the regiments was very good indeed.

The Emperor of Russia seems to have laid himself out most ably at Berlin to captivate the King, and the army, and the people.

Seymour's despatches are useful. He mentions small things, which show the character of men.

The Emperor does not disguise his desire of peace. ~~VOL. II. F~~

He wants no garanties matérielles at the Bosphorus for safe passage. He asks the principle of a pecuniary indemnity, but does not seem disposed to contest the details. Bernstorff observed truly, we could not get out of the Greek Treaty without the help of Eussia, and Eussia wanted us to get out of the way.

The Sultan begins to affect European manners. Calls upon ladies and talks about education! Dines with a merchant! After all, considering his education and his entourage. Sultan Mahmoud is the most remarkable man in Europe.

July 9.

Office at 2. Met Herries. Told him I should send him a statement of our Indian loans, and place Leach at his disposal. We could then talk them over, and see whether we could effect any financial operation. My idea is that by offering some little higher interest in India we might induce the holders of the remittable loan to give up that privilege of receiving the interest in England if resident here.

Saw Major Cunningham. He looks more than forty, well, certainly, but I should doubt his doing much hard work. He does not think himself a good person to command Irregulars. His Eohillas were almost in as good order as Eegulars.

He told me Lieutenant-Colonel Skinner was a man of large landed property. He had raised his corps very much from his own estate and neighbourhood, and was a sort of feudal chieftain. He has been educated like a native, though the son of a Colonel in the Company's service.

67   Saw Sir Murray Maxwell. [I]It seemed to me Sir Murray wanted to be sent with a frigate to try to open a commercial communication with Pekin. He thinks even Japan might be induced to trade. The instant the Chinese found the ship was gone and Lord Amherst meant to return by land they would have nothing to say to him. They probably took him for a spy.

Sir Murray thinks the Chinese might be led to give a port to the northward.

He describes the Spanish population of Manilla as being very small the native population large. It is but four days' sail, with a good breeze, from Manilla to Canton. Always a favourable wind. The harbour magnificent.

I think the whole object of his visit was to get a ship, and a sort of half embassy.

July 10.

Eeceived a letter from Lord Clare, who saw the Duke yesterday. He says the Duke was very kind and told him he should get all the information he could before the Committee of next year. I shall most willingly assist him.

July 11.

Cabinet. Talked of Ireland. The disposition to outrage seems increasing. The Duke said we were responsible for the success of the measure of this year, and we must put down the armed meetings. Warburton must be ordered to do so. The Duke said emphatically [1 He had commanded the ' Alceste,"which took out Lord Amherst. as Ambassador to China twelve years before.]

68   if we do not preserve the peace of Ireland we shall not be a Government. Peel is to write immediately. He thinks the first appearance of a determination to put down these meetings will have the effect of crushing them. We spoke of Poor Laws, Education, and Grand Juries. Lord F. Leveson despairs as to the two first. Upon both the Government will form its opinion. I am glad to see that the more the question of Poor Laws is considered the more the introduction of them appears unadvisable, or of any approach to them. I have ever held this opinion.

In Cabinet we again, having done so many weeks ago, considered whether any extension of time should be given to the Brazilians for the termination of their traffic in slaves.

Aberdeen seemed very indulgently inclined towards the slave dealers not so Peel and Fitzgerald. They seemed first of all to think it would be an awkward Parliamentary case, and Peel protested against our becoming responsible, as we should, for the horrible consequences which might attend the continuance of the trade for six months. The Chancellor thought a vessel leaving the coast of Africa, that is, engaging in the slave trade, at such a period as would afford a reasonable probability of her arriving on March 13, should be safe. I think February 13 was, after much desultory discussion, fixed as the day after which no vessel should leave the coast of Africa.

The Brazilians had offered as an equivalent for six months an agreement that in future vessels fitted for the slave trade, even if they had no slaves on board, should be seizable. It seemed to be the opinion, a little exaggerated, I think, that no prospect of future prevention of slave-trading could justify us in permitting fur an instant the immediate benefit we had within our grasp.

July 12.

The great day in Ireland; but I hope its happening on Sunday may break its effect. The orders for vigorous interposition, determined upon on Saturday, will have been of no use in preventing collision to-day, or even to-morrow, should the anniversary be postponed.

The Duke of Cumberland goes to Hanover, but he returns in October, and old Eldon meets him then in London. They had a regular Cabinet to decide whether he should go or not.

Eead the court-martial of Lieutenant Lewis, of the Bombay Artillery, who struck an officer in the presence of his wife. The Chairs wish to restore him. It is impossible. There is an end of all moral and gentlemanlike feeling if it be not understood that a man's person is sacred in the presence of his wife. We presume a wife to have feeling, and a man to respect it. The blow alone would have been a good cause of dismissal.

Had a letter from the Bishop of Calcutta, who, on offering to execute episcopal functions at the Cape, was told by Hay, of the Colonial Office, that the Cape was riot in his Patent, and he could not do so. This is a mistake. He can exercise episcopal functions, but not episcopal jurisdictions.

Had a letter from Mr. Joliffe, of Merstham, [1] proposing steam-boat navigation to India. [1 The seat of the Joliffe family, near Reigate, in Surrey.]

An application from Salisbury for a letter of recommendation to Lord W. Bentinck, in favour of Mr. Chester. Told him this was not a good time to ask a favour of Lord William, and it would be better to send the recommendation with the man, who does not sail till October.

July 15, 1829.

Office. Found a letter from Loch, suggesting the irregularity of my sending for his officers, and communicating with them on the subject of despatches to be sent to the Indian Government, and expressing a hope that nothing would occur to interrupt the harmony which existed between us.

I said in reply that I have expressed a wish to see Colonel Salmond, and afterwards to see Colonel Farant, merely from my desire to expedite business, and to do it well. That it was mentioned in conversation with Colonel Salmond and Mr. Wilson on Monday, that there was no irregularity in that course, and that I immediately determined to desist from it. That I believed I had so expressed myself at the time to Colonel Salmond.

I added that I could assure him I would not willingly, by endeavouring to extend the limits assigned by Parliament to the power of the Board, or by my manner of exercising that power, interrupt the harmony which so happily existed between the court and me.

Went to the Foreign Office. I fear the defeat of the Turks near Shumla was decisive; but still we have only Eussian accounts, and they do so lie! It seems certain the Russians took the opportunity of opening a negotiation. The carelessness of the Turks in not keep-ing a good look-out towards Silistria seems unaccountable, and they dawdled sadly before Pravady. The new Vizier is very inferior to old Hussein Pacha, whose caution would have avoided this catastrophe.

Dined with the East India volunteers. The officers of the regiment are all clerks in the Company's service. The non-commissioned officers and privates serve in their warehouses.

There are now 600 men. During the war they had three regiments, each 800 strong all their own servants.

When my health was drunk I spoke of the Duke of Wellington's natural fondness for India, of the high terms in which he always mentioned the gallantry of the Indian army, and the purity of the Civil Service. I said the Ministers were animated by his example, c.

The Speaker told me he thought Mr. Stanley[1] would never rise higher than he was' now. It had been a curious Session all men endeavouring to avoid committing themselves.

July 16.

Loch showed me two letters of Sir J. Malcolm, in which he deprecates the sending of more writers, and says numbers may be diminished, but not salaries, especially in the higher ranks; and if writers are sent they must be provided for. I believe he is right. I had already suggested the non-appointment of writers this year, and the Chairs seemed to acquiesce indeed, to have thought of it themselves.

[1 A curious instance of the failure of political prophecies, even by men of judgment and experience. Seventeen years later he was leader of a party, and twenty-three years afterwards Prime Minister.]

Recorder's Eeport. Before the report Madame de CayJa, the Duchess D'Escars, c., were presented to the King. I had some conversation with Rosslyn and Herries as to the Indian Question. Herries seemed to be afraid of the House of Commons. Rosslyn a little, too, of public opinion as to the opening of the China trade. They both seemed rather hostile to the continuance of the present system. I said I considered it to be a settled point that the patronage of India should be separated from the Government. The necessity of making that separation led to one great difficulty. The necessity of remitting home in goods 3,200,000*l* led to another difficulty, and to making the Government of India, wherever it might be placed, mercantile. The East India Company would not, and could not, without the monopoly carry on the concern.

Neither Herries nor Eosslyn seemed to admit the necessary separation of the patronage of India from the Government.

I said that, if it might not be separated, it would be easy to make a better and a cheaper government. I can see that Peel, Fitzgerald, Herries, Eosslyn perhaps Sir G. Murray will be against the Company.

The Duke said it was clear to him that the remittances must be made in goods, and could not be made by bills. He is for the monopoly.

In a few days the papers will be printed. A copy will then be furnished to each member of the Government, and I shall receive their observations.

The Eecorder's Eeport was a very heavy one. All the cases bad, and seven ordered for execution.

73   The King seemed very well.

Stratford Canning and Lord Strangford were at the Court, to be presented on their return.

Before the report we read the last Irish papers. The Duke of Northumberland and Lord F. Leveson seem to think rather favourably of the condition of Ireland. The belief of Peel and Goulburn, and, I believe, of the Duke, is that one example would settle all.

Lord F. Leveson says that the Brunswickers are encouraged from St. James's to expect that the Eelief Bill will be repealed. Many wish for an explosion, the Catholics less than the Protestants.

July 19.

Hardinge and Wood dined with me. Hardinge says the Duke of Cumberland has determined not to leave England, but to send for the Duchess and his son. The Duchess of Gloucester did not before, and will not now, receive the Duchess of Cumberland. Old Eldon wants a guarantee that no more Whigs will be admitted. I believe he would be satisfied with none but his own admission.

Hardinge seems to think we may not have a majority when Parliament meets. I think he is wrong. I trust to the Duke's fortune and to ' the being a Government," which is much, and to the others not being able to form a Government, which is more.

July 22.

Had a letter from Loch. He does not like the disbanding of the six regiments, but he says he brings it before the Court again on Monday, having promised every possible information.

Eead some of Colonel Tod's 'Rajastan." I had rather see Rajastan or Rajpootana than any part of India. It would really be interesting. Colonel Tod seems to be an enthusiast about the country and the people. He was there apparently at least sixteen years. The story of the beautiful Princess of Oudeypore [1] in Tod's book and Sir J. Malcolm's is the most romantic and the most interesting I know. That family of Oudeypore or Mewar seems to be the most ancient in the world. It far surpasses the Bourbons and the House of Hapsburg.

July 23.

Chairs at eleven. Told them of the danger in which they were, from the feeling of the mercantile districts and of the country; that we could not look Parliament in the face without having done all in our power to effect reductions in a deficit of S00,000. a year; that without a commanding case no Government, however strong, could venture to propose a renewal of the monopoly.

They were obliged to me for my information. I advised them to turn their attention immediately to all the great points.

On the subject of the six regiments the Court differ from the view I took. Loch gave me a long statement 1 Krishna Komari. She was poisoned by her father to avoid the hostilities of the rival princes who demanded her hand. The father was still living when Colonel Tod wrote. The House of Oudeypore was the only native reigning family who disdained to intermarry even with the Emperors of Delhi. See Tod's Rajasthan, i. 965.]

75   of facts, which I must read attentively, and then communicate with the Duke.

They are so enamoured of old habits that they hesitate about desiring their Indian Governments and the subordinate correspondents of these Governments to place upon the back of their voluminous letters a precis of their substance!

After the Chairs were gone I saw Bankes and Leach, and while they were with me Sir Archibald Campbell called. I saw him immediately. He is a fat, rather intelligent-looking man, well mannered, and sensible. I talked to him of the idea of exchanging Tenasserim. [1] He did not like giving up his conquest. I gave him one secret letter, and he will make his observations upon it.

He left Lord William at the mouth of the Hooghly. They had found out the removal of the Government was contrary to law. They had intended to be itinerant for a year or two.

It is only in the Bengal army that the officers are old. There they rise by seniority. In the Madras army they are made from fitness.

The Madras army, though most gallant, was quite unequal, from deficiency of physical strength, to face the Burmese. The Burmese soldiers brought fourteen days' provisions. All men are liable to be called upon. They never had more than 120,000 in the field.

The English army took 2,000 cannon, and it was believed the Burmese had 2,500 left.

[1 The furthest province of the British territory towards Siam, extending along the coast south of Pegu, and lately conquered from the Burmese. Empire]

76   Sir A. Campbell says there have been 60,000 refugees from Ava all now settled in Tenasserim. I had thought there had never been more than 10,000, and that some, about half, had returned.

Upon the whole, he seems enamoured of his conquests, but he did not adduce any good reason against exchanging it.

At the Cabinet room. Saw Lord Eosslyn there, as I used to be last year, desceuvre and bored, as all Privy Seals will be. He seemed dissatisfied with the state of affairs in Ireland and in England. At Manchester there is a fear of a turn-out of some more cotton-spinners. Every thing depends upon the harvest.

The negotiations with the Turks came to nothing. The Grand Vizier's answer to Diebitch is excellent.

The sickness amongst the Eussian troops continues, and Diebitch has not more than 40,000 men, even with Koth's corps.

The Ambassadors have been very well received at Constantinople. All are in good humour there, notwithstanding the losses near Shumla.

The Emperor does not go to the army.

Lord Heytesbury represents Eussia as being the least formidable of the great Powers for the purpose of offensive operations, and seems to think she contains many elements of convulsion.

Metternich is trying to cajole the Eussians by pretended fears of revolutionary principles.

They talk of a King in Columbia, and the French are intriguing to place a French prince on the throne, after Bolivar.

July 25, 1829.

Cabinet room. The Ambassadors seem to have been received most cordially at Constantinople. We know no more of the Grand Vizier's losses. That he experienced a complete defeat there can be no doubt.

In Columbia, the French seem rather inclined to place, after Bolivar, a Prince of the House of Orleans on the throne, and it does not seem unlikely that the Columbians may consider it their best arrangement.

The Emperor of Eussia seems to be desirous of Peru, and the King of Prussia has, at his request, sent the Baron von Muffling as his Minister to the Porte to mediate.

The Irish accounts are very bad. Lord F. Leveson seems now to think very seriously of the state of things. Doherty is come back much alarmed from Barris, where he has been with Blackie on a special commission.

July 28.

I recommended to the attention of the Chairs the establishment of steam communication with India by the Eed Sea.

July 29.

Read precis relative to Kotah.

These precis will make me thoroughly acquainted with the history and circumstances of the Eajpoot States, which are by far more interesting than others.

There is a looseness and a vulgarity in the East India House writing, the literature of clerks which is quite disgusting. Our clerks write better than theirs, but they do not write concisely and correctly.

July 30.

Eead Lord Heytesbury's letters. He is very Eussian. They have certainly got the plague at Odessa, and in all the stations of the Eussian army.

Met Peel at the Cabinet room. He said Ireland was in rather a better state. He agreed with me in thinking the Brunswickers were the cause of all the mischief. He believed the King had begged the Duke of Cumberland to stay, and that the Duchess was certainly coming over. They wish to attack the Ministry through the side of Ireland to make a civil war rather than not turn out a Government.

He had written to the Duke suggesting that we ought to have a Cabinet respecting Ireland, and he thought the Duke would come to town on his letter.

August 1.

Had from Sir G. Murray papers relative to the Canada question, upon which he wishes to have the opinion of the Cabinet to-morrow. The immediate question is whether a Bill passed by the Colonial Legislature for altering the state of the representation shall be confirmed by the Crown.

The state of Canada is such that I am convinced we ought in prudence to place the revenue collected under the 14th Geo. II. at the disposal of the Chambers, retaining, as they are willing to retain, a fixed salary for the Government judges, independent of the annual vote.

79   Sunday ⸱, August 2.

Cabinet at 4. Irish question. Lord F. Leveson seems to be much alarmed. He wants to use the Bill of this year for the suppression of an expected meeting at Derry, which meeting is to be unarmed, sing songs, drink toasts, make speeches, and petition for a change of Ministers.

It was considered that the powers entrusted to Government by the Bill for the suppression of the Eoman Catholic Association were never intended to be exercised for the putting down of such a meeting as that intended to be held at Derry. If the Brunswickers there come out of their houses and have a procession causing fear and threatening the peace, the common law can put them down. Care will be taken to have troops enough at Derry.

Lord F. Leveson likewise asks whether he shall proclaim martial law! Peel very properly asks him what martial law is. In fact it is the absence of all law and can only be endured when a country is on the eve of rebellion or actually in rebellion. [1] It seems to me that Lord Francis is unequal to his situation. I wish we had Hardinge there. He would never go wrong.

Herries told me he thought, after reading the papers I had sent him, that there was more of care for the Company than he expected.

Peel has written a very good letter to Lord F. Gower, [1 This was exactly the description given of it by Lord Beaconsfield with reference to Jamaica in 1866.]

80   telling him that the first thing they must do is to establish an efficient police, to be paid for by Ireland and of which the officers must be appointed by. Government.

August 3.

Saw Hardinge. He has perfected a very excellent system in Ireland by which all the 30,000 pensioners are divided into districts, in each of which is a chief constable who pays them. If they move from one district to another they have a ticket, so that the residence and the movements of all are known. Of 30,000 about 10,000 are fit for duty. Blank orders are ready at the Castle, directing the march of these men upon five central points, where they would be incorporated with the regiments, so that in a few days the army could be reinforced by 10,000 men. There are others who are not very capable of doing anything but mischief if against us. These would be ordered to the garrisons.

I wish Hardinge was in Ireland instead of Lord Francis.

August 6. Chairs at 11.

Astell does not seem to like my letters relative to the delay in answering despatches from India and in communicating events in India; and respecting the amount of military stores sent to India, and the expediency of enquiring whether their amount could not be diminished. Loch did not say anything. It was an attempt at bullying on Astell's part, which I resisted, and successfully.

81   August 10.

The Eussians appear to have passed the defiles on the northern side of the Balkans, and almost without loss. There is, I conclude, a force near Bourgas, but all that is to be hoped is that the Turks will be wise enough not to fight. It was an unlucky appointment, that of the Grand Vizier. Old Hussein never would have committed his fault.

R. Gordon has been magnificently received at Constantinople.

Polignac has been made Prime Minister of France. De Eigny is made Minister of Marine. The Government is Tory, and I should think very favourable to English alliance, not Greek, and certainly not Eussian. If it should be able to stand, it must be good for us.

Received letters from Colonel Macdonald from Tabriz. He says the Eussians at Tiflis talk as if they were going to war with us.

August 11.

Eeceived Persian despatches. The Persians will pay no more. They wanted to go to war. No one would go as Envoy to Petersburg but an attache. They all thought they should be beheaded. Macdonald seems to have kept them quiet.

Cabinet room. Met Lord Melville. Eead Gordon's letters from Constantinople. The Turks have not above 20,000 men there. They are not disposed to yield at all. Gordon thinks if we declared we would fix in any manner the limits of Greece, and maintain them, the Porte would not quarrel with us, and would, rather

82   VOL. II. C do anything than yield the point of honour by acknowledging the independence of the Greeks.

The Eussians mean to pass the Balkans with 60,000 men and march on Adrianople. They send a large force by sea to Sizeboli to turn Bourgas.

Lord Francis Leveson holds out the apprehension of a long religious contest in Ireland. [1] I believe he looks only at the surface and judges from first appearances.

August 12.

A victory gained by Paskewitz over the Seraskier, whom he has taken prisoner, with thirty-one pieces of cannon, c., near Erzeroum that is, three days after the battle, Paskewitz, still in pursuit, was within forty miles of Erzeroum.

Wrote two letters to the Duke one on the subject of Sir J. P. Grant, who has closed the Courts at Bombay because the Government would not execute an unlawful process, and the other respecting Persian affairs, giving the substance of the despatches which I enclosed.

We have a Cabinet to-morrow at 12 on Turkish affairs. I would not allow the Eussians to advance any further. I would send one from our own body, incognito, to Paris to talk to Polignac and endeavour to get him to join us in an act of vigorous intervention which would give character to his Government and save Constantinople. I would pass the English and French fleets through the Dardanelles, and give Eussia a leaf [Unhappily, like other pessimists, he seems to have judged Ireland correctly.]

83   out of the Greek Treaty. But I do not expect that this will be Aberdeen's course.

Drummond, whom I saw, said the Duke was delighted with the account of the Jaghirdars of the Kistna. Granville is gone to Ireland.

The Duke was gone to Windsor. It is the King's birthday.

August 13.

When the Cabinet was assembled the Duke said we were not to consider the state of things at Constantinople, and what we should do. He thought the Eus-sians would get to Constantinople, and into it. If they did he thought there was an end of the Ottoman Empire. He was doubtful whether, after the innovations introduced, the Turks would cordially support Mahmoud, [1] and already there were insurrections of the Greeks.

It was just what he predicted in his letter to La Ferronays, and what Lord Dudley afterwards said in a letter to Lieven; the success of the Eussians was the dissolution of an Empire which could not be reconstituted. It was too late to interfere by force, even if we had been disposed to do so alone.

He thought France, if we did nothing, would be quiet if we did anything, she would take the other line. Polignac was a more able man than people supposed, and he would adhere to the course he adopted. We might endeavour, at any rate, to ascertain his feelings and intentions.

As to the Greek question we must have a conference, 1 Sultan Mahmoud, as is well known, remodelled the whole internal organisation of the Turkish Empire. He was denounced as the Giaour Sultan by old-fashioned Turks

84 and consider the suggestions of the Ambassadors, namely, that whatever we chose to make Greece, should be declared independent, and guaranteed. Both the Duke and Aberdeen thought France and Eussia would both take the proposition into consideration. The former as to limits, the latter for delay. France had already told us that, provided we could agree upon the limits, she was inclined to adopt the suggestion of the Ambassadors.

We asked whether the permanent occupation of Constantinople by Eussia was to be submitted to? The answer was, No, to be opposed by war. It seemed to me and to Fitzgerald we had better endeavour to prevent, at a small expense, even if alone, a measure we could only retrieve if it took place at an enormous expense, if at all, and which would in all probability effect the ruin of the Turkish Empire. I did not think affairs quite so desperate. I thought the Eussians might get to Adrianople, but not to Constantinople, and that they could not maintain themselves at Adrianople without the command of the sea. We had six ships at the mouth of the Dardanelles, and these with the Turkish Fleet would open the Black Sea.

I was for passing our ships up to Constantinople and placing them at the disposal of the Ambassador, for from hence we cannot give orders adapted to circumstances. It was replied that would be war. If war were to be declared we should do as much mischief as possible, and go to Cronstadt, not to the Black Sea. We should have our ships beyond the Bosphorus when Eussia occupied the Dardanelles, and shut us in. This would make us ridiculous.

85 As the object is not to do mischief to Eussia, but to save the Turkish Empire, I should say that measure was to be effected at the Bosphorus, for Constantinople, once taken, and the Ottoman Power annihilated, it would be of no use to distress Eussia.

Fitzgerald seemed to be of my opinion that, however desperate the chance, we should do all we could to save Constantinople, and at any risk.

It was determined that our fleet in the Mediterranean should be reinforced by three or four line-of-battle ships, on the principle that wherever any Power had a large, force, we should have one not a very wise principle, it seems to me, if we are never to use force. I interceded for a few powerful steamers, with 68 pound carronades, and I think Lord Melville seemed inclined to acquiesce.

Questions are to be put to Polignac to ascertain what he would do in certain events. I said he never would open himself to Lord Stuart. It was then suggested by the Duke that Aberdeen could write a private letter. This will, I believe, be done. I said to

Fitzgerald, who was next to me, 'Neither letter nor Stuart will get anything out of Polignac. One of ourselves should go to Paris as an individual, see Polignac, and return before the Conference."

I suggested Eosslyn, as he had nothing to do. Fitzgerald said he could go and return in a week, and seemed to wish to do so. However, nothing was said openly; and with all the means of success in our hands, for, I think, Polignac might be brought into our views, we shall lose all bv not using proper instruments; just as we have lost the Greek question by persisting in keeping Stratford Canning.

We had a good deal of conversation as to the limits of Greece. The Duke was for adhering to the Morea. It was really the best line. It was what we had guaranteed. We had told the Turks we did not mean to go beyond it.

Aberdeen has always had a little private hankering after Athens, though he ridicules it. He had no scruple about annexing Athens, although not yet taken. I said I thought Polignac would be disposed to hold our language to Eussia, if we would make some concession on the subject of Greece, and enable him to settle that question with eclat. He would then be supported by France in any strong language he might hold, and would establish himself by the experiment of his first fortnight of office.

However, the Cabinet seems disposed to look at accessories, not at principles, at the minor objects rather than at the one great object, which is inducing France to act with us to prevent the occupation of Constantinople or to force its evacuation. Instead of yielding upon points of minor importance, in order to carry the question, we are to insist now on the minor points the evacuation of the Morea by the French, and then, I fear we shall weaken Polignac's Government, and lose our object.

Our foreign policy has certainly been most unsuccessful. We have succeeded in nothing.

The communication to be made to Polignac is to be made to him confidentially, and he is to know it is not to be made to Austria. It is considered that in any case Austria would support France and England if they acted together, and any indication Austria might give of moving alone would bring down Prussia upon her. This line, I think, well considered and prudent.

It seemed to be thought that, if the Turkish Empire should be dissolved, Austria might be inclined to share the spoils and be quiet; but if it were only weakened, she would feel she suffered.

It seemed to be admitted by all that we ought to have taken a decided step long ago. That we were too late, and that we were inexcusable.

I said a year ago Aberdeen would ruin us he would gradually let us down, not by any flagrant error, but by being always under the mark. The Duke, occupied as he is as Prime Minister, wanted an efficient secretary for Foreign Affairs, and he could not have had a worse.

Peel seems to think Ireland stands much better since the proclamation respecting the attack made by the Eibbonmen upon the Orangemen in Fermanagh. He seems to think the Irish Government ready enough when things are brought to their notice, but that they do not read or attend to the reports made to them.

August 19.

I am inclined to think from what Colonel Hodgson says that leather might be made in India as well as here. They have the hide of the buffalo. They want the tanning, and some one must be sent from this country to teach them. He told me of a Mr. Cotton who was long at Tanjore, where the iron is, and I have written to him.

August 22.

The Eussians have taken Erzeroum, and have quite dispersed the Turkish army in Asia. Every success of theirs in that quarter makes my heart bleed. I consider it a victory gained over me, as Asia is mine.

August 28.

The ' Courier' of last night throws doubts on the reported victory of Kirkhilissa. The Sultan is said to be now ready to treat. The plague is in the Kussian army, and in the country before them. Had a long conversation with Hardinge on Indian affairs.

August 29.

Eead a letter from Mr. Cartwright, the Consul at Constantinople, dated the 9th. The loss of Erzeroum is to be attributed to the Janizaries. In all Asia they seem to be rising. The Eussians are not expected to advance till they are joined by 15,000 men, coming by sea. Thus our fleet would have saved Constantinople.

Cabinet at half-past three. Before the Cabinet read Lord Heytesbury's and Mr. Gordon's despatches. Lord Heytesbury seems to be a mere Eussian.

August 31.

Mr. Gordon describes the Turkish Empire as falling to pieces. The national enthusiasm and religious feeling of the people seem to be gone. The Sultan is unpopular. The populace of Adrianople desires the advance of the Eussians, so scandalous has been the conduct of the Asiatics. The Pacha of Egypt gives no assistance, and thinks the weakness of the Porte constitutes his strength. The people of Trebizond have invited Count Paskewitz. Erzeroum was lost by the treachery of the Janizaries.

The Sultan has acceded to the Treaty of London. This accession is qualified, but not in such a manner as to preclude negotiation. He has consented to treat with Eussia, to give freedom to the navigation of the Black Sea, and to observe the Treaty of Akerman but he stipulates for the integrity of the Ottoman dominions in Europe and Asia. He has not, however, sent Plenipotentiaries.

General Muffling, the Prussian, is arrived at Constantinople. He reports the moderate views of the Emperor Nicholas, and states them.

The French Government, from the information it derived from its Minister at Berlin, lias instructed Count Guilleminot to declare to the Turks the terms on which Eussia will make peace. Eussia requires the execution of the Treaty of Akerman indemnity (but moderate) for the expenses of the war and the losses sustained by her commerce, for which indemnity, as it seems, she is willing to take Anapa.

She requires the free navigation of the Dardanelles for all nations. This cession to be secured by treaty, not by territorial occupation.

The terms of the Turks are not very dissimilar; but as Count Diebitch has orders to advance till preliminaries are signed, a catastrophe may take place still.

Mr. Gordon managed to get a paper into the Sultan's own hands, which may have led in some measure to this result. He naturally gave credit to the information contained in the Despatches of Count Guilleminot, but the French Government have no authority for their opinion as to the terms on which Russia will make peace. No communication to that effect has been made officially to them.

The French and Eussiaii Ministers at the Conference said they could not act on Mr. Gordon's letter, which is as yet uncorroborated by Count Guilleminot. They could not yet act as if Turkey had acceded to the Treaty of London.

The Eussians would now declare the independence of Greece within the Gulfs of Yolo and Arta, and they wanted Aberdeen to take that instead of the treaty. He thought he could get them to declare the independence of Greece within the Morea that they would be satisfied with that, and that, if they would, we had better secure that for the Turks now, than run the risk of the event of war and of the extension which might be given to the terms which might be forced upon them under the Treaty of London.

However, even admitting that the Eussians would be content with the independence of Greece within the Morea (with Attica [1] by-the-bye), it was the opinion of the Duke and of every one (but Aberdeen) that it would neither be generous nor honourable to force upon the Turks in their distress terms which they, attaching much value to the suzerainete, might think less favour-[1 Attica was still held by the Turks, having been reconquered after its first occupation by the Greeks.]

able than what they might obtain under the Treaty of London, and that we should be drawing ourselves into the embarrassment of what would be practically a new treaty at the moment that we were beginning to entertain hopes of getting out of that which had so long harassed us.

Upon the whole, I think the aspect of Eastern affairs is better than it has been since we have been a Government.

Diebitch is said to have 35,000 men, and a reserve of 40,000. I doubt the reserve being so strong. The 15,000 from Sebastopol have joined.

Paskewitz is made Grand Cross of St. George.

Diebitch will be so, of course.

The King, Peel said, is very blind. He has lost the sight of one eye. The Duke said when he was at Windsor last, the King was particularly civil to him, and Peel and the Duke were both of opinion that the King would be most cordial with the Government if the Duke of Cumberland were away, and was now more so than could be expected under his influence.

Aberdeen seems to have written the letter to Stuart, and Stuart to have communicated it to Prince Polignac. Stuart's idea is that Polignac has had too much to do in fixing himself to think much of foreign politics. He expressed himself, however, disposed to consult with England as to the measures which should be adopted if Eussia should break her engagements.

Several representations have been made to France for the withdrawing of the French troops from the Morea but hitherto without effect. These troops keep the country quiet, and enable the whole force of the Greek State to act offensively. Thus, assisted by French and Eussian money, the Greeks have acquired possession of everything within the Gulfs of Yolo and Arta, except the Island of Negropont.

September 1, 1829.

Bead with attention a paper of Courtney's on Leach's observations. Wrote some memoranda upon it, which I shall send with it to the Duke, when I have got from Shepheard a statement of the benefit derived by the territory from the fixed rate of exchange. It is a valuable paper. I have written to thank him for it, and to ask him to give me the result of his considerations on the mode of transferring the Government of India from the Company to the King, without materially increasing the patronage of the Crown; and likewise the view he takes of the alterations it would be desirable to introduce, if the Company should continue to govern India, in the powers of the Board of Control and in its relations with the Court.

September 3.

The Directors are much afraid of the Eussians. So am I, and the Eussians begin to threaten us. They hint that they have open to them the route to Bagdad, and they announce the presence in Petersburg of an Afghan Chief, and of Ambassadors from Eunjeet Singh.

[93 I feel confident we shall have to fight the Eussians on the Indus, and I have long had a presentiment that I should meet them there, and gain a great battle. All dreams, but I have had them a long time.

I have some idea of a secret letter to Bombay, directing the Government to take possession of the Island of Karak, [1] and of any other tenable point to seal the Euphrates, in the event of the Eussians moving down.

Loch wants to dethrone Eunjeet Singh!

September 4, 1829.

Saw Colonel Willoughby Cotton, who commanded en second in Ava. He has lately visited, as Adjutant-General of King's troops, all the stations of the army in Bengal. He says no army can be in finer order. Lord Combermere has weeded all the old men. The regiments manoeuvre beautifully.

Lord C. wishes to have two King's regiments cantoned under the Himalaya Mountains, where the climate is as good as in England.

Eunjeet. Singh has conquered Cabul and Cashmere. He has French officers at the head of his infantry and cavalry, and about five others. His artillery he keeps under his own family. He has of regular troops 30,000 infantry, and 10,000 cavalry, about eighty guns. All these easily assembled near the capital.

He is old, and when he dies his two sons are likely to quarrel and call us in.

The two ex-Kings of Cabul are living at Ludeana on pensions. Zemaun Shah, the blind King, and his brother, who was King in Mr. Elphinstone's time.

[94 Colonel Cotton speaks most highly of the Madras [1 A small island in the Persian Gulf to the north-west of Bushire] troops. They are more disposable than the Bengal troops, more free from prejudice of caste.

He regrets the reduction of the bodyguard which conducted itself nobly in Ava. I like a guard, and I would have an infantry as well as a cavalry guard, to be formed by picked men.

Colonel Willoughby Cotton says Colonel Skinner is about 55. His son is a merchant, and goes every year into Cashmere for shawls. Skinner has still about 1,300 men, and is quartered not far from Delhi. His people fire the matchlock over the arm at full gallop, and with correct aim. They strike a tent-peg out of the ground with their lances.

September 5.

Eeceived an answer from the Duke. He thinks the question of the six regiments begins to be serious, as the Court throw upon the Government the responsibility of running the risk of a mutiny in the army desires to see the paper, which I have sent him, and says it must go to the Cabinet.

I feel satisfied I am right. If the Cabinet give in to the Court, they weaken my hands so much that I shall be unable to effect any great reform. They make the Directors the real Ministers of India, and almost emancipate the Indian Government. So I told the Duke in my letter.

September 7.

Office. Saw Sir A. Campbell. He came to offer himself for a command in India. I spoke to him of his papers respecting war with the Burmese. He says large boats carrying 100 men could go up to Aeng, the troops need not land at Eamree. He was never an advocate for a diversion at Eangoon, and thinks they make too much fuss about the frontier of Munnipore.

Saw a Mr. Cotton, for a long time collector of Tanjore. He is against introducing the Eyotwaree settlement into that country, and by his account it seems very ill adapted to it, for according to him the Murassi-dars are there really proprietors, and with them the settlement is now made for the village.

I sent for him to tell me about the iron I had understood to be in the neighbourhood of Tanjore; but there is none, it is at Satara. He seems a sensible man, and I must see him again.

The Turks seem to have endeavoured to back out of their accession to the Treaty of London, or rather to clog it with insuperable objections. But Mr. Gordon has brought them back again, and on August 12 all was right, but no Plenipotentiaries sent. The Eussians were said to be moving on Adrianople. They had not above 35,000 men. There is a very bad account from Smyrna of the state of the population in Asia. In fact the Duke of Wellington's prediction is fulfilled. The Turkish Empire is breaking to pieces. By Lord Heytesbury's account the Eussians are very desirous of peace, and very apprehensive that a popular tumult may put an end to the Sultan. It is impossible to see the end of the calamities which would occur, complicated as they would be, if such an event as the dissolution of the Turkish Empire took place.

The new French Ministry is changing the munici-/palities. They hope to succeed at the next elections. Lord Stuart considers M. de la Bourdonnaye as the real head.

Polignac very prudently rests on his oars as to Greece, and properly observes it is idle to make protocols here when the march of events may have altogether changed the state of things before the protocols arrive.

September 8.

Office at 11. Went to the Duke. He read to me a long letter he had written on the question of the six regiments, in which he entered at length into the state of the Indian army such as he knows it to be, and concludes in favour of a revision of the line I had adopted with his approbation. He said the Government of India was wrong every line of the proposed letter abstractedly right; but there was to be considered the expediency of writing it.

I have written a letter to Lord W. Bentinck, stating confidentially the grounds of the change of opinion as to the disbanding of the six extra regiments. I added, 4 However, such an event will not happen in your time, nor I hope in mine," or something to that effect.

September 11.

Chairs at 11. Eead to them the Duke's letter on the six regiments. Told them I had written a private letter to Lord William to relieve his mind from the censure intended for former Governments (a very small portion of which is chargeable on him), and to caution him against similar errors. Gave them the alteration I had intended to make in the draft respecting pensions granted to King's soldiers enlisted into their army. They will consider it.

September 14.

Eead the papers containing the correspondence with the local Governments respecting the provision of stores in India. It is hardly credible, yet it is true, that till within these few years the Medical Board indented upon England for drugs which were produced in India! From Madras as late at 1827 they indented for file handles and blacksmiths' tongs! From Bombay in 1826 for wooden canteens and triangles! It is evident the local Governments have never displayed any energy.

September 16.

Eeceived from the Duke his ideas on the subject of a campaign against Ava. He would hold the great Dagon Temple at Eangoon, but only for the purpose of having vessels in the river to co-operate with the army.

September 17.

To-day has been an idle day. I have done nothing; but I have taken exercise, and so acquired health, without which I cannot do business.

September 20.

Met Mr. Conyngham of the Foreign Office. He told. e the Turks were ready to make the required con-ssions. Of the disposition of the Eussians nothing seems known. E. Gordon has of his own authority ordered up Sir Pulteney Malcolm from Yourla to the

VOL. II. II

Dardanelles. I suppose to carry away Englishmen and their property in the event of an insurrection or of some terrible catastrophe at Constantinople.

Lord Stuart, as I suspected, gives no opinion as to the probable result of the political contest in France.

I had a letter from the Duke respecting half-Batta.

September 24.

Cabinet room. Bead all the letters from Petersburg, Paris, Berlin, and Constantinople during the last fortnight, and the despatches sent during the last month.

E. Gordon seems to have done very well. He and Guilleminot have acted cordially together, and when they had induced the Porte to consent to make peace on the terms prescribed by the Russians, Gordon managed very prudently to get General Muffling to send his secretary to the Eussian head-quarters with the Turkish Plenipotentiaries.

Muffling would have gone with them to the Eeis Effendi had he been well enough; as it was, he sent his secretary, who afterwards went to the Eussian head-quarters and was thus enabled to state distinctly what had passed in the conference held with the Effendi. I think it very possible that without the intervention of the Prussian Minister, who was known to be acquainted with the feelings of the Emperor, General Diebitch would not have agreed to an armistice. The armistice seems to have been made on August 29. We know of it from Seymour at Berlin.

Polignac seems excellently well disposed. He would act cordially with us if he dared. At present he is obliged to cover all he does under the instructions given to Guilleminot by his predecessor under a different state of things, before the great Eussian successes. He talks of a Congress of the Powers interested, and of a joint declaration if Eussia should not adhere to her promise.

Eussia may be kept to her promises by the fear of a revolutionary movement in France. The French Opposition desire the success of the Eussians, the dissolution of the Turkish Empire, and the occupation of the Dardanelles by the Emperor Nicholas, because they know that such events would lead to a sotto sopra in Europe, a general scramble in which they would get the Ehine as their boundary. Generally, I have no doubt, young France wishes for confusion.

Austria is alarmed and would do nothing. The Prussians hold that the existence of the Ottoman Empire is not essential to the balance of power (that is, some of them do), and they would be glad to see Austria and Eussia divide Turkey, Prussia having her compensation in Germany. However, Muffling, going rather beyond his instructions, has been made to do good.

I think all things tend to the preservation of peace if there should be no explosion at Constantinople or in France. The Ottoman Empire seems, however, to be falling to pieces. The Government has been so oppressive that the people will not fight for it. Th. e Sultan has but 4,000 troops, and it is said the appearance of 10,000 Eussians would lead to the capture of Constantinople.

Diebitch seems to dread the catastrophe which might ensue, and the ambassadors have placed before him in strong terms the fatal consequences of an explosion at Constantinople.

I must say R. Gordon has done ably and well.

The rascally Russians have been intriguing with our Ionian subjects, and Aberdeen has written a very strong letter to Lord Heytesbury on the subject.

Polignac, desirous as he is of withdrawing the French troops altogether from the Morea, is at present afraid of doing so.

Aberdeen told me things were not going on well here. The King has quite lost the sight of one eye, and the sight of the other is indistinct. It gives him pain, too, and the fear of blindness makes him nervous. The Duke of Cumberland is always about him, as mischievous as ever, but pretending not to be hostile.

The Duke of Wellington gives the King up as a bad job. He sees him very seldom. At first he liked seeing him and setting things to rights; but he says he found what he did one day was undone the next, and he is in despair. The King has no constancy. There is no depending upon him from one day to another.

Aberdeen says the accession of Eosslyn has not produced the effect we anticipated that Lord Grey is very hostile. What we shall do for a majority next session I know not, but I think we shall stand, [1] although we shall not, I fear, be a strong Government. The [1 This might have been but for the events on the Continent in the year following, which formed a new starting-point in the politics of a large part of Europe.]

101   Catholic Relief Bill has destroyed our unity and the spirit of party. It has likewise destroyed that of the Opposition, who have no longer any rallying point. Thus the formation of a strong Government is difficult. The Brunswickers cannot form one, and the King cannot be persuaded to make one out of the Opposition. Indeed, that the Duke of Cumberland would never advise. The Brunswickers will endeavour to make terms with us as a body to make martyrs of some of the old Protestants, particularly of the Duke and Peel, and placing themselves at the head to go on as well as they could with the rest of us. This will

September 26.

The Chairs, or rather the Court, somewhat impertinently object to the addition I made to a recent draft, recommending an enquiry by practical and scientific men as to the powers India may possess of producing many articles of stores now sent from England. They say this is liable to misconstruction, and then misconstrue it themselves. They suppose these practical men, not being servants of the Company, to sit in judgment upon the proceedings of the military Board. I have corrected their intentional misconstruction, and have acquiesced in the substitution of a draft they propose to send instead, which will, I hope, practically effect my object, and therefore I have said we are willing our object should be attained in the manner most agreeable to the Court of Directors.

It is very lucky I had just sent them my letter about stores. It will appear to be [102 written subsequently to theirs. They think to humbug and to bully me. They will find both difficult.

September 30.

Eead the collection respecting the health of the King's troops. It is incredible to me that so many things should remain to be done nothing seems to have been done that ought to have been done. I fear our finances make the building of new barracks impossible at present. We could not build proper barracks for all the European troops in India much under a million. Still much may be done for their health.

October 5.

Arrived in London at 3. To the Cabinet room, where I found Lord Bathurst, come up to town for Seymour Bathurst's [1] marriage, and afterwards Fitzgerald came in.

Fitzgerald was a fortnight in Ireland, and gives a bad account of it.

A letter from Metternich says peace was actually signed. Sir E. Gordon's despatches give every reason to expect it soon would be. The peace cannot last. I am inclined to think it would have been better for the Russians to have occupied Constantinople, and for the Ottoman Empire to have been overthrown that we might have known at once where we were, than to have had such a peace as this. It is practically present occupation (for a year) of more than they now hold, [1 Hon. Seymour Bathurst, fourth son of third Earl Bathurst, married October 6, 1829, Julia, daughter of John Peter Hankey, Esq.]

for they are to have the fortresses ceded to them. They exact 750,000 for the pretended losses of their merchants, and five millions for themselves. The indemnity to the merchants to be paid by three instalments. On the payment of the first, Adrianople and a few places on the coast to be given up. On the payment of the second everything to the Balkan, and on the third Bulgaria. These payments occupy a year.

The five millions are to be paid in ten years, or sooner if the Turks can manage it. The Principalities to be occupied till the payment. The Turks to confirm the Government established during the ten years, and not to impose any taxes for two years more.

All the fortresses on the left bank to be destroyed. None of the islands to belong to Turkey. No Turk to enter the principalities. The princes to be for life. All payments in kind from the Principalities to cease, and instead the Turks and the princes to agree upon a compensation I It is unnecessary to go through the other articles relative to the Principalities. The treaty contains a real cession of them to Eussia.

The terms as to the navigation of merchantmen, their not being searched in a Turkish port, the refusal of acquiescence in the demands of the Eussian Minister where any injury is pretended, to have been done to a Eussian, to be just ground for reprisal, c., are of a nature intolerable to an independent Power, and not to be carried into execution.

On the side of Asia everything is ceded that can enable Eussia to attack either Turkey or Persia with advantage.

The terms imposed with regard to indemnities are extravagant and altogether contrary to all the Emperor's promises. He has not deceived us; but he has lied to us most foully. Sir E. Gordon seems to have done all that could be done. Perhaps he has saved Constantinople from conflagration, and the Empire from dissolution. He has managed to settle the Greek question, Turkey consenting to everything the allies may de 31 termine under the protocol of March 22. Sir E. Gordon has taken upon himself to order up the English ships, and Guilleminot has ordered up the French ships, but they were still at Smyrna when the dispatch came away. These ships, it is hoped, may be some check on the Eussians, and ostensibly they only go up to Constantinople to save Christians. However, if the Eussians advance they will probably lead the Turks to fight. Gordon and Guilleminot have very properly told the Sultan they will remain by him in any case.

The Turks declare the terms are, as regards payment, such as they have really no means of complying with. The allies will make representations to Petersburg to obtain a relaxation of these conditions.

In the meantime, while this was doing at Constantinople, Lord Heytesbury was asking Nesselrode what the terms he intended to propose were, and Nesselrode would not tell him. Lord Heytesbury's despatch and Gordon's are both dated on September 10. The 12th was to be the day of signature.

Lord Stuart by Aberdeen's directions has been pressing Polignac very hard to withdraw the French troops from the Morea, and Polignac has been obliged to plead the weakness of his Government, and to put off Lord Stuart by referring it to the Conference. I should say from what the papers show of Polignac that he will not stand. I do not know what his antagonists may be, but he is evidently not a powerful man.

A Liberal told Fitzgerald their object was now in France to make the King of the Netherlands King of France, and give Holland to Prussia, taking Belgium and everything to the Ehine to themselves.

I should say things looked ill everywhere, and unless we can make the Emperor of Eussia fear a convulsion in France, and determine to recede from some of his stipulations with Turkey to satisfy the rest of Europe, we shall have war, and war under the most unfavourable circumstances that is, if Austria be not as pusillanimous as she may be weak, for she ought never to consent to the establishment of the Eussians on the Danube.

The only line for the Turks to pursue is to promise everything; to endeavour to perform everything, and to withdraw to Asia, leaving the rest of Europe to settle who shall have Constantinople. Now they could not do that, as they are too weak; but six months hence they may.

We dine with the Duke on Wednesday and shall then, I suppose, determine what we are to do.

October 7.

Cabinet at 3. All present except Lord Melville.

Aberdeen read a paper he had written before the peace was known, the object of which was to show that the Ottoman Empire was dissolved, and that it could not be reconstituted; that our views with regard to Greece should now change with circumstances, and that we should endeavour to make it a substantive state. To Turkey it could no longer signify whether Greece had a more extended or more limited line of frontier, and our desire should be to place a fit man upon the throne. France is willing to propose in the Conference that to Turkey should be offered the alternative of a Greece with extended limits under Suzerainete, c., according to the Protocol of March 22, or a Greece with narrower limits, entirely independent.

The Duke said we must first have satisfaction for the insertion of the Article in the treaty of peace which bound Turkey to the Protocol of March 22; Eussia, as a party to the Treaty of London, having no right to settle that treaty herself. Next, we should insist on an armistice between the Greeks and Turks.

We must recollect that Turkey had bound herself to acquiesce in the decision of the Conference upon the Greek Treaty that is, to defer to our mediation. Could we, as mediators, propose to Turkey to cede Attica, Negropont, and other possessions she now holds? and would we willingly bring the frontiers of the Greek state into contact with our Ionian Islands?

If Greece were to have a sovereign, Prince Philip of Hesse Homburg would be the best man for us Austria would prefer him. France admitted that the wishes of Austria ought to be consulted.

France, however, rather wished for Prince Charles of Bavaria. Eussia for a Duke of Saxe-Weimar.

Aberdeen seemed to think there would be no great difficulty in carrying our point, and having Prince Philip of Hesse Homburg.

Peel said he thought we could not allow a treaty such as that signed by Turkey to pass without a remonstrance on our part. We referred to a letter of Dudley's, and to Aberdeen's recent instruction to Lord Heytes-bury, and likewise to the various declarations of moderation put forth by the Emperor Nicholas. Several ways were started of expressing our opinion a sort of circular to the Powers which signed the Treaty of the Congress a declaration to Parliament.

The Duke suggested a remonstrance to the Emperor Nicholas to be communicated in the first instance only to Eussia.

This seems likely to be adopted, but we are to have another Cabinet to-morrow.

In whatever we do we must endeavour to keep Austria out of the scrape, for there is nothing the Eus-sians would like so much as the opportunity of marching to Vienna.

Not only it would be romantic for us alone to go to war to maintain the balance of power, but it would, in this case, be absurd indeed, for, if our armies had driven the Eussians out of Turkey, we could not reconstitute the Turkish Empire. It is dissolved in its own weakness.

Great dissatisfaction was expressed, and justly, at the conduct of Lord Heytesbury, who has been humbugged by the Eussians all along.

The King has run up a bill of 4,000. for clothes in six months. All the offices of the Household, except the Chamberlain's, which has 1,900. in hand, are falling into arrear, and if there should be an arrear upon the whole civil list, it must come before Parliament.

Fitzgerald gives a very bad account of trade generally.

The King does not like us better than he did, and the Duke of Cumberland means to keep his son in England, and educate him here, taking the 6,000. a year. He wants to drive the Government to make him Viceroy of Hanover.

The Cabinet dined with the Duke.

October 8.

Cabinet at 3. A great deal of conversation of which the result was that a remonstrance should be made to Eussia on the subject of the terms of the peace. This remonstrance will temperately but strongly, more by statement of facts than by observations, show that the peace is not such as the Emperor had given us reason to expect he would require, and that it in reality threatens the existence of the Turkish Empire; that the destruction of that Empire would seriously affect the peace of Europe by changing the relative position of the several States.

Aberdeen wants a guarantee of the territorial possessions of Turkey, not of its Government. [I]I think no one 1 It is observable that this guarantee seems to have said nothing of the internal system of government, and so far to have been unconditional. It would therefore have gone considerably beyond the Anglo-Turkish Convention of 1878. It would also have applied to Europe as well as Asia. It is a commentary on the statement of Mr. Gladstone, in later days a colleague of Lord Aberdeen, that no statesman whom he had known in former times would ever have listened to the idea of such an engagement.

seems much inclined to agree with him. Such a guarantee would impose obligations without conferring rights upon us. It would be a guarantee which would give rise to infinite complications, and which would embarrass us very much.

Without a guarantee we may succeed in bringing the great States to an understanding that the distribution of the Turkish territories, in the event of the falling to pieces of that State, must be a subject for the decision of a Congress.

Austria has expressed herself very frankly. She is ready to do anything. She sees the danger and desires to know our view of it. The real view of France does not seem to be very different; but there is no dependence to be placed upon a Government trembling for its life. Prussia will be satisfied with the peace. Her sovereign is very weak, and the Prussians think their interest is served by the progress of Eussia in a direction contrary to them, and in which she menaces Austria.

The smuggling case is said to tell against Lord Stuart. He writes unintelligibly, and the French will not trust him so I shall not be sorry if we can get rid of him.

With Lord Heytesbury we are all dissatisfied, and have been from the beginning. There is a Council on Monday, and we have a Cabinet on Sunday at 3, when we are to hear Aberdeen's letter, and may probably have the Treaty.

There seems a determination to effect an armistice by force if the Conference will not order it in Greece.

We have nine good ships there. The Eussians seven bad ones, and the French two.

Before the Conference can proceed the 10th Article of the Treaty of Peace must be declared non avenu that which obliges the Porte to accept the Protocol of March 22 all negotiation upon that Protocol having been committed by Eussia to the French and English Ambassadors, and it having been expressly reserved to the Porte by us, that her objections should be fairly weighed.

The French have taken advantage of the peace to order their troops home from the Morea.

October 9.

Eead many of the Protocols of the early Conferences after the Eussian declaration of war. I shall to-morrow read these again carefully and sketch my State paper.

If I was in opposition I should describe the details relative to the Principalities, as showing the moderation of the thief who would stipulate that men should sleep with their doors open, till they have ransomed themselves by paying their uttermost farthing.

October 10.

Eeceived a letter from Sir J. Malcolm. He seems pleased with the secret dispatches relative to Persia and the Pacha of Bagdad. He seems upon the whole very much gratified, and very grateful.

He strongly presses the appointment of an Indian as his successor, and mentions Sir Ch. Metcalfe and Jenkins,

He likewise mentions a Mr. Chaplin, of whom I never heard. I take Jenkins to be a cleverer man than Sir Ch. Metcalfe, [I] who rather disappoints me.

Had three letters by Petersburg from Colonel Mcdonald, the last dated in August. The Persians, thoroughly alarmed, are doing all they can to satisfy the Emperor Nicholas by punishing the persons engaged in the massacre of the Eussian mission; but they had an insurrection to quell on banishing the High Priest, who was at the head of all. As they conclude all the bad characters had a hand in it they mean to take the opportunity of punishing them. Paskewitz is said to have from 20,000 to 22,000 men to have sustained no loss in the late engagements, but to suffer from the plague. At Erzeroum the Mahometans are not only satisfied, but well pleased. The Government of a Eussian general is better than that of a Turkish Pasha.

The Prince Abbas Mirza is at last doing something towards making an army. Major Hart, alone, however, keeps it together. The troops are as yet ill-armed, but they have their pay. Mcdonald thinks the King not likely to live long. He wants a cypher.

October 11, Sunday.

Came up from "Worthing to a Cabinet. Before we met read the last letters from Lord Heytesbury, which show a degree of infatuation respecting the Eussians, which is quite wonderful.

Before we began to talk Eothschild called out the Duke of Wellington, and offered at once all the money [1 Afterwards Lord Metcalfe]

to pay the Russian Indemnity. He said he only wanted the guarantee of England! If the Russians remained in the Principalities there would be a general war.

Irvine, an English loan jobber, saw the Duke yesterday with the same offer.

The joke is that Eothschild is to pay the money for the Turks, and to be made King of Jerusalem.

Aberdeen began by begging w e would first settle the Greek question. He brought a paper the Eussians were willing to deliver in containing a sort of apology for the 10th Article, and declaring that it by no means interfered with the powers of the Conference. We took a great deal of time in considering whether we should not suggest some alteration in this paper some is to be proposed not very essential.

We had a long discussion as to the name of the new State. At last it seemed to be thought ' Sovereign Prince of Greece' was the best.

Aberdeen thinks he shall have little difficulty about the Prince. The Eussians agree to the description given; but I dare say they imagine we mean to describe a different man. I suspect they think we want to give them Leopold.

Aberdeen read a letter he proposed sending to Lord Stuart, the purport of which was that we wanted to know what he meant to do towards redeeming France from the responsibility she had incurred and made us incur by giving instructions to Count Guilleminot, stating the terms of peace and the moderation of the Emperor instructions which misled our Ambassador, and in-/duced the two Ambassadors to give assurances to the Porte which events proved to be unfounded.

The letter, I think, likewise desired him to enquire in what form our joint representations as to the amount of the indemnity were to be made. To these the Ambassadors have pledged the two Cabinets.

There was a great deal more in the letter which is to be left out. It went into the details of the treaty, or rather of its effects.

The offer is to be made to the Turks of an independent Greece, from the Gulf of Yolo to Missolonghi, or of a Greece under Suzerainete, with Negropont, and the line from Volo to the Gulf of Arta.

I think we are all agreed that at the commencement of the war it was our interest to take as little as possible from Turkey that now it is our interest to make Greece substantive State, which may hereafter receive the debris of the Ottoman Empire. [1]

As to the really important matter, the remonstrance to Eussia, nothing was done. Nothing is, I conclude, written, and Aberdeen does not like Cabinet criticism, nor do I think the Cabinet at all agreed as to what should be said. Dudley's letters used to occupy us for days, and certainly they were the better for it although we lost a good deal of time occasionally.

Aberdeen said he would send it to me. I think I shall write an esquisse myself. We are to have no more [1 This may explain the apparently illiberal views of many of the Cabinet as to the Greek boundaries. They saw the difficulty of any halting place outside the Isthmus of Corinth, short of a wider boundary even than that ultimately adopted.]

VOL. II.

114 Cabinets for some time. The Chancellor wishes to have the remaining fortnight of his holidays uninterrupted.

October 12.

Went to town at quarter-past one. To the Foreign Office. The treaty arrived last night. Lord Aberdeen took it with him to Windsor. It differs materially from the projet. The Articles respecting indemnity are relegues to a separate transaction. The payment of 100,000 ducats is to lead to the evacuation of Adrianople; 400,000 form the next payment, then 500,000, and 500,000, making the sum originally demanded for individual losses; but, as I understand Mr. Backhouse, eighteen months must elapse before Turkey can be evacuated to the Danube. I had much conversation with him as to other points. On looking into the Act of the Congress I find the Powers adhering to it may be considered as binding themselves not to disturb the territorial arrangements that Act establishes; but they are not bound to maintain them. Thus if France appropriated to herself Spain, she would violate the treaty, but no Power signing the treaty would be obliged, by virtue of that Act, to make war upon France for doing so.

That the general treaty contains no guarantee is evident from the specific guarantee of the cessions made by Saxony to Prussia, which would have been unnecessary if the spirit of the treaty had been that of existent guarantee.

October 13.

Cabinet room. Found Lord Eosslyn there. Eead the treaty.

ATTITUDE OF RUSSIA TO PEKSIA. 115

115 The King was very well yesterday. The Eecorder's Eeport was so long that half was deferred.

The last dispatches from Persia, which arrived on Friday, were opened at the Foreign Office, and read by everybody. Aberdeen sent them to the Duke, who has probably taken them to "Walmer in his carriage. The Chairs sent for them, and could not get them. I must put a stop to this. I have written to Lord Heytesbury to beg he will in future forward letters to their address.

Wrote a ' proposed draft' to Lord Heytesbury, directing him, if he should have reason to think the Eus-sians intend to exact further concession from Persia, to intimate that such an attempt will be considered by his Majesty as unfriendly to himself as an Asiatic Power. I doubt my getting the Duke to agree to the sending of this despatch; but I shall try.

October 14,

Carried my proposed letter to Lord Heytesbury to Aberdeen, who agrees to send it with a trifling alteration, at least one not very important. Eead to him my proposed letter to Lord Heytesbury on the Peace of Adrianople. He seemed to approve of great part of it. He has done nothing at his yet, and seems to think there is no hurry!

We shall stand very ill in Parliament if we have nothing to show. I think mine is a good cadre of a letter, but that specific instructions should be given to Lord Heytesbury as to what he shall endeavour to obtain in a separate despatch.

Eead my drafts to Lord Eosslyn after dinner. He seemed to think the view I took was the right, and that much of what I had written was very good, but that it might be shortened. So I think.

October 15.

Henry copied the draft to Lord Heytesbury, for the Duke, to whom I sent it with a letter.

Showed the Chairs the draft to Lord Heytesbury on Persia. They were much pleased with it. So was old Jones. Sent it to the Duke. In little doubt his approving it.

Eeceived from the Duke the Persian despatches which I gave to the Chairs. The Duke had not read them.

Eeceived from him a letter on the subject of half-Batta. He says as an officer he should have thought there was a compromise in 1801. That it should be looked into as a question of economy. That above all things in dealing with an army you must be just

The Duke thinks the publication of the letter of Lord Combermere's secretary indiscreet and wicked, and is very angry with Lord Combermere.

A letter will be written to the Government on the subject, directing enquiry.

October 19, Sunday.

Eead Mcdonald's despatches from Persia, and sent them to the Duke, with a letter suggesting the heads of a letter to the Envoy.

The Eussians have given up one of the two crores due, and allow five years for paying the other. They mean, therefore, to rule Persia by influence. However, there is a good Mahometan and Anti-Eussian feeling beyond the Euphrates, and if mischief happens, it is our fault.

Eeceived a letter from Hardinge respecting half-Batta. He is for standing firm and giving some general boon, as an addition to marching money, to the whole army. That is my idea. I am sure it is the safest course.

Wrote to Loch, suggesting it, and at the same time advised him to answer the paragraphs respecting half-Batta, and not give misrepresentations too much head.

October 20.

Two letters from the Duke, written very hastily. It evident he did not like my making a sketch of a letter to Lord Heytesbury, and that he does not like, any difference of opinion as to the Batta question.

On the first point I still think I was right. He mentions some ideas of Eussia ordering Diebitch across the Balkan, and even the Danube, of her giving up the Principalities, c. In short he says all we know is that there is a peace we do not know what it is and it would be ridiculous to remonstrate against we know not what.

My draft was written before these reports were spread; and I only, from anxiety to have the despatch well written and soon, sketched what I thought would do.

As to the reports, I have told Aberdeen I cannot believe Eussia has on a sudden ceased to be ambitious, or to use perfidy as a mode of accomplishing ambitious ends. She may give out she will make these changes she may make some but her object is to prevent all combination on the part of Austria, France, and England If we do not remonstrate against what is signed, we shall lose all credit, if that which is executed should be comparatively favourable, and we shall incur great blame if no relaxation takes place. A remonstrance might be so worded as to do no harm to Turkey or to Europe, and to do good to us.

The Duke's other letter was on the Batta question, upon which he does not like contradiction, yet I think his course would lead to continued demands on the part of all the armies. I have told him I shall be in town to see the Chairs on Saturday, and will try to see him on Friday, and, if he wishes, bring the Chairs to him on Saturday.

October 21.

Keceived a long confused letter from Fitzgerald upon my project of a draft to Lord Heytesbury. He was at Sudborn, [1] where the Duke was. The Duke was not so much inclined to think the Eussians would make any considerable concessions as Aberdeen, but he thought, and had made Fitzgerald think, it would be premature to remonstrate. I have written to Fitzgerald and told him my opinion more at length than I told Aberdeen yesterday

October 23.

Cabinet room. Bead the despatches from Petersburg and Paris. All the hints of the Emperor of [1 Seat of Lord Hertford, in Suffolk] Eussia's intention of not retaining his army in Turkey come through Paris, Nesselrode having on September 29 spoken thus specifically to the Duke de Mortemart, and merely talked about taking less money and making some change in the guarantees to Lord Heytesbury. I did not see Aberdeen, who was engaged with the Spanish Minister.

I do not depart from my original idea that Eussia does all this to gain time, and with as much perfidy as she has shown throughout.

Polignac would take a loyal view if he durst.

I cannot see the Duke till Monday, as he does not return to London till Sunday evening.

I saw Hardinge and had a long talk with him about Batta, c.

October 24. Chairs at 11.

The Chairs say the Court have the matter entirely in their hands as to Batta. They wish to have the opinion of the Cabinet, and to be governed by that. I have written to the Duke to tell him so.

I am glad there is to be a Cabinet, because I think a Cabinet will take a more popular view of the question than the Duke, and, as I think, a juster view. I am for standing firm.

The Duke's letter on Persian affairs arrived while I was with the Chairs. I read it to them. The Duke suggests that Mcdonald should raise his escort in Persia an excellent idea. He objects to Major Hart having an assignment of land. He thinks Willock may be recalled. The officers not; but if the prince will pay them, so much the better. I think the Duke may be right as to the assignments of land. Upon all the other points I entirely agree with him. Eead last night a letter of Lushington's, or rather a minute, which shows he is determined to remain.

Cabinet room. Cunningham came in and showed me a draft of Aberdeen's to our Minister in Spain on the recognition by Spain of Don Miguel finding excuses for Spain, and saying we cannot do it. What I saw was the brouillon which had been sent to the Duke. It had his observations in pencil, and it seems Aberdeen sends all his proposed despatches to him and alters them at his suggestion. Certainly Aberdeen, left to himself, would be a very incautious writer.

October 26.

Office early. Saw Captain Hanchett on the subject of the navigation of the Eed Sea. He was there two years and a half. He says in going in you should make Aden and wait there for a wind. Water can be had there. Avoid Mocha, where the anchorage is dangerous and the water bad, and go to the Island of Cameran, then straight up in mid channel. All the dangers are visible, and in the mid channel there are none. Cosseir a good little harbour, the danger is going up to Suez; but that easy for a steamer. He worked with topgallant sails against the north-west monsoon. There is a breeze along shore at all times. The danger has been occasioned by the timid sailing of the Arabs, who always hug the shore, and anchor at night.

October 27.

I omitted yesterday to mention that at the Foreign Office I saw some despatches just received from Sir E. Gordon. I think the date of the first was October 2. He had the day before at last got the Turks to ratify the treaty, but it seems there was a hitch, and until the ratification the officers did not set off to stop hostilities in Asia. A Pasha had advanced on Philippopoli and General Geismar on Sophia. Diebitch threatened to advance on Constantinople. However, the day after he wrote his threatening letter he must have received the ratifications. The Sultan is very anxious to get the Egyptian fleet to Constantinople, probably as a pledge for the allegiance of the Pasha, and to show his greatest vassal obeys him. The Turks say it is the moral effect of the presence of the fleet on their own subjects that they want, that they have no idea of not acting faithfully. Sir E. Gordon assures me they mean to preserve the peace and must.

He has written the representation the Turkish ambassador is to present to the Emperor. It would be a good remonstrance for us, but it is not a good one for the Turks. It is very well written, but it is quite European in its style, and the Eussians will at once know, as I did, the author.

The Turks intended to send a splendid embassy to Petersburg, and Halil Pasha, once the slave of the Seraskier, now the Sultan's son-in-law, was to have been the ambassador. He is their least officer. However, Diebitch tells them they must not send it till they have the Emperor's consent. The Turks have ready the first 100,000 ducats, to get the Eussians out of Adrianople.

I should say from these despatches that things do not look peaceful.

October 28.

Had a letter yesterday from Mr. Elphinstone on Nazarre. It appears to be a fine on descents, c., of Jaghire lands. I think his opinion will be different from Sir J.

Malcolm's the latter wishing to make the Jaghires hereditary, or rather to give a fee simple interest to the actual proprietor. Mr. Elphinstone, on the contrary, thinking they should be resumed on death without heirs.

October 29.

Eead a work just published by Colonel de Lacy Evans, on the practicability of a Eussian invasion of India. The route would be first to China, across a desert from the shores of the Caspian from China by water up the Oxus, to within 550 miles of Attock. The great difficulty is between the end of the river, and the southern side of the Hindoo Koosh. This difficulty, however, has been often surmounted, and the road is constantly travelled by caravans.

I think it is clear that the invasion of India could not be attempted till the third year; but when should we begin to take precautions? A Government wholly Asiatic would not be still if the Eussians took possession of China; but ours, chained by European politics, would hardly move if they entered Cabul.

We ought to have full information as to Cabul, Bokhara, and China.

My letter of last year directed tlie attaining of information; but I dare say nothing has been done.

October 30.

Eeceived a Memorial from Mr. Fullerton, asking some remuneration beyond his salary for past services. He has a claim if we were rich. I think he should have 10,000 dollars. I dare say he thinks 20,000. Thoughtless extravagance is the destruction of generosity and even of justice.

Upon the subject of the invasion of India my idea is that the thing is not only practicable, but easy, unless we determine to act as an Asiatic Power. On the acquisition of Khiva by the Eussians we should occupy Lahore and Cabul. [1]It is not on the Indus that an enemy is to be met. If we do not meet him in Cabul, at the foot of the Hindoo Koosh, or in its passes, we had better remain in the Sutlege. If the Eussians once occupy Cabul they may remain there with the Indus in their front, till they have organised insurrection in our rear, and completely equipped their army. I fear there are passes from Balkh upon Peshawur. If these could be closed and the enemy poured upon Cabul we should know where to meet him. Istow we, being at Cabul, might be cut off from its resources by the descent of the enemy upon Peshawur.

There is some road from Eoondorg through Cashmere, but I do not fear that. The road an enemy[1 It may be remembered that Lord Ellenborougli strongly disapproved of any occupation of Afghanistan, or interference with its internal affairs, in 1840-42. At that time Russia had not advanced to Khiva. It is clear that he would not have held the same opinion as to our policy towards Afghanistan after the events of 1873-74] would choose would be that by the Valley of the Cachgu.

We know nothing of these passes, nothing of the country beyond them, nothing of the course of the Indus but we should have full information so as to be able to crush an advancing enemy, by making the whole country hostile, which money would do.

To meet an invasion we must raise every regiment to 1,000 men.

168 Regiments 360 1,008 504 60,480 Men, besides Artillery. 4,000 King's Inf. raised to 1,000 each Reg. 1,000 Do. four Regiments of Cavalry. 4,000 Four new Regiments. 2,000 Two new Cavalry.

Besides King's Artillery.

71,480

Besides the increase which would take place in the Irregular Corps, particularly in Skinner's.

A smaller increase than this would not be sufficient; for we should require 20,000 men at Delhi, 20,000 in Lahore, and 60,000 in Cabul. I speak of enrolled, not effectives but with these augmentations the Kegu-lar Army would only be 148,000 N. I. 24,000 King's.

172,000 20,000 Native Cavalry. 6,000 King's.

198,000

The out provisional battalions, local corps, c., of 198,000,1 do not think above 100,000 could possibly be disposable 4, and there would not be 70,000 effectives. The Artillery must be very numerous. I omitted the Company's English Kegiments, about 3,000 men.

Of all nations the Eussians are the least adapted for an enterprise of this nature. They have neither medical staff nor commissariat, and the men are without resource. A French army would be the best. I doubt the possibility of Eussia bringing more than 20,000 men to Cabul, and these could not descend the mountains till the third year, if Cabul was occupied. What I fear is an occupation of Khiva unknown to us. No preparation on our part no marching forward so that in three or four months from leaving Khiva the enemy might be at Cabul. I am sure we can defeat the enterprise. We ought to defeat it before the enemy reaches the Indus. If 20,000 Eussians should reach the Indus, it will be a sharp fight.

November 1, 1829.

A letter from the Duke. He returned the papers I sent him. He has doubts as to the expediency of making the Commissary-General of Stores I proposed; but he seems to have supposed I wished to do away with the Military Board. I have explained what I meant.

He approves of my suggestions as to correspondence, but thinks every paper must be sent home, and the collections formed here. I have explained that I always intended every paper should be sent home, and I have told him that I had the opinion of the clerks I consulted that the collections might be framed in India, with a saving of time, and without diminishing the check on the local Governments.

November 4.

Eeceived from Aberdeen his draft of a remonstrance to Eussia, which, it seems, must be sent at last. He has already shown it to the Duke and Peel.

There is no great substantive objection to it; but it is not very carefully written. I shall send it to him tomorrow with many proposed alterations. In the second box came Gally Knight's letter to Aberdeen; which is a poor, flimsy production. A peacock's feather in the hilt of a Drawcansir's sword.

November 5.

Altered, not only verbally, but substantially, Aberdeen's paper, and sent it to him.

Cabinet room. Eead a Memorandum by Lord Hey-tesbury, of a conversation he has had with the Emperor of Eussia. The Emperor expects the early downfall of the Porte and a Eevolution in France. Asks if another march to Paris would be possible?

Lord Heytes-bury saw Nesselrode afterwards and told him what the Emperor had said. Nesselrode said the Emperor always saw things en noir. He had a different opinion. He did not think the Porte in immediate danger, nor did he expect a French Eevolution.

[1 H. Gally Knight. Best known for his works on the Normans in Sicily, and Ecclesiastical Architecture in Italy.]

(2) The other guarantees they talk of are further cessions in Asia, specifically Batoum, or the occupation of Varna, or Silistria, instead of the Principalities. The latter is worse, and the Turks will probably consent to neither. They do not value the Principalities, and they know Europe does. [1]

November 6.

Saw Aberdeen. He is always gloomy about divisions. He is afraid of an attack on Foreign Policy. He thinks the two parties will unite in that. He hears there has been some approximation between Lord Grey (2) and Lord Holland. At the same time it is said there is a notion of bringing in Lord Grey. I suspect this report to have been fabricated by the Ultra-Tories to annoy the King.

He thinks the Duke is annoyed, more particularly at the King's not treating him well, and at his Government not being well supported.

In fact, however, it is a Government which will not fall, for the King hates the Whigs; the people do not regard them. He may like the Tories, but he knows they cannot make a Government, and the Duke's Administration has four-fifths of the country.

Eeceived a letter from the Duke, telling me he had settled Colonel Mcdonald's knighthood, and asking me if I should be ready to talk about India on the 13th. I [1 The Principalities, as commanding the lower course of the Danube, were all important to Austria especially. Thus, occupation by Russia, while it would have been felt as a menace to Central Europe, would have left Turkey a compact state beyond the Danube.

2 Lord Grey had been separated from the bulk of the Whig party since their junction with Canning in 1827.]

28 said about Batta certainly; about India I had rather talk first to Lord Melville and him.

Wrote to the Duchess of Kent telling her a Bengal cavalry cadetship was at her disposal for the son of Colonel Harvey.

There is a very interesting letter from an English officer at Adrianople with respect to the state of the Eussian army. It has suffered and suffers most dreadfully.

I told Aberdeen if I had seen the account of the conversation between Lord Heytes-bury and the Emperor Nicholas before I read his proposed letter, I should have suggested that much stress should have been laid upon the effect the downfall of Turkey would have upon affairs in France.

Polignac seems confident he can stand. He thinks he has the Chambers. The French behave ill in the settlement of the Greek business, and object altogether to our man, Prince Philip of Hesse Homburg. They equally object to Prince Frederick of Orange, and to Prince Leopold, whom Eussia would have had willingly. I wonder Aberdeen did not laugh when he was proposed. They want to settle the thing without a Prince. I suppose they want a Frenchman.

Aberdeen is for settling Greece as a 'tower into whose lap the broken parts of Turkey may fall. He gives up Eubcea. That is, the surrender of Euboea is to be proposed to the Porte, with a frontier limited in other respects, instead of the protocol of March 22.

The Turks who have left the Morea have no indemnity. The Turks who are in the other parts of the new Greece remain. It is altogether a wonderful business. These anti-revolutionary States combining to revolutionise a rebellious province of an unoffending ally!

November 11.

It seems the French do not like the idea of giving to the Turks the option of an independent State with smaller limits, or of a State under Suzerainete with extended limits, contrary to the treaty, and sending at the same time secret instructions to the Ambassadors to insist upon the entire independence of the new Greek State. The French seem likewise to have been offended at the protocol having been settled between Eussia and us, before they were called in to give their opinion. No wonder. Certainly our diplomacy has not succeeded. We have failed in all our objects.

November 13.

Cabinet. I was first called upon to say my say upon the general Indian question. I observed that the present prospective deficiency was one million a year. That until we could ascertain whether that deficiency could be diminished or done away with we were really not ourselves prepared to come to a decision upon the future government of India; nor would Parliament endure that the China trade should be closed upon the country for twenty years more without first inquiring whether it was necessary. The first question was, 4 Can we make such a reduction of expenditure, or effect such an increase in income as to enable the Government of idia to go on without any assistance direct or indirect VOL. n. K from England?" If it can, then we have the China trade in our hands. If it cannot, we have to decide whether the necessary assistance shall be found by means of a continuance of the monopoly or in some other manner.

I stated the increase of two millions in six years in the civil charges of Bengal; that the Court had issued the strongest instructions, and the local Government seemed to have a real intention to curtail expenditure. That I had done something, and should do all I could, investigating every item. Peel suggested a commission. I said that had occurred to me last year. The Duke, however, objected to a commission as really superseding the Governor-General and being the Government. Another objection certainly is the delay. Difficulties would be thrown in its way, and we should at last be obliged to decide without its final report, having thrown away our time here in waiting for it.

I mentioned that the character of the local Government was ' disrespect and disobedience." That nothing but a long continuance of strict rule could bring India into real subjection. It was this disobedience which was the chief source of increased expenditure. It arose in a great measure from the unequal hand which had been held over them the indulgence of the Court of Directors and the great delays in the communication with India arising out of the system of correspondence. I had endeavoured to remedy that, and hoped to get an answer to letters within the year. It was now two years and

[131] a half. I had likewise endeavoured to make arrangements for steam commu-nication by the Red Sea. I hoped to be able to send a letter to Bombay in sixty days.

The Cabinet seemed generally to acquiesce in the expediency of only having a Committee this year.

At first they all seemed to think the continuance of the government in the Company a matter of course. I told them that even with the China trade the Government could not now go on without great reductions of expenditure, and that I hoped the Cabinet would not come to a hasty decision upon a question involving so many important political and financial considerations. The present system was not one of great expense, but it was one involving great delay and delay was expense, and not only expense but abandonment of authority. It was in this point of view that I hoped the Cabinet would look at the question when it came before them.

I mean to go quietly to work; but I mean, if I can, to substitute the King's government for that of the Company. [1] I am sure that in doing so I shall confer a great benefit upon India and effect the measure which is most likely to retain for England the possession of India.

We afterwards spoke of the Batta question. I read Lord Wellesley's letter, and stated the opinions of Sir J. Malcolm, Sir Archibald Campbell, and Sir J. Mcholls.

I stated that it seemed the feeling in the army was excited more by the apprehension of further reductions than by the establishment of the half-Batta stations; that if concessions were made to the Bengal army, the [1 This was not carried out till 1858, [132] after the great mutiny.] & other armies would be discontented and further demands would be made.

The Duke said, as a soldier, and having been in India at the time, he must say he thought the orders of 1828 [1] a breach of faith but these having been issued, he thought we must stand to them. The general opinion was that as nothing could be said or done till the arrival of despatches, there could be no necessity for deciding.

I mentioned my Supreme Court Bill, which will be ready immediately.

I hope to save ultimately 60,000. a year in the Supreme Courts.

1,000 on each Judge 9,000 1 Judge at Calcutta 5,000 1 Judge at M. and B 8,000 Recorder's Court 8,000

Fees at Calcutta 30,000 60,000 Ireland is put off till Monday, that we may all read the papers. We dine with the Duke to-morrow.

The French oppose all the people we name for the Greek coronet. They have named Prince Charles of Bavaria, and the second son of the King of Bavaria with a regency till he is of age! However, this folly they did not press.

We first named Prince Philip of Hesse Homburg, whom the French would not hear of. Then Leopold!

[1 Orders issued by Lord William Bentinck, abolishing full batta or the larger scale of allowances to the military at stations where half-batta only had been recognised, before the Act of the Bengal Government allowing full batta in consideration of officers providing themselves with quarters. See Thornton's British India, pp. 221-25.]

[133] They did not like him. Prince Emilius of Hesse Darmstadt was thought of. The French have suggested Prince John of Saxony, second son of the King, a fine young

man, about 28, but unknown. His elder brother too may soon succeed to the throne, and he has no children. Otherwise there is no objection to this Prince.

It seems to me they are running after trifles. Eussia adheres to us as to the Prince, or rather remains neutral, thinking I have no doubt that France and England will quarrel about the feather.

The secret instruction which it was proposed to give to the Ambassadors is now abandoned, France having objected. They were to have been ordered to insist upon Turkey taking one of two things of which she was to have ostensibly the pure option. Now they are only clearly to intimate their wish. However, it seems Eussia will take a million of ducats less if Turkey will make Greece independent. That is, she will give up a claim to what she cannot get in order to effect that she has no right to ask.

The French Government have, by giving new rates of pension, got 1,600 old officers out of the army, and filled important stations with friends of their own. They think they shall stand.

I forgot to mention the Archduke Maximilian of Modena as one of the persons talked of for Greece. It seems uncertain whether any one of these Princes would take the coronet.

November 14, Saturday.

Cabinet room. Eosslyn and afterwards Lord Bath-urst there. Eead the Irish papers, that is, Lord Francis Leveson's private letters to Peel and Peel's to him, with a letter from Peel to Leslie Foster, asking his opinion as to education and Maynooth, and Foster's reply. The latter is important. He thinks the political and religious hostility of the two parties is subsiding. The chiefs alone keep it up. The adherents are gradually falling off. To open the questions of education, c., now, would be to open closing wounds, nor would anything be accomplished. The priests would resist everything proposed, and the Protestants would not be satisfied. The Kildare Street Society, however defective, does a great deal of good, more than could be expected from any new system we could carry at this moment.

As to Maynooth, to withdraw the grant would not diminish the funds, while it would increase the bad feeling.

The increased prevalence of outrage, arising more from a disorganised state of society than from politics or religion, and the assassination plan, must be met by an extensive police, directed by stipendiary magistrates; and the expense of this police, and the indemnity to sufferers must be paid by the barony in which the outrage takes place.

All Peel's letters are very sensible. Lord Francis Leveson's are in an odd style, rather affected occasionally, and his ideas are almost always such as require to be overruled. He is a forward boy; but I see nothing of the statesman in him. We ought to have had Har-dinge there.

Dined at the Duke's. A man of the name of Ashe is writing letters to the Duke of Cumberland threatening his life if he does not give up a book in MS.

This book of Ashe's is a romance detailing all sorts of scandals of the Eoyal Family, and of horrors of the Duke of Cumberland. The book is actually in the possession of the Duke of Wellington.

The King's violence, when there was an idea of Denman's 1 appearing for the Eecorder, was greater, the Duke says, than what he showed during the Catholic question.

Lady Conyngham has been and is very ill. There is no idea of the Court going to Brighton.

November 16.

Cabinet. France, Austria, and England to ask Don Pedro distinctly what he means to do. We certainly cannot go on as we are with Portugal for ever. Aberdeen fears France may acknowledge Miguel first, and thus take our place with Portugal.

The Duke says if we can keep Spain on good terms with Portugal, and with ourselves, the connection of France and Portugal does not signify, and we are much better off than with Portugal against Spain and France. This is true.

A long talk about Ashe, who has written a libel on the Duke of Cumberland, which the Duke gave to the 1 The King always resented an offensive quotation of Denman's as Counsel during the Queen's trial.

136   Duke of Wellington. Ashe wants it back, and threatens if he has it not returned to him; but in a letter, and in such terms that the Attorney-General does not think him liable to prosecution. He might be held to bail, perhaps, but that would bring out the case. It was decided to do nothing, but to take precautions against his doing mischief. The Duke of Cumberland has been cautioned.

The Insurrection Act seems to be popular with Fitzgerald. Peel says it is bad in principle, and has the effect of placing the higher classes in hostility against the lower. The decision seemed to be to have a powerful police stipendiary magistrates frequent trials constables appointed by Government counties paying for additional police.

Peel suggests the division of Ireland into smaller districts, and the acquiring a personal knowledge of individuals, and making the districts responsible.

I believe the country is too populous, and the population too wicked, for this plan to succeed.

The murderers will be brought in from a distance.

The state of demoralisation in which the country is is dreadful. Murders are held to be of no account.

November 17.

Eead, as I came down to Worthing, Colonel Mcdonald's last despatches, and his private letter, which I received last night. Sent them to the Duke, and asked whether under the circumstances we should let Abbas Murza have some thousand stand of arms, Colonel Mcdonald doing his best to secure ultimate repayment.

.? INVASION OF INDIA. 137

137   The Persian cavalry raised by the Eussians in their newly conquered territories seem to have fought as well as any troops in their service. Colonel Mcdonald says it is from a disciplined Persian army alone, commanded by Eussian officers, that he dreads the invasion of India. A European force would be wasted by the climate. The Pasha of Suleimania had too European a taste, and wanted to make regular soldiers without pay or clothing. So his soldiers turned him out, and made his brother Pacha.

Colonel Mcdonald describes all that side of Turkey as going au devant du conquerant. Such has been the wretchedness of their government.

Worthing, November 18, 1829.

At 11 P. M. received a letter from the Duke of Wellington by a messenger, telling me he regretted I had not met Lord Melville and him before the Cabinet, and proposing, as he and Lord Melville both wished to go out of town on Friday, that I should meet them either to-morrow, after 2, or on Friday morning.

I wrote to say I would be with him at 3 to-morrow.

November 19.

Met the Duke and Lord Melville.

After conversation on topics connected with the subject we came to the point, which was that the Duke wished both to preserve the monopoly and the Company as administrators of Indian affairs.

The Duke is much swayed by early recollections.

138 He is besides very desirous of having the City of London in his hands.

I admitted that the great and solid objection to placing the government of India directly in the hands of the Crown was the consequent increase of Parlia: mentary business, already too extensive to be well performed.

As to the China trade, if the Government of India can be conducted without the assistance derived from it, I saw no reason for its continuance; but I had rather continue the monopoly than lose the Company as a trading Company to China, for I thought the trade might be greatly endangered were their commerce to cease. I said that the continuance of the system of carrying on the government through the instrumentality of the Company was not inconsistent with giving to it the efficiency, the vigour, and the celerity of the King's Government.

Lord Melville admitted the cumbrousness of the present system.

The Duke seemed to have no objection to alterations in details, provided the principle were adhered to.

Both to-day and in the Cabinet on Friday last I was surprised by Lord Melville's inertness.

The Duke wishes Leach's paper to be ' the case to be proved." This may be done, and yet the necessary improvements introduced.

Met Seymour, who had been with the Duke. He is just come from Berlin. He seemed to say that the great success of the war was wholly unexpected by the Emperor.

139 November 20.

Wrote to Hylton Jolliffe to beg lie would turn his attention to the subject of steam navigation to India by the Bed Sea, as a private speculation.

November 21.

Eead a letter from Sir G. Murray. It seems the Duke, Lord Melville, and Sir George are to meet soon to consider whether some alteration should not be made in the rules of the Order of the Bath. I suggested that it might be an improvement to make civilians eligible to the lower grades of the Order. It might occasionally be very convenient to make a man a K. O. B. for civil service.

Sunday, November 22.

Told Bankes what the Duke wished respecting the Charter; but I likewise told him it had not yet been so determined in Cabinet, and that there was no objection to

our making the Government more rapid and vigorous, and less like the Tullietudlem coach. I desired him to consider this confidential to himself and the Commissioners.
November 25.

Eeceived a note from Bankes announcing that the Duke had accepted his retirement from the office of secretary, and had consented to make him an extra commissioner.

This has long been an idea of Bankes's, of which I never could see rational ground. Indeed, he seems to acknowledge it is not his own idea, but that of others, that on his return to the Government he should not have returned to the same office. In fact it is the influence of the Duke of Cumberland, and it is evident from the endeavour to detach Bankes from the Government now that the Brunswickers still have hopes. It is like giving notice to Lot and his family before the fall of fire and brimstone.

Bankes's letter is full of kind and grateful expressions towards me. Indeed, we have always been on very friendly and confidential terms. I have expressed my regret at his resolution. I told him I think he acts upon mistaken views, and I assure him that in whatever position he may stand towards the. Board, it will afford me much pleasure and advantage to remain on the same terms with him.

The Duke will be angry, and I do not think Bankes will soon get an office again.
December 2.

Kead for an hour at the Cabinet room. There is a curious account of a conversation between De Eigny and an Austrian friend at Smyrna. De Eigny thinks very ill of the Government, and of the state of France. He too wants the Ehine! He judges truly enough of the results of the treaty. ' England, Austria, and France will talk, but nothing will be done." He says Eussia was very foolish not to go on. She might have dared anything. However, the army seems to have suffered severely. They acknowledge the loss of 130,000 men in the two campaigns.

Diebitch has partly evacuated Adrianople, leaving there, however, 6,000 sick and a battalion. The plague spreads in the Principalities, and they do not know how to get the troops out of Turkey.

Zuylen de Neyvelt and others give a very bad account of the state of Constantinople. They say the Turkish Empire cannot hold together.

I do not like Lord Stuart's account of the state of the French Ministry. They will bring in Villele, who is an able man, and he may save them; but theirs is a desperate game.

The French seem to be disposed to go along with us in negotiating with the Emperor of Brazil for the recognition of Miguel, There would be a stipulation for amnesty, c.
December 4.

The Chairs talked of Lord William Bentinck. They are very much out of humour with him and heartily wish he was at home. He has neither written privately nor publicly, except upon trifling matters, for five months. He has declared his opinion in favour of colonisation. He is very unpopular. On the subject of Sir W. Eumbold he and Sir Ch. Metcalfe are very hostile, taking extreme views on the different sides. This hostility upon one subject will lead to difference upon others. The Government is not respected and certainly there has been no moment when it was of more importance that the head of the Government should be respected than when it is necessary to effect

[1 I. e. with the Emperor Don Pedro, father of the ultimately successful candidate for the Portuguese throne, Donna Maria de Gloria.]

a great economical reform. They describe the feeling at Madras as being still worse. There they did not think the governor an honest man.

The Chairs expect a letter from Macdonald to the Secret Committee with copies of his last despatches which I have already received through Petersburg, so they are unwilling to accept a communication of them from me. The letter, permitting Abbas Murza to purchase 12,000 stand of arms and to pay for them by instalments, will therefore go without any reference to the last despatches received.

Saw Aberdeen. He agrees with me in feeling much apprehension on the state of France as well as of Turkey. He seems, however, to think more of the state of parties here, and does not like the looks of the Duke of Cumberland (who was nearly dying last week) and of the King. It seems the King, although very well satisfied with measures of a public nature, is annoyed at not carrying some small jobs.

There was a great party at Woburn lately, and the world of course say there is an approximation to the Grey party. Aberdeen thinks the Woburn party showed good wishes, and Lord Grey, it is said, does not mean to come up to town. However, he is said to think he has been slighted, whereas the Duke of Wellington cannot do anything for him in the hostile state of the King's mind.

I told Aberdeen confidentially of Bankes's going out, which is an indication, no doubt, of continued hostility on the part of the Duke of Cumberland.

Saw Hardinge. Talked on various public subjects, and then told him of the probability that in three months Lord W. Bentinck would be recalled. I asked him whether he could be induced to go as Governor-General. He rejected the idea at first as unsuited to his rank in the army. I said we could make him Captain-General. He seemed to think it was a great field for a man who wished to obtain great fame, and if he was unmarried he would not be disinclined to go, but I should think domestic considerations would prevent him. I wish we had him as secretary in Ireland, but he is wanted everywhere. He is so useful. He would be most useful in Ireland.

Saw the Duke. I told him what the Chairs had said. He said he always thought Lord William would not succeed. Who could we get to replace him? He had always thought it did not signify as long as we had one man in India; but we must have one. I told him that, seeing the difficulty of selection, I had thought it right to tell him what was likely to happen. I should not be much surprised if he thought of Lord Tweddale, whom he thought of for Ireland. I do not know him at all.

December 6.

Eead Sir W. Eumbold's letters, and the minutes in Council on the Hyderabad case. Sir W. is a cunning, clever man. Sir Ch. Metcalfe shows too much prejudice against Sir W. Eumbold; but he was at Hyderabad at the time, and he may be right. I suspect it was a disgraceful business.

December 9.

Loch has got a cadetship for me. Colonel Baillie lends it. He postpones a nomination till next year in order to oblige me. I have thanked Loch, and begged him to thank Colonel Baillie.

Wrote to Lady Belfast to tell her Mr. Verner had his cadetship. Begged her to make his family and friends understand thoroughly that this was a private favour I had led her to expect long before the discussion of the Catholic question.

Wrote to Lord Hertford and enclosed an extract from my letter to Lady Belfast.

Eead a letter from Sir J. Malcolm, who is again troubled by Sir J. P. Grant. He enclosed a letter of his upon the subject to Lord W. Bentinck. The concluding paragraph of this letter refers to a letter from Lord William of June 18, at which time the spirit of the Bengal army continued bad.

Eead a letter from Jones, who will set himself to work about the navigation of the Indus. He says a Mr. Walter Hamilton speaks of the river being navigable for vessels of 200 tons to Lahore, and that from Lahore to the mouth of the river, 700 miles, is only a voyage of twelve days. And no British flag has ever floated upon the waters of this river! Please God it shall, and in triumph, to the source of all its tributary streams.

December 11.

Eead a letter from Lord Bathurst respecting the recall of Sir J. P. Grant. He had imagined I had said he had resigned. He seems surprised I should have supposed it possible a judge should be recalled without a formal meeting of the Privy Council. I reminded him of Sir T. Claridge's case, not half so strong as that of Sir J. P. Grant.

December 12. Eead Fraser's travels.

December 13.

A letter from Sir J. Malcolm, by which it seems that my letter to him of February 21 has been copied and become public: much to his annoyance. [1]

He sends me his letter to Lord W. Bentinck upon the subject. It seems by this letter, which adverts to other topics, that the spirit in Bengal is very bad that Lord W. has hitherto done nothing to check it, and that with the press in his power he has allowed it to be more licentious than it ever was before.

December 14.

Found at Eoehampton a letter from the Duke enclosing one addressed by Mrs. Hastings to the King, applying for a pension. The King recommends it to the consideration of the Court of Directors. I doubt the Court venturing to propose any pension to the Court of Proprietors.

I had another letter from the Duke enclosing a [1 This was the letter with the expression about a wild elephant between two tame ones which afterwards attracted so much criticism. It was intended as a private letter to Sir J. Malcolm, but by a mistake of one of his secretaries was copied as an official communication]

letter to him from Sir J. Malcolm and a copy of Sir J. Malcolm's letter to Lord W. Bentinck, respecting the unauthorised publication of my private letter the same I received yesterday. Sir J. Malcolm speaks of an intended deputation from the Bengal army to England, which Lord William was determined not to allow; but Sir J. Malcolm seems to think that Lord William by his conduct at first brought on much of what has taken place. He has relaxed the reins of Government too much. I am satisfied that, without a change of form and name, it will be very difficult to regain the strength the Government has lost in India.

I shall see the Duke if I can to-morrow and suggest the appointment of Sir J. Malcolm as provisional successor to Lord William. Sir J. Malcolm's sentiments are known, and his nomination would show the feeling of the Government here. It would be a hint to Lord William that we could replace him at once and make him do his duty. It would, in the event of anything happening to Lord William, guard against the mischiefs of an interregnum, which is always a time of weakness and of job.

December 15.

The Duke gone to the Deepdene. Wrote to him to say I would not fail to bring the question of Mrs. Hastings's pension before the Chairs; but I enclosed a memorandum showing all that had been done for old Hastings, and reminded the Duke that the Court could not grant above 200. a year without the sanction of two Courts of Proprietors.

Cabinet room. Lord Heytesbury seems to have shown Nesselrode the protocol about November 25. The Count was greatly agitated, and put himself into a furious passion. Asked the use of it? Perhaps it would be difficult to say. Supposed it was intended for Parliament which is very true. Said it would lead to a reply we should not like create a paper war, prevent the two Courts from remaining upon the friendly terms he had hoped were re-established. The more angry he is, the more right I think we must feel we were to send it.

There is a good paper of Aberdeen's to Sir E. Gordon, in which he considers the Turkish Empire as falling, and our interest as being to raise Greece, that that State may be the heir of the Ottoman Power. With this view he considers it to be of primary importance that the Government of new Greece should not be revolutionary, and the Prince a good one.

There is another good paper defending England against an accusation of Metternich that we should have spoken in a firmer tone to Eussia at an earlier period. The King seems much taken with these papers, and writes great encomiums upon them.

By Lord Stuart's account it appears probable that Villele will come in. The Government mean to avoid all questions upon which it is possible to have a difference of opinion, and to bring forward only measures of clear and undeniable utility. They think that, if their opponents should endeavour to throw out these measures, the Chambers will support Government.

France coincides with us entirely as to the Portuguese question; but wishes, and she is right, that questions more specific had been put to the Emperor Pedro. The intention seems to be to acknowledge Miguel on conditions, when Pedro admits he can do nothing.

December 16.

Eead Lord Ashley's memorandum on the judicial administration of India. I wrote a note on returning it in which I said he seemed to have taken great pains to collect the opinions which had been given by different persons upon the subject. Mine had been expressed by me in a letter to Sir J. Malcolm on August 7, in which I declared my general concurrence in the views entertained by him and intimated by him in his minute, giving an account of his tour in the southern Mahratta country. I had added that I was satisfied the more we could avail ourselves of the services of the natives in the fiscal and judicial administration the better, and that all good government must rest upon the village system. I told Sir J. Malcolm I had come to my office without any preconceived opinions, that 1 had kept out of the way of prejudiced men, and had allowed opinions to form themselves gradually in my own mind as I acquired more knowledge from pure sources. I could not, if I had written this passage on purpose, have had one more suited to my purpose. It showed Ashley I was not prejudiced, that my opinions were formed before I read his memorandum, and that I had formed them by abstaining from the course he has pursued for he allows all sorts of persons to come and talk to him, and to inoculate him with their notions.

1 afterwards said that he would see by Sir Thomas

149   Munro's memorandum of December 31, 1824, that he thought we had succeeded better in the judicial than in the fiscal administration of India, and in the criminal better than in the civil branch of the judicial government. This I said to show I had read Sir T. Munro's memorandum, which he did not give me credit for having done; and that it was not so much to the judicial as to the revenue branch that he should have directed his attention, with a view to improvements the field being greater.

I then said I did not doubt that there were capable natives to be found, but I did doubt that they would be selected, for that the European servants had disappointed me. The natives were better than I expected, c., c.

Saw the Duke. Suggested to him Sir J. Malcolm's being made provisional successor to Lord W. Bentinck for the reasons I have mentioned. He thought well of the suggestion; but said we must consider it, and mention it in Cabinet, as Lord William was a great card, and we must not do anything to offend unnecessarily him and his connection. The objection occurred to him that had occurred to me, that Sir J. Malcolm would die if he went to Calcutta. I hope he would not go there, that he would remain in the upper provinces. But I look to the effect of the nomination upon the conduct of people in India, and that of Lord William himself, more than to his actual succession.

The Duke then said we must look not to India only, but to all Asia, and asked me

150 if I had read Evans's book. I told him I had; that in forty-eight hours after I read it, I had sent a copy to Macdonald and another to Malcolm. I told him all the views I had with regard to the navigation of the Indus and the opening of a trade with Cabul and Bokhara. He said our minds appeared to have been travelling the same way. We must have good information of what the Eussians might be doing there. I reminded him I had desired the Government a year ago to obtain information as to all the countries between the Caspian and the Indus, and I intended now to give a more particular direction. He said Macdonald should have his eye upon the Caspian, and information as to those countries would be best obtained through natives. I reminded him that that had been the suggestion in my letter of last year. The Duke's opinion is that it is a question of expense only. That if the Eussians got 20,000 or 30,000 men into Cabul we could beat them; but that by hanging upon us there they could put us to an enormous expense in military preparation, and in quelling insurrections. They could not move in that direction without views hostile to us, and by threatening us there they would think to embarrass us in Europe. I proposed that in the event of the Eussians moving in that direction we should permit the Government of India to act as an Asiatic Power. By money at least, he allowed, without further orders, not to move in advance without instructions. But the Duke is ready to take up the question here in Europe, if the Eussians move towards India with views of evident hostility.

He approves of a message going at once with orders to Macdonald.

151   December 18.

Chairs. They will consider favourably Mrs. Hastings's case; but she must address her representation to them.

I told them of my suggestion of making Malcolm provisional successor to Lord William, and the reasons for it. They seemed to like the idea; but the same objection occurred to them which had occurred to the Duke and to me that if Malcolm went to Calcutta he would die. I said I did not want him to go. I did not look to his going. I looked to the moral effect of the appointment upon Lord William and upon all their servants in India. They want to get some political man of high rank and talents and determined character to go. They are heartily sick of Lord William. Whom they want to send I do not know.

I told them of nay conversation with the Duke and went over the same ground. They acquiesced in all I said. We shall have the missions to Scinde and to Lahore, and the commercial venture up the Indus, and the instruction to Macdonald. In short, all I want.

Despatches are at hand from Lord William, dated May l, in triplicate, and without the minutes which are referred to as containing the sentiments of the Government. These despatches merely refer the subject to the consideration of the Court.

One Jones, it seems, has written almost all the memorials, and is considered a rebel more than a Eadical.

We had a little conversation respecting the future Government of India. I told them it must be a strong Government, and I doubted whether in its present form it could secure obedience in India. It required more of appearance. They seemed to feel that. Astell acknowledged there was nothing imposing in the name of ' the Company," and that the present Government was fallen into contempt.

I told them I was satisfied that the patronage and the appeals should always remain where they were. I paid them a high compliment, which they justly deserve, upon the fairness of their conduct in deciding upon the claims of their servants.

They feel their Government is weak in its last year; but that the Ministers could not do otherwise than have a committee.

December 18.

Wrote a letter to the Duke, which he may send to the King, stating the result of my communication to the Chairs respecting Mrs. Hastings.

Eequested information as to the trade of the Caspian, that carried on by the caravans to Bokhara, and the general condition of that country, desiring likewise that means might be taken to keep us constantly informed of any movements made by the Eussians towards the Sea of Aral, and of any attempt to make establishments on the east coast of the Caspian.

Wrote to the Duke to tell him what was done and how entirely the Chairs entered into his views.

December 19.

Wrote to Loch to suggest that he should send Meyendorff's and Mouravief's books to Macdonald.

Read a clever pamphlet on the China trade, and in coming down to Worthing all the papers Hardinge sent me relative to the new pension regulations.

December 20.

Eead Meyendorff's 'Tour in Bokhara." It contains all the information I want as to the commerce between Bokhara and Eussia. We can easily supply Bokhara with many things the Russians now furnish, and with all Indian goods cheaper by the Indus than the Ganges; but what the Bokharians are to send us in return I do not well see, except turquoises, lapis lazuli, and the ducats they receive from Russia. We may get shawls cheaper by navigating the Indus.

December 21.

Read the memorandum the Chairs gave me respecting the application of steam navigation to the internal and external communications of India. It has been prepared carefully and ably, and is very interesting. It suggests the navigation of the Euphrates to Balis or Bir by steam, and thence the passage by Aleppo to Latakia or Scanderoon. It likewise suggests that it might be more expeditious to cross the desert from Suez to Lake Menzaleh, or direct to the sea.

December 22.

Wrote to Lord Hill, telling him of Sir G. Walker's dangerous illness, and intimating the importance, under the present circumstances of Madras, of having not only a good soldier as Commander-in-Chief, but a man possessed of good civil qualities.

Sent a copy of this letter to the Duke.

December 25.

Eead a memorandum of Jones on the last mission to Lahore, and a very long secret despatch in 1811 upon the subject of Eunjeet Singh's attempt to establish himself on the left bank of the Sutlege, and his retreat in consequence of remonstrances and military demonstration on the part of the British Government.

December 26.

Called by appointment on Lady Macdonald, who came here to speak to me about Sir J. Macdonald's salary and position at Tabriz. She says that after the letter he wrote, representing the inexpediency of Sir H. Willock's remaining as his first assistant and the non-existence of any necessity for two assistants, if the Bengal Government do not recall Willock Sir J. Macdonald cannot remain. She has likewise a good deal to say respecting the salary. I think 9,000 a year a proper salary. The Ambassador at Constantinople has 8, OOOZ. and a house; but Constantinople is on the sea, and the charge of bringing European goods to Tabriz through Russia is so considerable that 1,000 a year ought to be added for the charge.

December 29.

Eeceived three letters from Lord W. Bentinck, of July 6 and 8 and August 2. In that of the 6th he speaks of my private letter to Sir J. Malcolm, published in the ' Calcutta Newspaper." In that of the 8th he sends it to me, the names being altered, and all between brackets being interpolated, and in fact in the light of comment. In that of August 2 he speaks of the temper of the army, c., and all public subjects. I have sent the three letters to the Duke.

I was glad to have my letter. I can defend every word in it. It contains the simile of the elephants, which I am sorry for, as I fear those described as tame may be foolish enough to endeavour to show they are not so by affecting a degree of vivacity beyond their nature; but still I can defend it.

Lord William describes his position as not agreeable, having to effect the odious work of reduction. [1] He says that in India no man thinks of anything but MONEY, that the local government has incurred great odium by carrying into effect the orders of the home authorities. He recommends Sir Charles Metcalfe as a man standing by Malcolm's side, and fit for the government of Bombay. I a little fear Sir Charles Metcalfe. He is rather too vehement. I doubt whether he would be a safe man. I am quite sure Courtney would be a very unfit man. The Governor of Bombay ought to be an Indian, but who is there?

Lord William represents the Burmese Government as a barbarian Government. He says they have sacrificed all who assisted us, and that the difficulty in [1 Besides the burning question of 'Half-Batta Lord W. Bentinck's administration was regarded as hostile in spirit to that of his predecessors, and so disliked by those who had served under them, especially by the military.]

156 retroceding the Tenasserim provinces would be to know what to do with the 35,000 people who have sought our protection.

This report makes the wisdom of our recent policy yet clearer than it appeared before.

December 31.

Eead twenty papers on the opium treaties and management in Central India. The Supreme Government have decided upon no longer limiting the extent of cultivation in Malwa, and upon permitting the free transit of the drug. This was expedient because undoubtedly our restrictions led to the most hostile feelings on the part both of princes and people, to the injury of the traders, to violent and offensive interference on our part in the internal policy of foreign States, and to smuggling protected by large bodies of armed men. The smugglers would soon have been Pindarries. This system began only in 1825. It was forced upon the small States, and not upon that of Gwalior, so that smuggling defeated the object.

January 2, 1830.

Eeceived from the Duke a note to say the publication of my private letter to Sir J. Malcolm did not signify one pin's head, and it will have done good in India.

Wrote a long letter to Lord William Bentinck. I pressed upon him the necessity of making the home and the local authorities draw together. I told him he was suffering not for his obedience but for the disobedience of his predecessors. Assured him of 157 support, lamented the ungentlemanlike tone of society evidenced by the insult of the commanding officers to him, and by the publication of my private letter. I spoke in high terms of Lieut. W. Hislop's report on the opium arrangements (which on reflection I thought better than writing a letter to him), and I likewise spoke highly of Mr. Scott, the Commissioner in Assam. Acknowledged the Government could not have done otherwise than give up the opium treaties; but foretold a large falling off in the opium revenue from over-cultivation in Malwa.

January 3.

A letter from Clare on East Indian matters which I answered at length. Sent Prendergast's pamphlet to Jones.

Eead reports on the Delhi and Firuz Shah's canal, by which it appears my plan of joining the Sutlege and Jumna is not visionary. It has been done. The canal can still be traced. Delhi seems in distant times to have been like Milan, in the midst of canals. The grand canal sent a branch through the palace. The water has been again turned in the same channel. When the water flowed into Delhi on the opening of the canal on May 30, 1820, the people went out to meet it and threw flowers into the stream. In those countries nothing can be done without water, and with water, and such a sun, anything.

January 4, 1830.

Eead Eraser's journey and finished it. It is very interesting, and shows how completely the Persian monarchy is falling to pieces.

158   January 5.

Saw Wrangham. There is no news. The affairs of the Netherlands, he says, look rather better, and Polignac is very stout and says he is very strong. It seems great complaints are made of Lord Stuart, who gives little information, and what little he does give is incorrect.

January 6.

Vesey Fitzgerald will certainly not be able to attend the House this year. His physicians say he would die in five minutes if he got up to speak. I heard G. Dawson tell the Duke to-day. I rather suspect G. Dawson would like Vesey's place.

The Duke has been much occupied with the Greek question. I have not yet read any papers at the Foreign Office. He spoke to me of Bankes's going out, which he regretted.

He had had some conversation last year at Belvoir with Lord Graham upon Indian affairs, and had been quite surprised to find how much he knew. He had thought he only knew how to comb his hair. The Duke thinks of Horace Twiss for secretary. He had thought of Mr. Wortley, Lord Wharncliffe's son, a very clever young man, but he wanted a made man, not one to learn. I shall suggest Ashley's taking Horace Twiss's place, and Lord Graham being First Commissioner. This will force him to come forward. Then Wortley might be Second Commissioner. Horace Twiss is a clever man, but rather vulgar. However, he is a lawyer and a very good speaker, and will do very well.

159   January 7.

I told the Chairs my views as to an alteration in the Supreme Court Bill. They seemed to approve if the thing could be done. I had afterwards some conversation with the Chancellor upon this subject. He admitted the force of my reasoning, but desired to have a memorandum about it, which indeed will be convenient to me as well as to him. It should state all the new circumstances since the establishment of the Supreme Court which render its existence less necessary than it was, and more inapplicable than ever to the condition of India.

At the Duke's dinner I told the Duke and Eosslyn the substance of Lord William's letters. The Duke said the act [l]of the officers was mutiny.

The King is ill. He has lost a good deal of blood.

January 8.

The King quite well again. In the morning began and nearly finished a memorandum on the jurisdiction of the Supreme Court for the Chancellor.

Cabinet at 2. Conversation respecting the abolition of the Welsh judgeships, and the addition of a judge to the Courts of King's Bench and Common Pleas, or Exchequer. The two new judges would be Circuit Judges of Wales. The Welsh gentlemen seem to be favourable to the change. The attornies, who are numerous and powerful, very hostile. The Chancellor introduces again his Bill of last Session. The Equity [1 In combining to oppose the Half-Batta orders. See Thornton's India, vol. v.] is to be separated from the Common Law Jurisdiction of the Court of Exchequer. The subject was only talked of, and decision deferred till Sunday next.

We then talked of Ireland. The Grand Jury Presentment Bill is not yet prepared. The plan for a police is to place the nominations in the hands of the Lord-Lieutenant. To send stipendiary magistrates when and where they are wanted.

Peel's suggestions went much further; but Lord F. Gower seems to me to be only a clever boy. He has as yet proposed nothing worthy of adoption, and he has often been near the commission of errors from which he has been saved only by Peel's advice.

He wished to establish stipendiary magistrates in every county, the effect of which would have been to disgust all the gentlemen magistrates, and to lead them to the abandonment of their duty. He wished too to unite in all cases the inspectorships of police with the office of stipendiary magistrate, to avoid collision; but the duties of inspector are of a mere ministerial and inferior character, and would not agree well with those of a magistrate.

I must read to-morrow all the late protocols and despatches. The Russians and French have agreed to make Leopold Prince of Greece, but the King cannot endure the idea. Aberdeen thinks he has made a great conquest in carrying the point of Leopold's election. I confess I cannot understand the great advantage we derive from it. What an extraordinary scene! Those monarchical states, the most adverse to revolution, combine to assist the rebellion of a people against its sovereign, a rebellion commenced by murder and continued by treachery, stained with every crime that ever disgraced human nature! [1 They destroy the fleet of an unoffending Power in a time of profound peace in his own port. They thus facilitate the attack of an enemy, and in the extreme peril of the defeated sovereign they increase their demands in order to form a substantive State out of the ruins of his Empire. They then elect a Prince unknown to the people over whom he is to reign, and support him by equal assistance in ships and money! Those monarchical states set up a revolutionary government and maintain it in coparcenary! It was reserved for these times to witness such contradictions. I do not think any one is very well satisfied with them but Aberdeen. He is charmed.

Sunday, January 10.

Cabinet. Conversation first as to an intended publication by Mr. Stapleton of a ' Life of Canning in which he means to insert the substance, if not the copies, of public papers relating to transactions not yet terminated. He has had it intimated to him that he will do so at his peril. He holds an office under the Government during pleasure. I said he had no right over private letters relating to public subjects which only came to the knowledge of the writer by his official situation. He should be told it was a high breach of [1 The massacres by the Greeks at Tripolitza and Athens, the latter in direct breach of a capitulation, had, according to a not unfavourable historian, cast a dark stain on the Greek cause and diminished the interest felt for it in foreign countries. (Alison, Hist. Europe, 1815-52, iii. 150.)

162   VOL. II. M public confidence, and lie should be displaced if lie was guilty of it. He will have a hint, but I fear not one sufficiently strong. It is Lady Canning who thinks she can injure the Duke of Wellington, and so publishes these papers. Stapleton is her editor. She demanded from Aberdeen official letters of Canning's, and actually threatened him with a suit in Chancery if he did not give them up. The Duke says he has copies of all Canning's letters, and he shall publish if they do. [1]

We had Scarlett and afterwards Bosanquet in upon the Welsh Judicature question. It was at last decided that the Equity Jurisdiction of the Courts of Great Session should be sent to the Court of Exchequer, that power should be taken to the King of directing the circuits to be held where he pleased, and that the two new judges of the English Courts should do the duty of the Welsh circuits. The proceedings to be assimilated to those of the English Courts.

The saving by the reduction of the Welsh judges, after allowing for their pensions, will leave an ample fund for the compensation of the officers reduced.

I read Lord Stuart de Eothesay's last despatches and Lord Heytesbury's. There seems to me to be great over-confidence in their strength on the part of the French Ministers. I cannot help thinking they will fall. Villele will have nothing to do with the Govern- [1 Augustus Granville Stapleton had been private secretary to Canning, and published about 1830-31 The Political Life of George Canning, and nearly thirty years later, George Canning and his Times. The latter work contains much correspondence the publication of which might have been objected to at the earlier date.]

163   ment under this House of deputies, which declared his administration deplorable. He seems to stipulate for their dissolution.

Halil Pacha takes to Petersburg fine presents for the Emperor and Empress, and other presents he is to distribute ' selon son gre et en son nom," which are enough to bribe all the ladies in Europe. There is a list of them extending over seven pages.

It seems to be doubtful whether the French have not been endeavouring to induce Mehemet Ali to revenge their quarrel with Algiers by marching along the whole coast of Africa. The French are much out of humour with their Algerine follies, and heartily tired of their expensive gasconade.

Mehemet Ali does not seem much inclined to send his fleet to Constantinople, although he has honour enough to send the Sultan's.

The Kussians have launched two large ships (120 and 74), and they have bought a double-banked frigate built in the United States.

Monday ', January 11.

At the Cabinet room, where I met Sir George Murray; read the letters relative to the alterations in the judicial system of Scotland.

Bead a letter from Loch, allowing me to show to the Cabinet Lord William's letters. He wished them to be read, not shown, or rather not circulated; but it is contrary to all rule, so I left them to-day on the Cabinet table.

164   The Duke told me yesterday he felt no concession could now be made, although it was a mighty foolish thing to have had a quarrel about.

Got home at 5, dressed, and was going to business, when I found a note from Drummond, desiring me to call on the Duke as soon as I could. I ordered the carriage and went. Found the Chancellor there.

It seems there is a great hitch about Prince Leopold's nomination as Prince Sovereign of Greece. The French have now proposed it. We desire it. Eussia acquiesces. We have always declared we did not care who was Prince Sovereign of Greece, but we were resolved never to acknowledge as such a man in whom we had not confidence. Some time ago the King of Prussia applied through the Grand Duke of Mecklen-burgh to the King for his vote in favour of Prince Charles of Mecklenburgh, the brother of the late Queen of Prussia and of the Duchess of Cumberland. This application was made through the Duke of Cumberland to the King, and the King returned an answer through the Duke of Cumberland. What this answer was is not known; but the King having mentioned the circumstance to Aberdeen, and he to the Duke, Aberdeen, by the Duke's desire, wrote through Sir Brook Taylor to the King of Prussia, and civilly put him off. This letter of course the King saw, and approved. The Duchess of Cumberland complains the answer of Aberdeen was very different from that given through the Duke of Cumberland by the King, and says it is an intrigue.

The King has been put up to this, and tells Aberdeen he knows his own ground that the people of England will not bear that 50,000. a year shall be paid by them to the Prince of Greece. He does not care whether Leopold goes or no, but he is determined he shall leave his annuity behind him.

The articles in the ' Standard' and other papers, a few days ago, are supposed to have had reference to this then intended rupture. Aberdeen goes to the King to-morrow, and the Duke having seen all the Cabinet, Aberdeen will, if it should be necessary, declare their concurrent opinion. The Duke thinks the King will yield to Aberdeen; to avoid seeing him if he is obliged to go down, he will declare distinctly to the King that his Majesty had better name whatever Minister he may wish to give his confidence to; but that to whatever Minister he may choose to have, he ought to give his confidence.

Certainly nothing can have been more scandalous than the King's conduct to the Duke. He has never given his Government the fair support. Say what the Duke will, he of Cumberland is believed.

The Duke had a note about the King the other day from Lady Conyngham, written only to tell him the Duke of Cumberland had been four hours with His Majesty.

That Prince Leopold will make an efficient King of Greece I do not believe; but he is not likely to be hostile to England. Prince Charles of Mecklenburgh, named by Prussia, would be really Eussian, and the tool of States not friendly to us.

Prince Leopold hopes, if he goes to Greece, that Government will purchase the lands he has bought, for which he has given 40,000. or 50,000.

Determined to have my letter respecting the acquisition of information in Central Asia and the navigation of the Indus sent to the Chairs to-morrow, that it may be sent, and be on record as mine, in the event of His Majesty turning me out the next day, as he will very possibly do.

January 12.

Henry [1] copied for transmission the letter in the Secret Department, and I took care it should be sent to the India House in the course of the day, that if I should be out to-morrow, I may have the credit of having originated a measure which, if effected, will be of incalculable value.

Cabinet at 2. Aberdeen was gone to the King at Windsor. It seemed to be expected he would do nothing, and that the Duke would be obliged to go down to-morrow the Duke thinks he shall succeed and no one seems to dread a turn out. I am not quite so sure. The mischief is that these secousses make a weak Government.

I found in the box of drafts the letter to Sir Brook Taylor respecting Duke Charles of Mecklenburgh, which the King says he never saw or sanctioned. It bears his initials and approval, which have been traced out in ink over his pencil.

The Duke of Cumberland wants, if it be but for a week, a friendly administration that he may get out of the Exchequer 30,000. set apart for the annuity for his son's education, but to which he is not legally entitled, his son having been educated abroad. It is out of [1 The Honourable H. S. Law, Lord Ellenborough's brother.]

167   revenge for a hostile cheer, and to get this money, to which Lord Eldon and Lord Wynford have told him he has no right, that he is endeavouring to overthrow the Government.

January 13.

After I came home read the minutes of the Governor-General and Council on the college at Calcutta. There is nothing so important as to preserve young men, who are to govern an Empire, from idleness, dissipation, and debt. This must be done. The Governor-General's own superintendence may effect much. The suspension of the incompetent may do more; but while the habits of expense are given at Hayleybury, and continued by their residence without any control in the midst of a dissipated capital, nothing will reform the system.

Cabinet dinner at Aberdeen's. He was an hour and a half with the King yesterday. The King was much agitated in dressing himself for the interview. The man who shaved thought he should have cut him twenty times. He had taken 100 drops of laudanum to prepare himself for the interview.

Aberdeen says it is a real quarrel not a plot to get rid of us the King thoroughly hates Prince Leopold, and he has been made to think the Ministers have slighted him in this matter. The Duke goes down to him to-morrow. He can show the King that Leopold was first mentioned by France that he was made acquainted with the proposal or rather suggestion made by France to Leopold on November 9, that he was then told we could not hear of it till our candidates, Prince John of

168   Saxony and Ferdinand of Orange, were disposed of. The subject was again mentioned on November 24.

In point of fact the earliest day on which it could have been made known to the King that France had distinctly proposed Leopold was Monday, and he was told on the Tuesday.

The King seems to have been violently agitated. He said sneeringly to Aberdeen," If I may be allowed to ask, is Prince Leopold to be married to a daughter of the Duke of Orleans?"[1]Aberdeen said he had seen it in the newspaper and knew nothing more of it. The King alluded to the possibility of Government going out, admitted the inconvenience just before the meeting of Parliament, but said he was immovable. Leopold might go to the devil, but he should not carry English money out of the country. In the morning, talking to the Duchess of Gloucester, he said, 'If they want a Prince of my family, they might have had the Duke of Gloucester," upon which the Duchess burst out a-laugh-ing.

The King seems thoroughly out of humour. He says ' Things seem going on very ill in India. Do not you mean to recall Lord William? ' He had been made very angry in the morning by the ' Times' calling upon him to pay his brother's debts, and this morning the ' Morning Journal' places in juxtaposition the paragraphs in the ' Times," and those for which it was lately prosecuted.

Lady Conyngham is bored to death, and talks and really thinks of removing. She was to make a grand [1 This marriage took place in August 1832, when Prince Leopold had become King of the Belgians, and the Duke of Orleans King of the French.]

169

attack on the King to-day. I suppose she finds the Duchess of Cumberland gaining influence. Her note to the Duke the other day, to tell him the Duke of Cumberland had been four hours with the King, was intended to put him upon his guard.

The Duke does not mean to resign to-morrow, but to request, if he should not succeed (which Aberdeen thinks he will not do), that the King will allow the Cabinet to put their opinions in writing which the King cannot refuse. We shall then meet on Friday and decide what we shall do.

The Chancellor took me aside and said it would be a foolish thing to go out about Leopold. So it would; but if we allow ourselves to be beaten in this, we may be beaten round the whole circle of public questions.

When the Duke has proved the proposition was not made by us, that it came from France, the King will say, ' Well, if you did not think it worth while to propose him, why should you not reject him? Why adhere to him? ' I feel very indifferent about the result.

Dr. Seymour, Fitzgerald's physician, represents him as very ill indeed, and in danger if he does any business; but Peel, who saw him to-day, thinks that much exaggerated.

January 14.

Chairs at 11. I asked them to find out when Eoths-child sold out his Indian stock.

170

It seems (by a note I received in the evening) that he began on October 15, and at different times sold out 42,000. stock. I sent the Chairman's note to Goulburn.

About ten received the promised circular from the Duke. He was an hour and a half with the King, when he was obliged to leave him in consequence of his being unwell and the King afterwards sent to desire he would come again on Saturday.

For the first hour the King was in a state of irritated and contemptuous indignation. However, the Duke thinks he brought him to feel he had nothing to complain of in the conduct of his Government. He finished by getting into better temper and a good tone; but the Duke thinks he should have brought away his assent if he had been with him another hour. The Duke wishes to hear the opinion of the Cabinet upon some points, and we meet at two to-morrow.

January 15.

The Duke gave the Cabinet an account of his interview with the King. The King was with Munster and the Duke of Cumberland when he went; but the Duke was admitted in about forty minutes, which time he passed with the Lady Conyngham, who told him he must expect a storm.

The King was in bed, looking very ill. He said, ' Well, what is your business?" and seemed at first most indignant. The Duke, however, corrected his misapprehensions showed him the dates, and proved that he had known from the first that it was probable Leopold would be proposed by France. The proposition was made by us to Prince Frederick of Orange on November 13, his final answer received on August 11 (there may be a slight error in these dates, as I write from memory). In the meantime the King of France had about November 29, when Leopold took leave of him, told him he would propose him. This was known here immediately, and Leopold distinctly told he could not be heard of till our own candidate was disposed of. The regular proposal of Leopold did not arrive here till January 1, and was communicated to the King with the pro jet of a protocol, for it was no more, on the 9th.

It was still only a proposition, and the Government now come to advise the King to consent to it.

The Duke showed the King that there had been ten candidates in all:

Prince Philip of Hesse Homburgh, Prince John of Saxony, Prince Frederick of Orange, Prince Charles of Bavaria, Prince Otho of Bavaria, the Archduke Maximilian, Prince Paul of Wurtemburgh, Prince Leopold, Prince Emilius of Hesse Darmstadt, and Prince Charles of Mecklenburgh.

The seven first either declined or were rejected. Prince Emilius of Hesse Darmstadt was an aide-de-camp of Bonaparte, and the King would not have him, and with regard to the last, Prince Charles of Mecklenburgh, the Duke showed the King he was much more nearly connected with Prussia, and so with Eussia, than with England. The King admitted this, and seemed to have been brought into good humour, when he became so ill that he was obliged to beg the Duke to leave him, and soon after sent him word he would see him in two days.

The Duke says he was really unwell, and in fact was taking physic all the time he was with him.

The Duke showed the King that he alone had not the power of nomination. He had one voice out of three, and there were ten candidates.

' At any rate said the King, ' Claremont reverts to the Crown." The Duke, fearing he might wish to give it to the Duke of Cumberland, or somebody, asked the Chancellor to-day to look at the Act of Parliament and tell us what becomes of Claremont in the event of Leopold's being made King of Greece. The Chancellor looked and thought Claremont would certainly remain to Leopold, and if he died or gave it up go, not to the Crown, that is, not to the King, but, by specific enactment, become a portion of the revenue under the Woods and Forests. Of course Leopold will give up Claremont, which is in fact a source of expense. The Duke said Leopold would be at least innocuous, and he might be of use, The King asked how we could be such fools as to think he would be of any use.

While the Duke was with the King the Duke of Cumberland was with Lady Conyngham, and told her, amongst other things, that the ' Times' was the Duke of Wellington's paper.

The ' Morning Journal' is his paper, and uses the expressions he puts into the King's mouth.

Aberdeen says Leopold is quite aware of all he will have to go through.

He has written to Lord Stuart to ascertain whether there is any truth in the report of his being engaged to the daughter of the Duke of Orleans.

I cannot help thinking that is so, and that the French proposition originates in that.

January 16.

Eead last night a very interesting report by Captain Wade of his mission to Runjeet Singh in 1827.

Eeceived a box from the Duke with a circular note saying the King is not well enough to see him before Tuesday. He has seen no one since he saw the Duke, and the Duke hears he was not mistaken in his judgment of the effect he thought he had produced upon 'the King's mind; so I suppose this matter, which looked threatening at first, may be considered as settled, although not yet formally terminated.

The King will, I dare say, make another plunge when he finds Claremont will not be at his personal disposal, as he seems to have imagined.

January 19.

Eead all day Sir Thomas Munro's Life, which contains a great deal of interesting and valuable information. He was a very great man.

Talked to Hardinge of various matters. He was at Stowe when Lord Chandos in the middle of the night received a note from his father, communicating one from Sir. W. Fremantle, which informed him that the King was going to turn us all to the right about. Lord Chandos said to Hardinge he would never belong to a Government of which the Duke of "Wellington was not a member.

January 19.

Eead the rest of the ' Life of Sir Thomas Munro," a most valuable book. I believe there are no books so really useful as the lives of great and good men.

On my arrival in town, found a note from Hardinge, who thinks the despatch as to watching the Eussians and navigating the Indus quite perfect.

The Duke went to-day to Windsor. About eight he sent round a box containing a note, saying that the King consented to Prince Leopold's being King of Greece. So for the present, at least, we are safe again, I never had much apprehension.

January 20.

Cabinet dinner. Lord Bathurst not there. We had very little talk upon public matters. The Duke had a bad cold. The opinion seemed to be that the press of the session would be upon domestic matters, for the reduction of establishments and taxation.

The King wrote to the Duke and grumpily acceded to Leopold's appointment. Leopold is very uppish upon the subject. He was at Cobham to-day and yesterday.

I am to see Peel on Sunday at half-past one on Indian matters.

January 22.

At one, Privy Council to consider the petition of the E. I. C. for the recall of Sir J. P. Grant. The Lord President, Lord Chief Baron, and Lord Chief Justice of Common Pleas present. The committee reported that they did not consider themselves warranted at present in advising

175   Sir J. P. Grant's removal, but they thought it right he should be directed to proceed home that the several matters objected to him might be investigated.

I took the opportunity of the presence of two judges to get a legal opinion as to Sir J. Malcolm's conduct in resisting the service of the Habeas Corpus ad testifi-candum.

I took the opportunity likewise of laying before the two judges the change of circumstances since the institution of the Supreme Court, and the present reasons for making their jurisdiction without the limits of the Presidency the exception and not the rule.

The judges seemed to enter into my view. The Lord Chief Baron suggested that there might be a previous enquiry before the Country Court, which might for that purpose be a sort of grand jury.[1]

Lord Hill showed me a letter from Sir F. Watson addressed to Sir B. Taylor, as the King's first aide-decamp, and directing him as such, by the King's command, to intimate to Lord Hill the pleasure it would give His Majesty to know that Lord Hill had given Captain Scarlett, the son of the Attorney-General, an opportunity of purchasing a majority. Captain Scarlett is a very young captain and Lord Hill feels the thing asked cannot be done. He was going to see the Duke of Wellington about it. Not very long ago the King gave away a regiment without asking Lord Hill however, that was settled; but it is clear that, unless Lord Hill is allowed to exercise the fair patronage of his office, he will resign.

[1 I. e. when the case was to lie transferred to the Supreme Court.]

176   January 26.

Cabinet. It seems the French have acceded to the proposals of the Pasha of Egypt, and finding 50,000 men would be required to take Algiers, prefer his operating with 40,000 of his own. He pretends to have made arrangements which will secure an easy conquest, and promises to place Tunis, Tripoli, and Algiers under regular governments, nominally under the Sultan, whose consent he reckons upon, and capable of preserving the relations of peace with other Mediterranean Powers.

The Pasha's army is commanded by French officers, and the annexation of these States to Egypt would be their practical annexation to France. When his army is disseminated along the coast of Africa, I might realise my dream of taking Egypt from India.

We considered the proposed order in Council relative to the slave regulations of the King's own ceded colonies. The Duke was evidently not well, and he was rather out of humour. We were three hours and a half in Cabinet. He made various objections to the proposed regulations. He impressed upon us the danger of tampering with the rights of property. We were doing that with property of an odious character, which we should not do in England. He pressed the effect in the West Indies and the example everywhere. He seemed to complain that the regulations were different from those agreed to in the summer. Sir G. Murray was very quiet. He is a very sensible man, but he is overawed by the Duke, having been under him so long.

177   Poor old Tierney is dead, for which I am very sorry. He was a very good friend of mine.

January 27.

Cabinet at four. There can be no Council to-morrow, as Greville has the'gout and Buller is in Cornwall.

There is to be an intimation sent to the Pasha to the effect that we disapprove of the proposed attempt to conquer Tripoli, Tunis, and Algiers. France is to be told the same. I wished conditional orders to be given to the Fleet, and that the Pasha should be told orders had been given. It being doubtful whether French vessels might not convoy the Egyptian fleet and transports, I thought we had better now consider what we should do in that event; that we had better not threaten without determining to execute our threat, and that we should consider how we should deal with the French ships if we stopped the Egyptian in short not take a first step which might make a second necessary, without knowing in our own minds what that second step should be. The Duke thinks the French will back out when they know our disapprobation, and that at any rate the Pasha would. I rather doubt this of either of them.

The French say they have a sort of quarrel with Tripoli, but none with Tunis, and they enter into a scheme for conquering both as stepping-stones to Algiers. Tunis in their hands would be more dangerous than Algiers.

Hardinge told me he had had a long conversation ith Peel the other day on the state of the country. c thought Peel seemed to have apprehensions, and to ~~VOL. II.~~

178 ᴎ think that if the King, through some intrigue of the Brunswickers, got rid of the Duke, things would go very ill indeed; that the authority of the Duke alone kept things quiet. England is in a bad state, because the country gentlemen have ill-paid rents; but Scotland and Ireland do very well, and the trade of the country is not depressed.

Cabinet dinner at the Chancellor's. The Duke of Montrose there, as it was to have been a dinner for the sheriffs. I told the Duke of my notion of altering the law of succession to property in India, and enabling all existing proprietors to leave their estates as they please.

January 28.

The Times ' publishes my letter to Malcolm to-day, with comments.

Upon the whole I am glad the letter has been published. I think no one can read it without seeing I am actuated only by public views, and that I am determined to do my duty.

The editor of the ' Courier' called at the Indian Board and saw Bankes, and asked whether he should say anything. Bankes said he would see me before he gave an answer. I do not care about the publication, and the letter will defend itself.

January 29.

Chairs have received very bad accounts of the temper of the Madras army, which has no cause of complaint. Lord W. Bentinck has been at last obliged to lay his hand

179 upon the press, and, as might have been expected, is much more abused than if he had done so at first. The Eadicals had begun to consider him one of themselves, and so think him a traitor when he refuses to go any further with them.

I went to the Duke and told him what they said. He is, as usual, sanguine, and thinks it will blow over.

I told the Duke I thought he had better look out for a Governor-General, for it might be necessary to recall Lord "W. Bentinck. The objection to making Malcolm provisional successor is that he would stay till he died in order to be Governor-

General one day. Otherwise his provisional appointment would strengthen the local Government very much.

At the Cabinet they had all read my letter in the 4 Times," except the Chancellor. I told him to read it.

Peel was indignant at the publication. Lord Eosslyn said Joseph Hume had had the letter some time in his possession, and must have sent it to the ' Times."

Peel said it was a very good letter. I said I was not ashamed of it.

They all laughed very much at the simile of the elephants.

Cabinet. Much discussion as to the terms of the speech. Aberdeen's part was very ill done indeed. It underwent much alteration and was improved. That regarding distress and remedies was postponed. There is no remedy, and it is best to say so.

In the meantime the export of almost all manufactures is increased largely in quantity, but the value is diminished. Still this proves continued and increased employment, although at low wages. This is a state of things in which we cannot try to make corn dearer or wool either. Nothing but the extreme cheapness of our manufactures makes their export possible.

Aberdeen read his letter to Consul Barker respecting the Pasha's designs. The last paragraph, which intimated that the Pasha's persistence ' would too probably lead to our decided opposition," was omitted. It was thought that the recommendation, to weigh well the serious consequences of a measure highly objectionable to us, and to which other Powers could not but be unfavourable," was thought sufficient to stop the Pasha.

If the first words had stood, we must have used the same to France, and the threat might have led to collision. In any case the Pasha would have communicated the expressions to France.

The Duke and the Chancellor were to see Leopold to-morrow.

Another Cabinet to-morrow at four for going on with the Speech.

January 30.

Hardinge called. He told me all was not settled as to Lord Chandos having the Mint. He referred to the Duke of Buckingham, [1] who would rather have it himself, with a seat in the Cabinet.

Lord Mountcharles goes out to annoy his father, and force him to give him a larger allowance, unaccom- [1 He had, as appears from the Wellington correspondence, pressed for years his claims to a seat in the Cahinet, with an importunity to which the Duke of Wellington expressed his objection. His large parliamentary interest, which almost made him the chief of a party of his own, made him. appear entitled to expect it.]

panied by the condition of constant attendance in the House of Commons.

Kead the Duke of Northumberland's letter to Peel on the state of Ireland. The Duke represents the Catholic Belief Bill as having produced none of the evils anticipated by its opposers, if it has not produced all the benefits expected by its supporters as having upon the whole worked better than could have been expected in so short a time and under such circumstances.

The disturbances he thinks confined to the counties of Tipperary, Clare, and Eoscommon; in the first produced by too high rents; in the second by late collision and the want of proper management on the part of the gentlemen; in the last by attempts to convert the Catholics, and the zeal of new converts. The Catholic Union is dissolved. The great body of the Catholics have abstained from the ostentation of triumph.

Monday, February 1.

Bankes called this morning, but I did not see him. He saw Henry. He came to say he was out, and S. Wortley in his place. When he understood Lord Chandos did not take the Mint, he went to the Duke and offered to remain, thinking his going out, with Lord Chandos's declining to come in, might, taken together, embarrass the Government. However, the arrangement was already made.

Eead Lushington's minute on the Neilgherry hills. He wants to make an English colony there. If he had, every man would make some excuse, desert his duty in the hot months, and go to the Neilgherry hills.

Eead the first volume of Gamba's ' Travels in South Kussia." He was Consul of France, but writes like a Eussian. He talks of restoring the commercial communication with Asia by the Phasis, Caspian, and Oxus. All this is absurd. Unless indeed the Eussians, after occupying China, turn the Oxus into its old course, and thus enable themselves to carry goods by water carriage to the foot of the Himalaya, or rather within 250 miles of Cabul.

February 5.

Eeceived last night a note from the Duke asking me, if I could, to have a Cabinet to-day on Batta. If I could not, to send Peel the letters of Malcolm, c.

I determined to have the Cabinet. Peel had not read till the day before yesterday the Batta papers, and, although inclining to the opinion that the present orders must be maintained, he thinks it, as it is, a serious question for the Government to decide after the minutes of Lord William Bentinck and the members of council, with the apprehension of a mutiny as the possible result of our standing firm. I said if we gave way the other armies would bring forward their demands that it was a question, not only between the Home Authorities and the army, but the Home Authorities and the Local Government which had for sixteen years resisted the orders sent to them.

The Duke cautioned the Cabinet as to the character of the Indian army, which he said was a mercenary army, retained in obedience by nothing but the wish to return to England; but lie thought after what had taken place we must resist, and adhere to our present orders. Peel wished all the members of the Cabinet to read the minutes before they decided, and there is to be a Cabinet on Sunday.

It was determined that if a question should be asked to-night, Peel should say ' the orders had not been countermanded." Peel observed very justly on the state of things which seemed to exist in India. An army sending such memorials to the Government, and the members of the Government writing pamphlets against each other. In point of fact, years will be required to restore a proper tone to the Government of India.

I mentioned to the Duke the mission of two Russian Poles to India and Manilla, and that I suspected Eussia of a wish to purchase Manilla. Neither the Duke nor Aberdeen seemed to think the Spaniards would or could sell the Philippines. However, Aberdeen will write to the man at Madrid to find out whether any proposal to that effect has been made by the Russian Government.

The members of the House of Commons consider their majority last night fortunate. The House is very loose. In the majority and minority were the most opposite parties. O'Connell went out with Sadler. The Brunswickers are in high glee, and have sent for their valiant champion, Falmouth. In our House they made a poor show.

Prince Leopold is not by any means disposed to take Greece without Candia, and it was thought, from Lord Lansdowne's speech, he and others had advised him to take this line. Aberdeen is very much embarrassed to find a substitute.

February 6.

Spring-Bice asked Bankes in the House last night whether the letter to Sir J. Malcolm published as mine was mine. Bankes said that I had no copy of it, and therefore could not say it was correctly given. It was a private letter. Brougham, and Mackintosh, and that ass, M. A. Taylor, spoke in reprobation of it. Mackintosh most unfairly and disingenuously pretended to understand I endeavoured to get off by saying it was a private letter, and said it would be an extenuation of my offence if I would disavow the sentiments contained in it. What must he be himself to suppose I would disavow what I had written! Upon the whole, the tone taken by Peel and Bankes, but more especially by Peel, was too apologetical. I shall be obliged to go to the House on Monday to have a question put to me by Lord Lansdowne. I shall distinctly declare he may consider the letter as mine, and that I am ready to defend every line of it. Wrote to Lord Wellesley to offer to put his name upon the Committee on East India affairs if he would attend. He declines on account of ill-health.

Eeceived a note from Peel begging me to have the Chairs to meet him on the appointment of the committee. I sent to the Chairman, and he came and met Peel; but Astell was out of the way. We are to meet at half-past one to-morrow. Peel did not seem to have looked much into the subject, which the Chairman observed.

Saw Bankes. He is not certain of succeeding now to the secretaryship of the Admiralty, but he expects it ultimately. He thinks the Duke of Buckingham had nothing to do with Lord Chandos's rejection of the Mint: but does not know how it went off. He thought that Lord Chandos had accepted, and the Duke seems to have thought so too.

A very good account from Ireland. The country gradually and quietly coming round.

Sunday, February 7.

Cabinet. First, Batta. The Duke gave his decided opinion in favour of adhering to the present order. After some conversation, but no opposition, the Cabinet acquiesced unanimously in that decision, which has been mine from the first.

I had a moment's conversation with Peel about the letter to Sir J. Malcolm, and told him I would defend every word of it, elephants and all.

Then we had a good deal of discussion respecting the policy to be pursued with regard to Cuba, against which the Mexicans are preparing to organise a slave insurrection, for which purpose they have sent a Minister to Hayti. It seems to be generally believed that Canning, about the year 1823, issued a sort of prohibition to the Mexican and Columbian States to attack Cuba, but no trace can be found in the Foreign Office of any such prohibition.

Sir E. Wilson means to ask a question upon the subject to-morrow. He says, if you prohibit the Mexicans and Columbians from attacking Cuba, you should prohibit the Spaniards from attacking them which is fair in fact the expedition of Barradas was undertaken before we knew anything about it, and if we had wished we could not have interfered.

The question as to what answer should be given to Sir E. Wilson, and what policy pursued, was deferred till to-morrow.

In the meantime it appears that Mr. Sobertson, who is at Mexico, remonstrated strongly with M. de Bo-caregna, respecting the objects of the embassy to Hayti, and he was told by Aberdeen that he did quite right, and that not only ourselves but other states might view with disapprobation an attempt to excite a warfare of an uncivilised character in Cuba.

The French have assembled 35,000 men to attack Algiers. They promise not to keep it. [1] They intimate their intention of assisting Mehemet Ali with a fleet; but in the meantime they are satisfied at Constantinople that Mehemet Ali will not move.

Aberdeen told Laval that we had informed the Pasha of Egypt that we should view with disapprobation his attack upon Tunis and Tripoli without the consent of the Sultan. Laval begged this might be repeated to him three times.

Much conversation as to the state of the House of Commons. The Tories are most radical. Sir E. Vyvyan told Holmes or Planta his object was to reduce the Government majorities as much as possible, and to make the Government as contemptible as possible. Sir E. Knatchbull leads about twenty-three. I think the probability is that, unless we make some coalition with [1 This promise was repudiated by the Government of July.]

the Whigs, we shall go to the ground between the two parties, [1] both uniting against us upon some point (upon my letter to Sir J. Malcolm as likely as any other).

I took home Sir George Murray. He expressed his surprise the Duke should cling to the hope of reclaiming the ultra-Tories, whom he would not get, and who were not worth having.

I confess I think he carries it on too long, although I am not surprised he should have wished it at first.

Prince Leopold has given no reply to Aberdeen's letter, or to the offer of the ambassadors.

Lord Holland gives notice to-morrow of a motion about Greece, and Lord Melbourne moves for some papers respecting Portugal.

Lord Melville gives notice for me of the committee on East Indian Affairs, and I am not to go down till Tuesday, that we may have out the letter to Malcolm and other Indian matters all at once.

February 8.

Wrote a memorandum for Peel and Bankes to this effect: ' That I had neither copy nor recollection of the letter; but that I had no doubt the letter published as mine was substantially correct. It was a confidential exposition of the motives which induced me to recommend two judges to the King. [2] It was never intended to be published, nor did I expect it would be. The [1 This eventually occurred on the Civil List question after the accession of William IV.

¶ It was suggested that with these colleagues Sir J. Grant would be like a wild elephant between two tame ones. Alluding to the method of taming captured elephants in India.]

expressions, therefore, were unadvised, but the sentiments were and are mine, deliberately formed upon full consideration of the official documents before me.

Cabinet. It appears on looking into papers of 1825 and 1826 that so far from our having prohibited Mexico and Columbia from making any attack upon Cuba, we uniformly abstained from doing anything of the kind. The Americans declared they could not see with indifference any state other than Spain in possession of Cuba, and further their disposition to interpose their power should war be conducted in Cuba in a devastating manner, and with a view to the excitement of a servile war.

We offered to guarantee Cuba to Spain in 1823 if she would negotiate with the colonies with a view to their recognition.

Subsequently we were willing to enter into a tripartite guarantee of Cuba to Spain with the United States and France.

The United States seemed not unwilling, but France held back.

Peel is to say there was no record of any prohibition, but that the United States declared so, and it was possible Mr. Canning may have intimated a similar disposition on our part. This is to keep open to us the faculty of interfering if we please.

The Duke thinks my letter does not signify one pin. The simile of the elephants evidently means no more than that an indiscreet judge wae placed between two discreet ones.

The Duke told me he had offered a Lordship of the Treasury to Ashley, who had declined it. He then told him to make himself master of the Batta question. Ashley said he had not seen the papers. He said, let him see the papers. I told him I had sent them the moment I got them to him, and he had desired me to send them to the Cabinet room, which I did. When they were taken from the Cabinet room they went to the India Board, and Ashley might have seen them. I had never kept any papers from him. We then talked about the speech to be made in moving the committee. The Duke seems inclined to have little said. Peel seems disposed to say little; but he knows little. I think they are wrong. I am sure it is necessary to correct the erroneous notions which have been propagated with respect to the trade. They will otherwise acquire so great a head it will be impossible to beat them back.

However, this we are to talk over with Peel tomorrow.

General King, who voted against the address on Thursday, is turned out by the King himself; the Duke having only mentioned the fact. I dare say the King may be alarmed by the spirit shown by the House of Commons.

The suicide of. on account of his wife's seduction by the Duke of Cumberland, will drive the Duke of Cumberland out of the field.

February 9.

Called on the Duke. He advised a very narrowed statement in moving for the committee. I rather doubt his judgment upon this point. I fear the opinion of the country will become settled, and that when the strength of our case is brought forward it will be found unequal to the driving back of the stream. However, I made a speech as he desired. Lord Lansdowne said a few words.

Lord Durham then questioned me as to the authenticity of my letter to Sir J. Malcolm. I acknowledged it was substantially correct, and declared I could not have entertained any other sentiments without a dereliction of duty. He expressed disapprobation, considering the letter as evincing a determination to control the independence of judges. The Duke replied then Lord Melville then Lord Holland I last. I declared that, as my father's son, I was the last man capable of harbouring a thought against the independence of judges; but I would resist their usurpation, more especially when they usurped powers withheld from them by Parliament as dangerous to the peace of India and to the stability of the British power.

I said India could not bear the collision of the Supreme Court and the Local Government. If we did not support the Government we should lose India.

I was determined to maintain the integrity, the dignity, the authority, and the unapproachable power of the Local Government, and especially to support a man who, at that distance from England, acting in the faithful discharge of his public duty, incurred the highest responsibility and the greatest personal risk in defence of what he considered essential to the stability of the British power in India. I believe I did well. They all told me I should hear no more of it.

191

February 10.

Saw Bankes. He says the House of Commons is loose indeed; but he thinks Ministers will have a majority on the East Eetford business. The worst of it is that those who ought to be the friends of Government will not stay out a debate. Last night Peel and Goulburn were left with a decided minority, but the House was counted out.

Saw Hardinge. He seems to think there is no great danger, and he thinks the House is in so loose a state that the accession of an individual or two would not draw others; that Brougham may be quieted, and that the others do not much signify.

In the meantime Abercromby has been made Chief Baron of Scotland. Another Whig gone. A very valuable intimation to those who remain.

Lord Lansdowne brings in Zachary Macaulay, son of the old saint. [1]They say a very clever man indeed, at least as a writer.

Hardinge told me the Duke told Mrs. Arbuthnot I spoke very well last night. At dinner the Chancellor and Sir George Murray congratulated me on what had taken place.

After the Cabinet dinner, much talk and nothing settled. The motion of Sir J. Graham will, I think, be amended and easily. There is a disposition, very properly, not to give Portuguese papers. As to the Lord Holland's motion on Friday no decision is come to.

[1 The late Lord Macaulay. He is erroneously described by his father's Christian name.]

192

Gave the Duke the petition of the Bengal half-castes.

Mr Jenkins, who was for many years resident at Nagpore, called upon me and offered himself as successor to Sir J. Malcolm. He said the Chairs were disposed to him, if the Government had no objection. I said I was aware of the services he had rendered, but that there were many distinguished servants of the Company, and likewise persons of ability who had not been in India, whose several qualifications must be considered. It was further a point upon which I must of course communicate with the Duke of Wellington. The man is a person of dry cold manner, not prepossessing.

I am disposed to think Mr. Chaplin the best Indian for the situation.

February 11.

I think Polignac's Ministry must fall, and really, as regards himself, I cannot feel regret, as he is the greatest liar that has exercised diplomatist functions for a long time. I had thought better of him. If their expedition ever sails for Algiers they will find what it costs to send an expedition over sea. I think, however, they will succeed, and, if they do, they will keep Algiers.

Sir R. Gordon entertains a very different opinion from that expressed by Aberdeen as to the future fate of the Ottoman Empire. He thinks the events of the late war prove little, and that the Sultan has learnt a lesson which will induce him to treat his rayas better that the war once over, all men will return to their duty. However, he gives no good reasons for his opinion. He states very fairly the difficulty of his own position. He says he has hitherto believed it was the intention of his Government to support Turkey. He has therefore had influence, because where he has advised concession the Turks have understood we meant it should not be hurtful to them but now, how can he advise the Turks to yield to what is asked, when he knows the Government think that the more is taken from Turkey, the more is saved from Eussia? Sir E. Gordon says his colleagues are by no means of opinion that the Ottoman Empire is falling, and that France allows their officers to go in numbers to serve with the Turkish troops.

Eeceived a letter from Sir J. Macdonald in which he tells me the Turkish Asiatic provinces are falling away from the Sultan.

He encloses a letter from a Mr Sterling, giving a very interesting account of his journey by Meshed and near Balkh to Cabul. He took a new road to the north of the Paropamisan ridge. In Cabul he experienced no difficulty.

February 12.

House. Lord Holland's motion of a resolution that the House would not be satisfied with any plan for the pacification and settlement of Greece, which did not secure to that state the means of independence by sea and land, and leave the Greeks free to have their own Constitution. His information was most inaccurate. Yet on this he founded his distrust of the Government. Notwithstanding this distrust he was neither with them nor against them, nor did he wish to turn them out.

He made an indifferent speech. Aberdeen a fair one ill delivered. The Duke spoke admirably. The brains were beaten out of the motion. No division. Goderich and Clanricarde and Melbourne spoke; Lord Melbourne poorly.

On the East Eetford question last night we had a majority of twenty-seven in a House of 226 members the high Tories voting with Government.

Bankes has now the offer of a Lordship of the Admiralty till Croker can be got rid of; but he will not go. Castlereagh will have the Treasury Lordship that is, 600Z. a year more for having been careless.

February 13.

After seeing the Chairs spoke to the Duke about the Bombay succession. He asked what I meant to do with Elphinstone? I considered he had left India altogether, The Duke thought he must return that he would go to Bombay again with the expectation of afterwards going to Madras. I think the Duke has an idea of making him Governor-General. I mentioned Mr. Chaplin. The Duke mentioned Mr. Jenkins, of whom he thought highly. He had done well at Nagpore, and he had had some correspondence with him when in India which gave him a good opinion of him. The Duke spoke of Mr. Eussell, but thought he had been mixed up with the Hyderabad transactions. I then mentioned Clare. The Duke thought him better than any of the others mentioned. That it was a great thing to have a⌐l It will be remembered that tins question had led to the resignation of Huskisson and his friends⌡

man of rank; he must be well supported; lie had not a very strong mind. However, on the whole he seemed better than the others, and I am to propose him.

I am very glad to have Clare. I have a great respect and regard for him but I have a little hesitation as to his fitness. He will, however, be a most zealous and honourable servant of the public, and his good manners will keep people in good humour and in order.

Leopold has sent in his answer. I have not seen it yet. He accepts on conditions.

The debate last night in the Commons is considered very favourable. Dawson's amendment was adopted and Planta and Holmes say the temper of the country gentlemen is much improved. They are quite in spirits again.

A hint of Peel's, but a hint that the Government did not fear an appeal to the country, seems to have had a good effect.

February 14.

Cabinet. On Thursday Peel, in opening the Compensation Bill, will detail the various legal reforms.

He is disposed to diminish gradually the number of crimes for which the punishment of death is awarded. The Duke seemed reluctant and so did others. However, the Chancellor did not object.

My father considered that where a man could not protect his own property the law ought to protect it for him by higher penalties. However, now it seems a man must protect his own property, and punishments are to be proportioned more to the extent of the moral offence than to the necessity for preventing crime.

Then we considered Leopold's answer. The man accepts provided 1. There is a guarantee of the new State.

2. That the frontier is slightly altered.

3. That the three powers protect the present insurgents in Samos and Candia.

4. That a loan of 1,500,000*l* is guaranteed.

5. That he may have troops furnished to him.

6. He stipulates that the Greeks should have the power of declining him, le soussigné, as their Prince.

A guarantee there will probably be, and therefore the alteration of boundaries, which Leopold knew could not be listened to, is in fact unnecessary.

Each power separately and individually may use its good offices with the Porte for the protection of the Greeks in Samos and Candia, and indeed, under the agreement as to an amnesty, each would be bound to do so; but no triple agreement will be entered into, the object being to get out of the Treaty of July 6.

Aberdeen seemed disposed to allow 1,000 men of each of the three Powers to go to Greece. This would continue the triple action, and as these troops would go, not against any external enemy, but against Greeks, the measure would be somewhat in contradiction to the declaration the other night that the Greeks and their Prince might make what Government they pleased. After some conversation it seemed the general opinion that it would be better to pay the cost of the troops than to have our own there, and in fact the same money would enable Greece to have twice the number of Germans or Swiss that she could have of British. This I thought. But I suggested that Greece could not want a large sum down. A sum might be required for outfit, but then an annual sum. Peel proposed the whole loan guaranteed should be 700,000., of which 100,000. to be paid down as outfit, and then 100,000. a year for six years at 5 per cent; the three Powers guaranteeing each a third part of the interest. It is better to guarantee the loan, then to pay money down. The loan, they say, can be made at three. Aberdeen says the Greeks give a most flourishing expose of their future finances, and he thinks they will become a rich State, and the Powers be exposed to no danger of being called upon for the payment of the interest. I think he begins to love his Greek progeny.

The Duke only desired we would get out of the treaty. I suggested the inexpediency of our joining in the guarantee. A guarantee gave no right of intervention we should not otherwise possess, and it obliged us' to interfere when we might not desire to do so. However, I fear there will be a guarantee.

February 16.

Cabinet. There seems to be little doubt that the Emperor Pedro means to direct an expedition from Eio against Portugal, Terceira being the point of rassemble-ment. This is a practical answer to the question recently put by us conjointly with France and Austria as to the intentions of the Emperor, and therefore we are at liberty to act as if a specific answer had been received. It seems Austria will be very unwilling to recognise Don Miguel; France not.

The object of recognising him is to prevent a revolutionary war in Portugal and the entrance of Spanish troops into Portugal to oppose it.

Whenever Miguel is recognised, I think Lord Boss-lyn will be made Master-General of the Ordnance, Lord Beresford going to Portugal as Minister, and then the Privy Seal will be disposable. I dare say the Duke, out of good nature, will offer it to Lord Westmoreland.

Aberdeen read the remonstrance he proposed sending to Spain against the proposed expedition to Mexico.

Leopold met the Plenipotentiaries, and Aberdeen thinks he would have acceded, but he evidently required the sanction of another person. The French Ambassador used very strong language, telling him his Court would be very much hurt indeed at finding him make these difficulties after all that had passed, c.

Peel told me he was disposed to grant the motion for any correspondence between the Board of Control or any member of it, c., with a direct negative. To move the previous question was an admission of some error. I was telling him the circumstances when it was necessary to attend to Aberdeen's business. I must tell him to-morrow.

February 17.

At the Cabinet dinner at Lord Melville's, talked to Peel and gave him a copy of the report of the Privy Council and of my letter to Sir J. Grant. He is disposed to take a high tone, and thinks men will follow him better when he does than when he temporises. I am sure they will.

He says he would reduce everything so low as not to be beat upon establishments. If he is beat upon unimportant questions he does not care, and will not go out. They will not get a majority for stopping supplies, and if they can agree upon motions, he is prepared to play the game of '83[1] with them. I am sure he is right.

February 18.

House. First a question from Lord Holland whether the orders to the Admiral respecting Greek slaves, c., would, after the settlement of Greece, apply to Candiot Greeks. Then Lord Melbourne's motion for Portuguese papers. He did not speak well but very bitterly. Goderich spoke pathetically against the Terceira affair Lord Wharncliffe well with us Lans-downe wide and loose the Duke very excellent Aberdeen worse than usual, and very imprudent, abusing Miguel and making awkward admissions.

It was quite established that Canning had nothing to say to the Portuguese Constitution, and I think we shall hear no more of Terceira. Fifty-two to twenty-one no proxies.

February 19.

Cabinet. Leopold's answer. He wants troops and money. After long talk it was resolved the French troops might stay a year, till he could raise others, and money should be given.

[1 Alluding to Pitt's course at the beginning of his first Ministry. He retained office a whole Session in spite of the motions carried against him, and in the general election of 1784 obtained an overwhelming majority.]

February 20, 1830.

In riding with Lord Eosslyn had a long conversation with him upon Indian matters. He had just been reading the despatches from Lord Stuart and Lord Heytes-bury upon these subjects. I told him I had anticipated all Lord H. suggested and had done, I really thought, all that could be done. I am to send him the secret letter. He thinks, as I do, that Aberdeen is in a great hurry to get rid of the Greek question, and disposed to incur future embarrassments to avoid present inconvenience.

Lord Eosslyn does not much like the division of last night, but I believe it was a good one.

February 21.

This morning looked through the finance accounts of the three years, ending 1819, and the three ending 1828, with a view to comparing the state of the country with what it was before Peel's Bill. The increased consumption is astonishing. The increase of British tonnage and in the number of seamen since 1819 is equal to the whole tonnage and to all the seamen in the foreign trade with Great Britain, although that is increased nearly in the same proportion with our own.

The increased consumption of tea and coffee is 50 per cent. The number of pounds in 1819 being about 30,000,000 of pounds, and now 45,000,000 pounds.

The import of foreign raw produce is much increased of that produce which competes with the landed produce of England.

Hardinge called. He thinks the Government quite safe now. Indeed, he never had much apprehension. He regrets Sir James Graham's divergence from the road which leads to office. He thinks he came up to London intending well; but that he thought under present circumstances he could be a more considerable man out of office than he would be in a subordinate situation.

The Duke of Northumberland says the salary of the Lord-Lieutenant may well be reduced to 20,000. a year.

February 24.

Lord Eosslyn, who called upon me at the office, thinks I may go a little too far in my directions with regard to Eussian spies, that is, in a public despatch. I had directed that if it appeared danger was likely to arise from their return to Europe or from their passage into any Asiatic country, their persons should be placed under restraint, and in all cases their papers and letters got possession of. He suggests that this might be mentioned in a private letter, or left to the discretion of the Local Governments.

We had a long conversation on Lord Stanhope's motion for to-morrow, when Whigs and Tories are to combine to beat us.

The division last night in the House of Commons on Lord J. Eussell's motion for giving two members to Manchester, Birmingham, and Leeds, was not satisfactory. There were 140 for it, and only 188 against it. The Tories stayed away.

February 25.

House at 4 and until 2. Lord Stanhope's motion for a Committee of the whole House on the internal state of the country. He made a weak speech, because to get votes he abstained from stating the cause of distress, which in his opinion is currency, or any remedy. Goderich and Lansdowne made good speeches. Kose-bery not a bad one, though as usual pompous. All suggesting some remedies all for reducing taxation, but against a Committee of the House. Lord Eadnor made a good vulgar speech. King spoke better than usual. He proposed, but afterwards withdrew, an amendment for a Committee upstairs. The Duke, who alone spoke on our side, did not speak well, and some of his statements were hazardous. Lords Darnley and Bute declared there was no distress near them.

We divided well. There being but fifteen present for Lord Stanhope's motion, and ten proxies.

February 26.

Chairs at 11. Went over with them the letter on Batta.

Lord Wharncliffe intends on Tuesday to propose examining the Chairman of the East Indian Company.

February 27.

Wrote a note to Loch to tell him of Lord Wharn-cliffe's intention. He does not like the idea at all, and wishes to see me before the Committee sits. I have named Monday at eleven. I told him my feeling was against his being examined, as I thought it unfair; besides, lie was not the best witness. I told Lord Wharncliffe he should examine Lord Amherst.

At the Cabinet room I attempted to read the papers respecting Irish education. My opinion is that it would be better to let the matter rest for the present; the agitation of it may revive animosities, and if any good be attainable, it may be attained at a more favourable period than the present. I rather doubt whether it might not be yet more safely left to the people themselves, as education in England and in Scotland.

March 1.

Cabinet. We were to have talked about Irish education, but more important matters intervened. There is a motion on Friday of Mr. Davenport's for a Committee on the internal state of the country. Peel thinks there will be a union of parties in favour of it. He feels it must be opposed. Some of the friends of Government have said they must vote for it. He proposes that Goulburn should to-morrow give notice of his intention of explaining his views as to taxation on Monday week. Peel thinks that he can procure an adjournment of the debate till after Goulburn's expose.

Goulburn suggests taking off the whole of the beer tax, and remitting the hop duty for this year, as well as remodelling it. He likewise proposes lowering the duties on East and West India sugar, the former from 37s. to 25s., and the latter from 27s. to 20s.

As the revenue is decreasing, these reductions cannot be taken from it. There must be a commutation. This he proposes to be a modified property tax, to apply to landed property, all fixed property, and the funds as well 'as all offices, but not to the profits of trade.

March 2.

There seems to have been some incivility last night on the part of Sir Charles Burrell and Sir E. Knatchbull against me, with reference to my opposition to the Duke of Eichmond's motion on the wool question last year.

March 3.

Peel's. Met Bankes, Graham, and Ashley. It was, after talk, agreed that the papers asked should be refused, unless in the course of the debate it should appear that the granting of Grant's petition and the report of the Privy Council would improve the division. I expect a regular attack upon myself from all quarters. I would give a year of the House of Lords to be there to throw grape-shot amongst the small lawyers.

Cabinet room. Eead despatches relating to the expedition to Algiers, which is certainly going.

Cabinet dinner at Peel's. The affair of the vacated offices becomes serious, for it seems certain that it is necessary to take the declaration again upon any new patent, and the Board of Admiralty should have taken the declaration as well as Castlereagh the Board of Control as well as me.

The Chancellor continues to have no objection to reducing the salaries of the Supreme Court Judges.

March 5.,

Chairs at 11. I got rid of them as soon as I could, as I wished to go to the Committee.

Loch showed me a letter from Lord William Ben-tinck, by which it appears that the officers of the Cawnpore division of the army wished to have a general meeting for the election of delegates to England. Sir J. Whittingham forwarded their request to Lord Combermere, highly disapproving of it. Lord Comber-mere directed the

Adjutant-General to write a letter coinciding with Sir J. Whittingham's opinions, and adding that he would be the advocate of the army both in India and in England. Lord William (Bentinck) is going up the country with the Government and wishes to take Lord Dalhousie with him. He expects very uncivil treatment, and says the discontent is deep-seated. The same account is received from other quarters.

The debate was adjourned last night. E. Grant made a speech in a moderate tone, but disingenuous. Lord Ashley spoke good stuff apparently, but Henry says he could not hear him. Lord Graham was unembarrassed and did well; but the l Times' hardly gives him ten words.

I sent a note to Peel to-day observing upon the disingenuousness of Grant's speech. He told me he had been reading the papers, and saw it was no question of judicial independence, but of judicial aggression, and he thought the tone of the Governor who was in the right much better than that of the Judge who was in the wrong. So I hope he will make a good speech.

March 6.

Eead letters from Sir J. Macdonald. They came by Constantinople. The only news they contain is that the Eussians certainly have the intention of conquering Khiva and Bokhara. This comes from Chasanes Murza.

I told the Duke, who seems disposed to make it an European question.

I showed the Duke a most atrocious libel on royalty which has been published in the ' Calcutta Gazette." If the King saw it he would recall Lord "William by the Sign Manual. A letter must be written immediately in the press. It is in such a state that our Government cannot stand if it be permitted to go on uncontrolled.

I asked the Duke as to taxation. He said he thought it could be done without income tax. To lay on income tax would be to weaken ourselves in the opinion of all foreign Powers. Besides, it would prevent our reducing the Four per Cents.

He calculated the loss of the beer duty at 3,500,000. and, marine insurance, cider, remission of hop duty, c., would make the loss 4,500,000.

To meet this he expected

Surplus of last year 1,700,000

Additional from general improvement. 400,000 Additional malt by reducing beer duties. 500,000 Increased duty on spirits. 500,000

Keducing Four per Cents 750,000

Savings 1,400,000 Ireland, soap, c 450,000

Stamps 200,000/5,900,000 4,500,000/1,400,000‖

There may have been more; but he spoke, and I write from memory.

I told him I thought that with a diminished duty on beer and an increased duty on spirits he could not expect an increase of 500,000. on spirits. He admitted that was the weak point. He said he was sure we could not carry an income tax while we had a million surplus. If we have a good harvest, I have no doubt the increase on malt will be great; but I apprehend there must be a repayment of beer duties, and if there should be, the loss will be enormous.

March 8.

Sent Mr. Elphinstone a letter giving an account of the travels to the North of the Paropamisan range into Cabul.

The Duke said we really must look out for a new Governor-General. I suggested Hardinge. He said Hardinge had not as yet station enough in the opinion of the public, in the army, or in Parliament. He wished him to be Secretary in Ireland. It would have been much better if he had gone there instead of Lord F. Gower, and Lord F. to the War Office. To be sure, then we should not have had the reductions Hardinge had effected. He had, as I knew, always wished Hardinge to go to Ireland.

I observed that Hardinge was rising every day in public estimation, which the Duke acknowledged, and I added that I was sure none would do the duty better, for he had firmness and habits of business. The Duke seems to think of Elphinstone. He said he was a very clever man. I told him I had been an hour and a half with Elphinstone last night. I told the Duke all my notions respecting individual responsibility, members of Council, c., and that I had begged Elphinstone to think of them. The Duke seemed generally to approve of them. It seems Lord Wellesley never would go to Council. I do not wonder at it; but the Duke used to tell him he was Governor-General in Council that he ought always to go there.

March 10.

Dined with the Duke. Cabinet dinner. Only the Peers there. The others detained by Lord Palmerston's motion on Portugal, on which there was a majority of two to one, 150 odd to 70 something. Huskisson made a very bad dull speech. We talked about a successor to the Speaker. They seem to think he will not resign now, as he would not get a good pension in the present temper of the House.

The candidates are Sir J. Beckett, Littleton, G. Bankes, Wynn of course. I mentioned Frankland Lewis as a good man, which he would be. I dare say the Chairs will think he should be elected unanimously.

It seems there must be a Bill of Indemnity for not taking the declaration, two Bishops, Chester and Oxford, not having taken it. The Duke finds he has at Dover, as Lord Warden.

We had some little conversation about the income tax, which the Duke is very hostile to, and I am glad we shall not have it.

March 11.

The Eussians have at last sent their reply to our expostulatory note. I have not had time to read it. Lord Heytesbury calculates that the last war cost them 12,000,000., but they endeavour to conceal the amount.

Peel told me the House was quite excited against the Bombay judges, and that the division fairly represented its real opinion.

March 12.

There was but one black ball in the election of Lord Clare, and the Chairs think that was put in by mistake; no one objected.

March 13.

Eead Sir H. Parnell's pamphlet on taxation.

Cabinet room at two. I had only got half through the Kussian answer when the Cabinet met for the subject of taxation.

I rather expected to find that the Duke had had communications with Goulburn, and that the idea of a property tax was given up. However, that seemed not to be the case. It was determined the whole beer duty should be given up in any case.

The expected revenue is. 50,250,000

The expected expenditure 47,930,000

Surplus 2,320,000

Add by reduction of Four per Cents 777,000

By Is. Qd. on British, and 2d. on Irish and Scotch Spirits 400,000

By stamps in Ireland. 220,000 3,717,000 Deduct beer tax, 3,200,000, but the loss to the revenue from the probable increase of malt, calculated at. 2,500,000 1,217,000 Probable increase of revenue 450,000

Sinking fund. 1,667,000

VOL. II. P

The conversion of stock into annuities is proceeding at the rate of 1,000,000. a month, and the increased annual charge already is 250,000. Certainly to this extent the estimated three millions of surplus might be fairly reduced; but to reduce the surplus to 1,200,000. or 1,600,000. would be an entire abandonment of the system adopted by the Finance Committee and the Government.

It seemed to me that the members of the House of Commons were all in favour of the income tax; all the Peers against it. The Duke was strongly against it. He apprehended the reduction of establishments, and particularly the pressure of the tax on men of 1,200. a year, and under.

If I imposed the income tax, I would make it the means of a thorough reconciliation between the higher and lower classes. In this manner only would it be effectual and make a strong Government.

I object greatly to Goulburn's deductions from the old income tax. He excepts occupiers; that is, as regards land occupiers, quite right; but he excepts manufacturing capital and capital engaged in commerce. Now, why should the man who has 100,000. in a manufactory, and makes 10 per cent, on that sum, pay nothing, while the man who invests his 100,000. in the funds gets only 3 per cent, and pays 5 per cent, out of that reduced profit? The man who has a manufacturing or commercial capital is a saving man. He can afford to pay something to' the State, and why should he not? So the lawyer who may be making 10,000. a year is to pay nothing. If he takes 5,500. a year and becomes a judge, he pays 137. 10s. Yet his interest is still for life.

In all this there seems to me unfairness.

If the tax be imposed as it is proposed, it will be very difficult to include afterwards the classes now exempted. It will be impossible to take off the tax, and whenever a tax is unpopular, those upon whom it presses will say, ' Take it off. It is only adding J or per cent, to the income tax."

A real property tax is the fairest of all taxes but an income tax is the most unfair even when it affects all income; but when it affects the income of some who have a life interest, and not the income of others in the same situation, it is most unfair indeed.

It is quite erroneous to suppose that those who pay an income tax are the only persons who suffer from it. The reduction of establishments, the diminished consumption, the increased economy in every article of expenditure on the part of those affected by it have necessarily the effect of reducing the wages of labour. The labourer may buy some things cheaper, but he has less wherewith to buy.

Sunday, March 14.

Saw Hardinge at two. Told him how we stood as to the question of taxation. He said he thought the income tax would be popular, but agreed with me in thinking it should be established on strictly just principles.

Cabinet at three. Goulburn read a new statement showing the surplus this year, if we reduced beer and leather, and next year too. The surplus this year is about 2 millions. Next year about 1,500,000.

The income tax reaches the funds, and the Irish, and the parsimonious, and the rich so far it is good, but it likewise reaches the man of 100*l* a year. It tends to diminution of establishments, to diminished demand for labour. To create an alteration in demand generally.

It was proposed to exempt professions and trades. This was unjust, and it would have led to an entire separation and hostility between the landed proprietors and the united body of labourers and manufacturers.

These last would have joined on all occasions in urging a further and still a further increase of income tax, and would never have consented to a tax on consumption. The income tax would finally absorb all other taxes.

Another great objection to the income tax now is that it would have the effect of perilling the reduction of the 3 per cents.

The Duke, Eosslyn, and I were decidedly against income tax. Lord Bathurst and Lord Melville, as well as the Chancellor, less decidedly so, but still in favour of abiding by the reduction of the beer and leather tax. Aberdeen said nothing, neither did Sir G. Murray, so they were understood to go with the majority.

Goulburn acknowledged the discussion had to a great extent changed his opinion, and that he was not then prepared to propose the tax.

Herries seemed much in its favour; but more, as it seemed to me, because he wished to maintain a large surplus according to the decision of the Finance Committee than for any good reason. Peel was decidedly for a property tax. He wished to reach such men as Baring, his father, Eothschild, and others, as well as absentees and Ireland. He thought too it was expedient to reconcile the lower with the higher classes, and to diminish the burthen of taxation on the poor man. I accede to the principle; but I doubt whether taxes on consumption do really press more heavily on the poor man than an income tax. What he has to look to is not the actual price of the article he wants, but the proportion which his wages bear to that price. It matters little to him what the price of candles may be, if he has not money wherewith to purchase them. That system of taxation is best for the poor man which most tends to increase the funds for the employment of labour; and every disturbance in the system, every alteration of demand, does intrinsic mischief.

After this matter was decided, Peel behaving most fairly, and declaring he would support the decision of the Cabinet whatever it might be, and that in this case the decision of the Treasury was to be principally looked to, we talked of Queen Donna Maria, in whose name Don Pedro has established a Eegency in Terceira.

I read Leopold's letter to Lord Aberdeen, in which he refers to his letter of February 11, for the statement of his views in taking the Greek coronet, saying that he only acceded from courtesy, and as a matter of form, to the protocol, and further urging some alteration in the frontier. He has made an application for a joint guarantee by the three Powers of a loan of 60,000,000 paras, or 2,400,000. Now we only agreed to guarantee 50,000. a year, and that for troops. Nothing will be said upon this point till he has withdrawn his letter. He seems to be Aberdeen's pet. I do not think, had the Greeks searched Europe, they could have found a man whose character was more congenial to their own.

March 17. Leopold has withdrawn his obnoxious letter.

March 18.

House at five. Debate on the Duke of Eichmond's motion for a select Committee on the state of the labouring classes, and the effect of taxation upon the productive powers of industry.

A most dull debate, till Lord Holland spoke. I answered him. Lord Lansdowne next, then the Duke. I spoke, showing the impracticability of the Committee. I however showed up Committees rather too much. This Lord Lansdowne took hold of, not very fairly, but he did it well.

We had in the House 69; they 39.

With proxies we had 140 to 61. My uncle voted in the minority, and so did Coplestone. Dudley, Lord Malmesbury, Lord Gower, voted with us.

The Whigs, Brunswickers, and Canningites were in the minority. The Duke of Cumberland was there.

I find we have some recruits in proxies Lord Lauderdale, Duke of Bedford, Downshire, Lord Wilton; and Lord Jersey sits behind us. He has now Lord Lauderdale's proxy. All this is consequent upon Lord Rosslyn's accession. Lord Grey has now no one left. No one expressed a wish to turn out the Ministers.

March 19.

It seems that in the House of Commons Huskisson made a friendly speech, finding he can do no harm, and Lord Althorp a very friendly one. In short, everybody seems to be of opinion that the worst thing that could be done would be to turn out the Government.

Peel says, and so does Herries, that the House is in favour of an income tax. That what we have determined upon is the best for this year, but that next year there must be an income tax.

Cabinet. Leopold wants more money. It was agreed he should have 70, OOOZ. a year loan guaranteed to him for seven years, instead of 50,000.

The holders of 4 per cents, are to have the option of 100. stock 3, or 70Z. stock 5 per cents. Trustees may only convert into the 3 per cents.

March 20.

Chairs at 11. They have made some alterations in the letter to the Indian Government respecting their conduct, and have praised Lord William for his perseverance, c. This is contrary to the Duke's view and to mine. I shall see whether I can allow their amendments.

I find they have likewise altered much in the letter relative to Batta.

March 23.

The Duke, Lord Bathurst, and Rosslyn went away at 2 to the Cabinet, where they decided against the

216   Jew Relief Bill. The bishops have intimated that they must unanimously oppose it.

Debate on Lord Clanricarde's motion on the eternal Terceira question. The Duke spoke very well. The House was flat. The division with proxies 126 to 31, 4 to 1. We have now of Whig proxies Bedford, Lauderdale, Wilton, Downshire, Belhaven, Meldrum, and Lord Jersey.

March 24.

Cabinet dinner at Sir J. Murray's. Considered what course should be adopted upon P. Thompson's motion for a committee to revise taxation. Peel still hankers after the property tax, and rather unwillingly opposes this motion. However, it will be done on the ground that the remission of such a question to a committee would derange, by existing apprehensions and hopes, the whole industry of the country. In fact it would likewise vest the Government in the committee. Peel, Plant a, and Holmes all think the division will be close. I do not apprehend that, if the debate be well conducted.

Had a long conversation with the Duke upon Indian matters. The recollections of his youth are strong upon him, and he still clings to the old forms.

March 25.

Kead some evidence before the Commons on the China trade.

Committee. Examined Mr. Elphinstone. He gave very good evidence.

House. A flat discussion on the Kentish petition.

217   March 26.

We had two to one last night. The House not very full. It seemed by no means the wish of the House to have a property tax; quite the contrary.

Mr. Elphinstone re-examined by Lord Lansdowne and others. He gave a very good evidence, and quite knocked up colonisation.

Monday, March 29, 1830.

Office at 2. Looked over regulations, c., relative to the half-castes and considered their question. Came to a decided opinion against their admissibility to offices which can be held by natives.

When Lord Carlisle presented the petition I said very little, expressed compassion for their situation, and a wish to relieve it in any manner consistent with the conservation of our empire and the well-being of the great body of the native population. I said what they asked was not equality of rights, but privilege.

Lord King's resolutions on the Corn Laws. A dull debate which lasted till nine no division. The Duke did not speak well, and it was unnecessary for him to speak at all.

March 30.

Committee. Examined Mr. Chaplin, who gave a very good evidence. He is decidedly against the employment of half-castes.

I told the Duke at the Committee that I had written to the King immediately on Clare's appointment, and afterwards to Sir F. Watson, when I sent the warrant and had

218   got no answer. The Duke said he would enquire about it. He thought he should have spoken to the King before. However, he would settle it.

March 31.

Committee at 1. Examined Mr. Eicketts, the half-caste, when Lord Carlisle had examined him in chief. Mr. Eicketts did not seem to know much about the law. It was odd enough to observe him looking round to me after every answer.

We had afterwards Mr. Baker, a strong contrast indeed with Mr. Eicketts. He gave very curious evidence relative to the trade of the Arabs of Malabar with Scinde, the Persian Gulf, and the Eed Sea.

April 2.

Cabinet. Question whether the French should be allowed to hire 9,000 tons of transports now in the river for the expedition against Algiers. The Duke was strongly against it. The French had behaved so ill to us, concealing their objects from us, and revealing them to other Courts, besides intriguing with the Pasha of Egypt.

Aberdeen was for giving the permission. He thought the French would consider it quite a hostile measure if we refused permission. However, permission will not be given.

Leopold is still negotiating about the money, and it seems doubtful whether he will not resign at last.

April 3.

The Company have got into an awkward scrape. It seems they have not made out their account of the prime cost of their tea as merchants do, that they have charged all losses whether from fixed rate of exchange or other causes, whereas merchants in general state prime cost on a calculation of the price in the place where the article is purchased, the other calculations going in diminution of profit.

I begin to think the maintenance of the monopoly will be impossible. I have long thought it very inexpedient. It would leave a sullen, settled feeling of discontent in the minds of the manufacturers and merchants of England.

April 6.

Wrote to the Duke to tell him I had not yet received the Duke of Devonshire's memorandum respecting Sir W. Eumbold, and that in the meantime I was getting into as small a compass as possible the information he desired.

I added that the liberation of the Nizam changed our position with respect to Sir W. Eumbold, and I should be glad to speak to him about it.

I reminded him of Lord Clare's appointment, not yet approved by the King.

April 8.

Cabinet at 2. The Committee on the Bank Charter to be taken out of Huskisson's hands.

The King was not well yesterday. The Duke recollected Clare's appointment, and thinks I shall have the warrant in a day or two.

April 9.

Wrote to Wrangham, begging him to send me the Cabinet box I desired the Cabinet messenger to take to my house yesterday. I think it contained the papers relative to Eussian projects against India.

I have been so unwell the last two days I have been unable to do any public business.

April 12.

Had some conversation with Hardinge. He thinks the Duke will not remain in office above a year more, and that Peel will then be Minister, and that Peel looks forward to that now. I said I feared he would be a very Eadical Minister.

Hardinge thinks Sir G. Murray would be very well satisfied to be Master-General, that he feels the Colonial Office is above him. I doubt, however, if he would like leaving it. If Peel was Minister he would have all the Ministers he could in the House of Commons.

From what Hardinge heard from Croker I am inclined to think that foolish fellow and others imagine they could go on without Peel.

I do not think it impossible we may have a dissolution of Parliament if there should be a good harvest.

April 12.

Sent the letter and list of Eussian papers about China to the Duke. Wrote to Aberdeen and told him so. Observed at the same time that I should be very glad to make some arrangement with the Portuguese for excluding opium from their Indian ports; but I feared the present state of our relations with Portugal was not favourable for our doing so.

April 13

Found in London the papers I had sent to the Duke. He says he is sorry he has read them. He had thought better of Sir Ch. Metcalfe. The only one of the four who writes common sense is Elphinstone.

April 15.

The King was apparently very ill indeed yesterday.

Eeceived a medal struck for the native troops engaged in the Burmese war from Loch, and another to be transmitted to the King.

April 16.

Saw Hardinge, who called upon me at E.

The King has really been very ill, but certainly not worse than the bulletin made him.

Sir H. Halford does not go down to-day, nor will there be any more bulletins.

Hardinge seems to be dissatisfied with Peel, who he says is cold and never encourages any one. All this is very true.

I think Hardinge rather looks to the Colonial Office. He thinks Sir G. Murray does not do the business well, and that he would be perfectly satisfied with the Ordnance. Hardinge does not like Ireland, yet, I think, he will find he goes to Ireland. The Duke certainly wishes it.

The Duke of Clarence is very fond of Hardinge, and tells him all lie means to do when he is ' King "William This seems much confined at present to changes in uniforms. He means to make the Blues red, and to have gold lace for all the Line, and silver lace for all the Militia.

April 17.

Saw Sir A. Campbell at 1. He came about his claim upon the Company. I told him I transacted all business of that nature in writing. I gave him information as to the proposal of the Chairs, which is to give him staff allowances for a year, instead of Batta, by which he would gain about 15,850 E., or about 1,580. What he wants is about 25,000., or the difference between that and the value of his pension of 1,00(W. a year that is, 15, OOOZ.

Went to the Foreign Office. No news there or at the Treasury of the King. The report is that he is better.

Eead there for an hour and a half.

Polignac offers, if it were desired, to sign a Convention upon the principles laid down in Aberdeen's despatch as to Algiers.

He seems out of humour altogether with Leopold; Yillele seems to have no great disposition to come in, although his friends have. He says the Opposition will in any case have 180 votes in the new Chamber.

Spain will withdraw her Minister and have only a Charge d'Affaires at Lisbon if Don Miguel will not grant the amnesty.

France does not remonstrate against the abolition of the Salic Law in Spain, as she precluded herself by

~~THE SALIC LAW~~. 223 treaty from the succession. The law was otherwise in the old Spanish monarchy. [1]The abrogation of the Salic law is directed against Don Carlos, c., and the King naturally wishes his own child to succeed, be the child male or female.

Saw Mr. Downie on the part of Mr. Chippendale, the man who was removed by the Sign Manual from the service of the India Company. The Court and the Bengal Government did not view his offence in the same light. The poor man is ruined, but the feelings of humanity must not interfere with the interests of the public service. His removal was a good hint to the whole body of civil servants, and did good.

April 18.

Brought Lord Clare home after church, and showed him my letter to Mr. Elphinstone respecting the chiefs of Kattywar and the Guicowar. Talked over the policy to be pursued with regard to them.

He is to leave England in September, and means to go to Marseilles.

April 19.

Lord William seems to have been much gratified by my letters in May and June affording the pledges of my support and the assurances of my confidence. Afterwards, however, he received my letter of July, intimating censure for the relaxations of the rules restricting the residence of Europeans, and a difference [1 The Salic law was introduced by Philip V. of Spain, the first Bourbon king, whose own claim was through his mother, daughter of Louis XIV., who had renounced the succession.]

of opinion as to the Government leaving Calcutta. His letters are in a very good tone and temper. I sent all the letters to the Duke.

April 20.

Drove to the Foreign Office and saw Aberdeen. Went to enquire how the King really was, for the bulletin of yesterday says his difficulty of breathing continues. Aberdeen said the King really was not so ill as the bulletin represented him to be. There was no present danger. The Duke thinks he understands the King's case exactly, and says he has no water on the chest, as is reported, but is rather fat. It is said the seat of pain is the prostate gland. The people about him are seriously alarmed.

Advised Hardinge, who dined with me, to come forward on the Terceira question, which he seems inclined to do. Peel will be much obliged to him. I told him I thought the strong position was this: ' We are at liberty to prevent that which, if we permitted, would be a cause of war." I think I shall write a memorandum for him.

April 21.

Wrote to Astell to ask if he would buy the Eussian China papers. I told him at the same time that a Eussian ship was going at the charge of the Eussian Government to India, Swan Eiver, and China as a commercial feeler.

Cabinet at 2. The King is rather better, but in a precarious state. The embarrassment in his breathing comes on in spasms. His digestion is good, and they think there is no water. The Duke will urge him to have regular bulletins published. He goes down tomorrow. He has not seen him since this day week. The King is in excellent humour with everybody, and never was more kind to the Duke.

There has been a short difference between the King and Peel. The King having sent a pardon to Ireland for a Mr. Comyn, who burnt his house to defraud his landlord, c., Peel insisted, and the man will be hanged; the Lord Lieutenant having taken upon himself to give a reprieve only, and not to promulgate the pardon.

The Duke described the King as a bold man, afraid of nothing if his Ministers would stand by him, and certainly neither afraid of pain or of death. I did not think this of the King. In general he has been supposed to be a coward.

In Cabinet it was decided to authorise and advise the Lord Lieutenant to put into execution the law for suppressing the association against that which O'Connell is now endeavouring to organise, and at the same time to give silk gowns to Shiel and two or three other Roman Catholic barristers, omitting O'Connell. However, this last measure will be mentioned to the King, although a King's letter is not required.

We had afterwards a talk, and a long one, about Algiers.

Prince Polignac sent a despatch to the Due de Laval, giving explanations satisfactory upon the whole, but mixed up with matter accusatory of us. Of this despatch the Due de Laval was not authorised to give a copy. We want a written declaration of their views, none other being official. They are afraid of their Chambers, and of giving a pledge to England different from that which they have given to other Powers, and with which other Powers have been satisfied. Peel thinks they will promise to abstain from permanent occupation, and exact an amount of indemnity so large, with occupation as a security, as to make that occupation permanent. If they got possession of Algiers, I do not believe they will ever give it up say what they may.

Peel objected to me saying what declaration would satisfy us, as in the event of their deceiving us, or quibbling, it would then seem to be our folly which had led to it.

All seem to view the comparative statement of the prices of teas in the same light that I do, as fatal to the monopoly.

April 23.

Eode to the Treasury to enquire after the King; but there were so many waiting to see the Duke I did not wait. The King is rather better.

April 24.

A letter from Lady Maodonald enclosing one from the Nain Muhan to herself, very complimentary and really pretty. She is to be at Tabriz in October.

The King has had two good nights.

[227]   Peel's letters to the Lord Lieutenant respecting the suppression of the new Association and the appointment of Catholic King's Counsel was circulated.

Sunday ', April 25.

Eead Aberdeen's and the Duke's speeches on the Terceira question, and afterwards wrote a memorandum for Hardinge's use, bringing into a short compass all the strong points of the case.

Mr. Sullivan called upon me after church, and told me his son remained in India. It is very extraordinary that he should be glad of this, as he must be without the hope of ever seeing him.

April 26.

Cabinet at 3. The King has had another good night. He has, however, had another attack. His pulse is in a weak state. He seems oppressed by fat. He is become alarmed about himself, which much increases danger in such a complaint. Consequently all the entourage is alarmed too.

The drawing-room and levee are to be postponed sine die. Trade and agriculture are both flourishing. The only embarrassment arises out of the uncertainty as to the King's health.

Leopold is to have a loan of sixty millions, guaranteed in equal portions by the three Powers. The loan to have a sinking fund of 3 per cent, to be paid in equal portions in eight years. The guarantee is to Leopold and his descendants, being sovereigns of Greece.

Thus he has obtained almost all he asked, and what he most wanted, the money.

228   Peel seems to think the King's death by no means improbable. If it should take place, Parliament would adjourn till after the funeral, and then be dissolved.

In the House Lord Durham, in presenting a petition against the East Indian monopoly, said he gathered from what had fallen from His Majesty's Ministers that they were determined to maintain it.

I said,; I cannot admit that anything which has fallen from me, or, in my presence, from any of my noble colleagues, can justify the noble lord in assuming that His Majesty's Government have formed any determined opinion upon the subject."

April 27.

House. East Eetford case. The Duke showed me a letter from Halford which gives a very alarming account of the King. He went on much the same till half-past three this morning, when Halford was sent for and remained till half-past eight. The embarrassment of breathing was considerable. The King was rather better at half-past ten, when the bulletin was dated. Halford says he can tell more than he can write. He does write that there is water, and it is evident the King is very much alarmed.

From the letter I should say he could not live many weeks.

In the House Lord Strangford told me that Sir W. Seymour [1] was dead. He died in December a short time after the birth of his son.

Eeally the mortality amongst judges is awful.

[1 Recently appointed a judge at Bombay.]

229 April 28.

"Went to Guildhall to be present at the trial of Serjeant Kearney for the assault on As tell. I was not called as a witness. The man was very intemperate indeed, and abused Astell very much. He spoke of my kind interference, c., but made a mistake in imagining that I had advocated with the Chairs the loan he asked of 250. I came away as soon as the Eecorder began to sum up. It was curious to see how justice was administered. The Eecorder, an old twaddle, who talked half the time with the accused, and allowed him to make speeches instead of putting questions, and Sir C. Hunter, Sir J. Shaw, and another alderman!

Went to the office at 3. Loch, with whom I had some conversation at Guildhall, told me he had heard the explanation Melville intended to give of the matter of prime cost, and he thought it satisfactory. Wortley said Arbuthnot by no means thought it satisfactory, but was to put the questions. Wortley said Arbuthnot told him the Duke had read the evidence and was himself satisfied the monopoly could not be maintained.

Cabinet dinner at Lord Bathurst's. The Duke was at Windsor this morning. He did not see the King because the King refused to see the Duke of Cumberland, and begged the Duke would not see him unless it was very pressing, that the rebuff to the Duke of Cumberland might be less. Accordingly, the Duke sent in on paper what he had to say, and he got two signatures, although they were given very reluctantly. The King says it is unkind in those about him to urge him to sign, as they know how distressing it is to him. In fact yesterday it would have been death to move his arm. We are to meet on Friday to consider what shall be done. Some means must be devised of getting signatures, for his state may last some months. He was ill for four hours yesterday evening. Halford was with him all the time, and held his hand. Halford says he is sure the King would have died had he not been there. He was nearly dead as it was. However, after this attack, which began at half-past two, he had a solid dinner and slept well, and this morning he woke much relieved, but with a dropsy that is, an external dropsy, the water being between the skin. Knighton thinks some must be upon the chest; but the two others are inclined to think not. He may live days, weeks, or even months; but I doubt his living weeks. On Sunday he saw the women, and on Monday too. He was then alarmed about himself. Now he mistakes water for gout, although his legs are swelled to double their usual size. The physicians do not undeceive him. However, the public will find it out. He has not read the newspapers for two days He is much relieved by the effusion of water.

It seems the medical men when they read the first bulletin said, ' It must end in water."

Lord Eosslyn has looked into the Acts, c., and finds there is no difficulty at all about the money vote on the Bills. They all went on at the accession of the present King.

The Duke was requested by the physicians and the people about the King not to mention Shiel's proposed appointment; to make it, if he thought it essential, but to spare the King all discussion. Of course, as it is thought the King would be agitated, the Duke has neither mentioned it nor done it.

There was in circulation a letter from the Duke of Northumberland expressing his extreme satisfaction at the decision of the Government with respect to the putting down of the new associations, and likewise with respect to the making of the Catholic silk gowns.

The bulletins are to be now shown at St. James's; a lord and groom-in-waiting will be there.

Eeceived a letter from Sir J. Dewar[l]to inform me of the death of Sir W. Seymour. He died more of the fear of dying than of fever. His apprehension for Lady Seymour affected him very much. She was confined the day he was taken ill.

April 29.

Halford thinks worse of the King. There have been other attacks of embarrassment of breathing. I do not myself think he will live a fortnight.

There was an excellent division on Terceira about 2 to 1. Hardinge was not wanted.

April 30.

Cabinet. The King very ill yesterday. The least exertion brings on an attack. Halford thinks he has water in the abdomen and chest. He had some sleep, and was better in the morning when they issued the l Chief Justice of Bombay and a colleague of Sir W. Seymour. They were the two judges referred to in the letter to Sir J. Malcolm.

bulletin, which says his symptoms were alleviated. However, the bulletin so little corresponds with his real state that they think he saw it. It seems to be now more an affair of days than of weeks. It may happen at any moment.

Peel suggested the possible case of both Kings dying before an Act appointing a regent, and we may be called upon to provide for it. The Duchess of Clarence would be Queen Eegent.

We talked about a Bill for enabling the King to give authority for the affixing of the Sign Manual.

To avoid delay and the examination of physicians Eosslyn proposed that, if the King would sign it, there should be a message.

It will be arranged that there shall be two Ministers present one to countersign, the other to affix the stamp.

The Attorney- and Solicitor-General were called in. They evidently thought the King's mind was gone as well as his head, for they proposed a delegation of the Eoyal authority.

Planta called upon me to ask more particulars as to the office of Signer of the Writs. It seems it comes in lucky time to oblige Lord Chandos, who has long wanted something for a Mr. Wentworth, and nothing could have happened more conveniently for the Government.

Met Lord Eosslyn, who told me he and Lord Bat-hurst met every committee day Lord Londonderry and

Lord Durham on the Coal Committee. Sometimes they could not get a fifth, and then they adjourned joyfully. Both Lord Londonderry and Lord Durham continued most wrong-headed upon the question.

I rode as fast as I could to town as soon as church was over (for the Duke had wished to see me before he went to church, thinking I was in town), and in Brompton met Lord Eosslyn, who told me there was no Cabinet, and that the Duke had found the King better than he expected.

Eode at once to Apsley House. The Duke was gone out, having left word he should be back soon if I came. I waited an hour. When he returned he told me he had no idea

I was out of town, or he would not have written. Lord Combermere had asked to see him, which he could not refuse.

The Duke said that on Friday the King was much better. The miracle which the physicians had said could alone save him seemed accomplished. Great quantities of ether quantities much greater than are usually given had apparently restored him, and all were in good spirits, when, feeling himself much better, he drank a great deal and was actually sick! Thence the indifferent night of Friday. On Saturday he was better again, and when the Duke saw him, seemingly very well, quite alive in very good humour with everybody, and quite without nervousness. However, he passed a bad night, as the bulletin says, probably in consequence of having drunk again. Sir H. Halford was quite in tears on Saturday, not more on account of the King's state than on account of his own professional disappointment. He had thought on the Friday that he had accomplished a miracle. They have treated the King as if he had been a hospital patient, and have epuise'd the resources of art boldly applied to his case.

The King did not express the least apprehension to the Duke; but to the women he speaks of his danger, and as if he was a dying man. The Duke thinks he does this to try and vex Lady Conyngham.

The thing most surprising to me is the Duke's opinion of the King's firm courage. He said he had seen him not only now, but before, when he was considered not to have twenty-four hours of life in him, yet he, knowing his situation, was perfectly firm.

Before the Duke came I had some talk with Holmes, whom I met with Drummond. Holmes said they could finish the session by the end of July if they acted with that view. I fear it will last much longer if the King-lives, and if he dies, that we shall have a six weeks' session in August and September. Holmes said he did not think the King's illness by any means diminished the strength of Government. He thought the friends of Government were rather mere disposed to come down, and he could on any great question get 300.

He had gone round on Wednesday to the reporters, and had told them they would never have a holiday if they reported speeches on a Wednesday, so they did not, and they will not. This will put an end to all speechifying on holidays.

May 3 Cabinet. Saw a letter from Halford to the Duke. The King was ' in a most distressing, not to say alarming, state' from eight to-day evening to half-past three. He cannot get sleep. Halford says it was ' a gigantic struggle."

The Duke saw Lord Combermere to-day, having received the letters I sent him before the interview. The Duke told him the Government were parties to the disapprobation expressed by the Court of Directors.

Lord C. threw the whole blame upon Lord W. Bentinck. He had carried the order into execution without communication with him, ' and had told the army if they objected to it, they might memorialise."

This I do not believe.

Lord C. said the army was not in a state approaching to mutiny, and never had been.

He had not said it was in his minutes (but he did in a letter); as to the minutes of the other members of Council, he was not responsible for them. They were civilians. Besides, Lord W. wished to go up the country. He had received in July a letter telling him he was not to go except in a case of emergency, then the Government was not to move from Calcutta, and he endeavoured in his minute and the others in theirs to make an apparent case of emergency that they might move.

As to the last point there is an anachronism, as the orders not to leave Calcutta as a Government arrived after the minutes were recorded.

236 The Duke told Lord Combermere that all the orders for reduction of expenditure having proved inefficacious, it was necessary for the Government here to take reduction into their hands, and it was very natural and obvious to enforce an order twice repeated and already obeyed at the other presidencies.

When the army assumed the tone which appeared in the memorials, it was impossible for the Government to do otherwise than insist upon the enforcement of the order. They had expected from him that his whole influence would have been used to strengthen the Government and to prevent any ebullition of feeling on the part of the army. Lord Combermere left the Duke very angry. If the King had been well he would have joined Lord Anglesey. As it is, I expect he will oppose the Government. Lord Hill saw him for a few minutes, and had only some unimportant conversation with him. He told Lord Hill he had made thirteen or fourteen lacs. He made seven lacs by prize money at Bhurtpore.

The French have not yet given a written explanation as to Algiers. Their army is said to be in very fine order.

Leopold seems to have insinuated that our yielding on the subject of the loan was sudden and late, c. Aberdeen understood him to allude to the King's illness, and to impute our concession to the wish to get him out of the way. He took no notice of it, and treated the thing as settled.

Preparations have been made for the event of the King's death.

Peel has been obliged to leave London, as his father is dying.

237 *May 4* Committee. No witnesses. Walked with Lords Bathurst and Eosslyn to the Duke's. The bulletin is good. The King had some sleep and is better. Hal-ford's account, too, is better. The King slept six hours, but the water was so much increased about the legs that they have made punctures to draw it off. Upon the whole the account leads one to suppose the thing will be protracted.

In the House of Commons last night, Goulburn was obliged to withdraw the vote of 100,000. for Windsor Castle and refer it to a Committee upstairs. The expectation of a dissolution is acting powerfully on votes, and he would have been beaten. The Duke approved entirely of his having withdrawn the motion.

The continuance of the King in this state would be highly inconvenient indeed. There would be no possibility of carrying on the money business in the House of Commons.

In the House of Lords we had a motion from Lord Mountcashel for an address for a commission to enquire into the abuses of the English and Irish Church. No one thought it worth while to reply to him.

May 5' Read and altered a letter relative to the new arrangement of civil allowances.

Elphinstone approved generally of what I proposed which is.

1. To depose every chief who shall harbour banditti.

238 2. To oblige them to give up refugee criminals under the same penalty.

3. To engage as many as possible to abandon their heritable jurisdictions.

4. To remit the arrears.

5. To form a local corps in which the chiefs and their relations should be officers (with only two or three Europeans) to maintain order. This corps to be a sort of bodyguard to the Eesident. The robbers to be admitted as privates.

6. Troops to be brought if necessary from Cutch.

7. Every measure to be adopted to encourage the growth of cotton.

These things I shall throw into a letter, which, however, will not be sent till Clare goes out.

We talked of native education. I read to E. my alterations of the letter of last July relative to his plans for education, with which he seemed satisfied.

He seems generally to approve of my views upon that subject, particularly of uniting the English with the native classes at the several colleges, and teaching the natives useful knowledge.

They should be examined in the regulations of the company.

Office, but first saw Hardinge, who seems full of the Duke of Clarence, with whom he is high in favour, as having, urged by Wood, had several things done for the young Fitzclarences.

He said the Duke thought the King might live four months.

Cabinet dinner at the Chancellor's. The Duke saw the King, who looked very well, and seemed cheerful and in good humour.

He was very ill yesterday. Black in the face, and the ends of his fingers black. They think he will go off suddenly in one of these attacks.

Little water came from one leg, and they will scarify it again.

O'Eeilly, who probably performed the operation of scarifying, and who must know the state of the King, whom he saw daily, declared positively yesterday to Lord Maryborough, and with a face of surprise, that there was no water.

The Duke of C. saw the King on Sunday, and was at Windsor and probably saw him to-day.

The Duke of Sussex has lent the King an easy chair, and affectionate messages have passed between them.

The Bishop of Chichester is now at Windsor, the Lord and Groom and Equerry in waiting, two physicians, besides O'Eeilly and Sir Wathen Waller and Knight on.

When they told the King they must make a puncture in about four hours, he desired it might be made at once if it was necessary.

The Duke told the King he had told Sir H. Halford he would always find him intrepid with which the King was much pleased.

He said when he saw a thing was necessary he always made up his mind to it.

Wortley told me the Household betted the King would be at Ascot.

By-the-bye, Wortley did very well last night in not allowing Wynne to lead him into a speech on the half-castes. He spoke very officially and properly. I complimented him upon it. In fact it is an act of forbearance in any man, but especially in a young man, to throw away a speech.

Precedents have been looked into, and every necessary step is known, should the King die.

The Duke will immediately go in uniform to the Duke of Clarence and advise him to come to his house in town.

A sketch of the speech will be prepared, but kings like making the declaration to the Privy Council themselves, as it is the only thing they can do without advice.

Peel's father died on the 3rd.

May 6 Left my card with Lord Combermere, who called yesterday.

The bulletin states the King to have been better yesterday, but to have had a bad night.

The private letter to the Duke says he passed the night wretchedly, and with much inquietude. They find it necessary to make further punctures, and have sent for Brodie.

The King spoke to Halford for some time with much composure and piety as to his situation.

Lord Bathurst looked into the precedents in Queen Anne's reign, and at the declarations of several kings on their first meeting their Privy Council.

[241 House. A good and useful speech from Lord Gode-rich on the funded and expended debt. He showed that the receipt from taxes was about the same as in 1816, although 9 millions had been taken off, and that the interest of the National Debt would, in 1831, be reduced 4i millions below its amount in 1816.

Cabinet at half-past ten at Aberdeen's. A letter from Leopold, endeavouring to throw upon us the blame of delay for two months, and treating acquiescence in his terms of loan as a sine qua non. Now the terms we propose are not exactly the same, as we make a payment by annual instalments a part of it, and I expect he will break off at last; but he will wait till the King is actually dead.

May 7 A very good account of the King. He has passed twenty-four hours with mitigated symptoms.

Dined with Sir J. Murray. I must next year have an Indian dinner.

May 9 Read as I went to town to Cabinet, and returned in the carriage Cabell's memorandum on the Hyderabad transactions.

The Duke read the letter he had received from Sir H. Halford. It gave a bad account of the King. Yesterday was a day ' of embarrassment and distress," and he is swollen notwithstanding the punctures made by Brodie. He is anxious about himself, and must know his danger, yet he talks of the necessity of having a pew dining-room at the Cottage ready by Ascot.

We had much conversation respecting the law

242 ~~VOL. II. E~~ asserting his power of disposing of his property by will.

The Chancellor was not there. He went to Windsor.

The other matters considered were merely the mode of dealing with several questions to be brought on next week. It seems to be clear that no dependence whatever can be placed in the House of Commons. Every man will vote for his constituents.

No answer has been received from Prince Leopold.

My apprehension is that the King cannot live ten days.

Lord Londonderry went to Windsor yesterday and saw the physician. He had a dinner afterwards at his villa, and told every one, the Lievens being there, that the King was much worse than he had ever been. This was untrue, for the Duke left Windsor after Lord L., and when he left the Castle the King certainly was not worse, but rather better. I have no doubt Lord L. managed to tell Wood, [1] and Wood would tell the Duke of Clarence, who would think he was ill-used and deceived.

May 10 The Duke will read the Hyderabad memorandum as he goes down to Windsor on Wednesday.

I told him of the alteration in the treaty with Nag-pore.

The Chancellor was at Windsor yesterday. He did not see the King. The physicians seemed to think [1 Lord Londonderry's brother-in-law, having married Lady Caroline Stewart, also sister-in-law of Lord Ellenborough] it could not last a week. He is greatly swollen, and generally.

Lord Bathurst went to Windsor to-day. His account was a little better, but his expectation did not go beyond a fortnight. In the meantime the physicians are afraid of telling the King of his danger.

Sir W. Knighton sat up with him last night, and was much alarmed by one of the attacks, not having seen one before. However, he did not call Sir H. Hal-ford.

The probability is that the new Parliament will meet in the last week in July.

The Speaker says the House of Commons is like a school two days before the holidays. They do not know what mischief to be at.

Lord Eosslyn seems to think all sorts of intrigues are going on, and has some little doubt as to the Duke of Clarence. I have none.

House. E. Eetford again. Wrote to Lord Holland when I came home to call his attention to the Hickson Nullity of Marriage Bill. I cannot take a part; but lie must do so if he wishes to preserve his grandfather's clause.

May 11 Heard from Lord Holland, who is fully alive to the consequences of the Bill. He thinks I am right not to take a part.

There was an indigo-planter before the Committee to-day. It seems, as I supposed, to be just as unnecessary for indigo-manufacturers to be indigo-growers as it is for maltsters to be great farmers.

This man took out no capital and he had no licence; yet he was permitted to reside and take a lease, and the agency houses lent him money at 10 and 12 per cent.

The judge, Sir T. Strange, was a sensible man. He deprecated the introduction of English law into the provinces.

The King is getting weaker, which the physicians dread more than his spasms. It is thought he can hardly last a week.

Bead the memorandum on Hyderabad a second time, and sent it with the proposed letter and alterations to the Duke.

Prepared materials for Lord Stanhope's motion about shipping on Thursday.

May 12 Cabinet dinner at Lord Eosslyn's.

The Duke saw the King to-day. He said there was a decided alteration since Wednesday last. He was now in appearance an invalid, but not a dying man. His body is very much swollen. They took several quarts of water from his feet yesterday. He is good-humoured and alive. His eyes as brilliant as ever. His voice a little affected. His colour dark and sodden.

The Duke thinks he may die at any time; but may live a fortnight or ten days Knighton thinks so too. The other physicians think worse of him.

He called for the ' Eacing Calendar' yesterday. They were afraid he would call for the newspaper.

Knighton found he was not aware there were now any bulletins.

245 Knighton proposed to him the taking the sacrament, as he did not take it at Easter. He said he would think about it, but to be better before he took it. His taking it now might lead to the publishing of more bulletins.

He continues to take the greatest interest in the improvements at the lodge.

After dinner we talked only of the things necessary to be done on a demise.

Lord B. seemed to say we could not have the Duchess of Clarence as Eegent, because there was no precedent. I trust this will be got over.

Leopold has written an unsatisfactory answer to the last letter about the loan. However, he goes.

The Porte has acquiesced in the arrangements of the protocol, so Leopold is Prince Sovereign of Greece.

The Duke read Cabell's memorandum to-day. He thinks Cabell proposes doing more than should be done. He has a strong feeling as to the scandalous nature of the whole transaction. Lieutenant-Colonel Arabin has been infesting the Chancellor upon the subject.

May 13 Dined at four. Eode to the office and back, and to the House.

Prepared for Lord Stanhope's motion for returns on shipping, c.

The Duke had a great deal of information, and answered Lord Stanhope. I spoke, however, afterwards, as I had some new facts. Then E. Eetford till nine.

246 Eead letters from Sir John Macdonald and a paper he enclosed from 'Blackwood's Magazine' in 1827 on the invasion of India by the Eussians.

May 14 Colonel Briggs called. He is a clever man. He will prepare for me a memorandum on the composition of the native army. He seems equally conversant with revenue, judicial, and military matters.

House. E. Eetford as usual. The King is much relieved by the draining of the water from the punctures; but the wounds gave him much annoyance last night. The fear is they may lead to mortification. Lord Eosslyn and I go down on Sunday to Windsor to enquire.

May 15 Astell has sent to Lord Combermere the letter lately despatched to India in which the conduct of the several members of Government is commented upon as regards the Batta question. Lord Combermere only asked, as far as I recollect, to know upon what grounds his conduct has been censured. I told Astell to tell him the censure rested entirely on official documents with which he must be acquainted. The Duke was very angry with Astell, when I told him of it after the Cabinet, and expects a question in the House of Lords.

I told Astell the letter ought not to have been given. It reveals what has been done with regard to the Batta question, and the news may possibly reach India through the press before the Government obtain it.

Cabinet at half-past four. Not only have the Turks acceded to the arrangement for 247 Greece, but the Greeks have done so too. Leopold adheres to his memorandum of March, and wants the power of drawing as much as he pleases of the loan at any time.

He will be invited to meet the Plenipotentiaries or to send a person to meet them to discuss this point. The people about him say he means to break off. If he should, Peel thinks we could not do it upon a better point, and he is right.

The King is decidedly better. The Duke saw him to day. He was looking more healthy. He has had some refreshing sleep. He is more likely to live than to die. The only danger is from mortification in consequence of the punctures; but his constitution is so good that in all probability he will avoid this danger. This wonderful recovery quite changes our position. In all public business we must now calculate upon his living at least till the end of the Session.

Lord Morpeth is to make a motion for the repeal of the Banishment Clause in the last Libel Act. To the repeal of that clause, which is inoperative against the common libeller, we have no objection, and the Attorney-General is pledged to it; but the House of Lords would not like, and the King would not endure, the repeal of that provision without the substitution of some other security. That proposed by the Attorney-General is the requiring security to the amount of 500. from two sureties that the editor shall pay fines on account of libels. This is reasonable, and would to some extent prevent the putting up, as is now done, men or women of straw as editors, who ⌊248 have no means of paying fines. The other proposal of the Attorney-General,⌋that the types should be seizable to whomever they may belong, is objectionable and would hardly be carried. Peel is very sorry the question is stirred at the present moment. The press is generally with us or quiescent, and the 'Morning Journal,"⌈1⌉a paper instituted to oppose the Government, has within these few days been given up altogether from the want of support. Certainly this is not the moment at which it is desirable to appear to commence an attack upon the Press and the Attorney-General can do nothing that will not be suspected by them.

The Duke has written a memorandum on the Hyderabad affair.

May 16 Read the Duke's memorandum; he mistakes the law. However, I cannot write notes upon his memorandum without the Act of Parliament. The King had an indifferent night, but still feels better. I only met Lord Bathurst, who told me so. He had not seen the private letter.

Had a long conversation with Lady C. Wood at Lord Camden's about the Clarences. It seems there has been a great deal of hope excited in the Spencers.

They expect Lord Holland to be made Minister, and their son Bob or Lord Darnley to be first Lord of the Admiralty! Nous verrons.

It seems the Duchess of Clarence and the Duchess of Kent were and are great friends, and the Duchess of Clarence is very fond of the young Princess.

⌊1 It had been obliged to pay heavy damages for a libel on the Duke of Wellington.⌉

249 Monday, May 17.

At eleven set off with Lord Eosslyn for Windsor. We drove to the visitor's entrance. After a time Sir A. Barnard came. Lord Eosslyn said we did not presume to ask to see the King, but we were anxious to know how His Majesty was, and to present our humble duty to him.

Sir A. asked if we would see Knighton? Lord Eosslyn said it would be very satisfactory. However, no Knighton came, but a message through Sir A. Barnard that Sir Wm. Knighton had gone in to the King and had mentioned we were there, and His

Majesty had expressed himself very sensible of our kind attention. This I conclude is Knighton's own message, and that the King will never hear we have been. Sir A. Barnard seemed in excellent spirits about the King. He had a good night, and is certainly much better. He talks of being able to go to Ascot and to stand up in the carriage, though he could not go up into the stand.

We met the Bishop of Chichester going back to town. I suppose he thinks he shall not be wanted.

Eode down to the House. East Eetford.

The Duke's private account of the King is excellent.

May 18 Committee. Examined Colonel Briggs, who gave very good evidence indeed. Ordered the attendance of six witnesses for Tuesday, whom we shall endeavour to despatch, and that will enable everybody to go to Epsom on Thursday and Friday.

250   The King much better. All his symptoms alleviated.

To-morrow the Duke will get from him his signature to the message for a stamper. There are to be three signatures of Ministers, that is, of Privy Councillors, to authorise the stamper, who is to be nominated by the King to affix the royal stamp to instruments in the King's presence.

By the account from Marseilles, it appears that there are 11 sail of the line and 28 frigates in the French expedition, in all 97 sails about 350 transports, carrying 75,000 tons. There will be 30,500 infantry, besides a very complete equipment of artillery, c., 75 battering guns, 4,000 horses. The Duke of Angouleme's (the Dauphin's) visit has delayed the expedition four days. They will probably be on the sea to-day.

Eosslyn was talking yesterday of the danger from this expedition, and the annexation of Algiers to France. I do not fear it we can, if we manage well, make it very costly by bringing forward the people of Tunis and Morocco, not near the coast, but almost from the desert. We must take care to secure Tunis, and then the French will be no gainers by their move.

Lord Londonderry made a very foolish speech about foreign policy in putting off his motion, which stood for the 25th. Aberdeen promised the Greek papers on Monday next.

May 19 The Duke saw the King to-day and found him looking better than he did at the last Council.

251   The drain from the legs is now very small. He was annoyed last night by them and sent for Halford, who sent off for Brodie; but there was nothing of importance. They cannot yet say that he will not ultimately die of this complaint. Knighton thinks he will be an invalid all his life. Tierney says they cannot tell for a week whether there is any mischief remaining about the chest. The Duke wished to speak to him about the stamp; but he made an excuse about his legs requiring some dressing, and the Duke, seeing he did not choose to talk about business, went away.

It seems clear that Leopold means to abdicate.

The Attorney-General has made his libel preventive measure a poor weak inoperative thing, ridiculous, and unconciliating.

The French Chambers are dissolved as a coup de theatre on the sailing of the expedition, and they are to meet on August 3, by which time they expect to hear of its success.

A union of parties is expected on the Greek affair. I am not sorry for it. The Huskissonians and Whigs are drawing nearer together. The Tories, on the other hand, are rather approximating to us so that by the beginning of next Session men will be at last in their right places.

May 21   The King had a bad night. The private letter gave a bad account. He has been drinking again, very irritable, intolerably so. Halford says, would neither sit in a chair nor lie in a bed, c. Halford at last held strong language, and I believe told him his life depended on his obeying his physician.

252   I am very much disappointed indeed at this. I hoped he was really getting better and would live.

Aberdeen is to allow the instalments of the loan guaranteed to Leopold to be paid in four instead of eight years if he can keep him to his principality by doing so.

The French were off on the 18th. There is a partial change in their Ministry.

May 23   Eode to the Cabinet at three from Eoehampton. The bulletin is that the King had had embarrassments in his breathing.

The Duke waited two and a half hours before he saw him yesterday. The King signed the two messages, and then said c the Duke has just caught me in time!" and in an instant there was a gurgling in his throat. He seized Knighton's arm. The Duke ran for Halford, went out into the gallery where he did not find him, then into another room where he was. Hal-ford immediately took a bottle from the table and gave the King something which seemed to relieve him.

The Duke thinks the King was in pain three or four seconds; but it was a minute and a half before he was relieved. He then did not speak; but made a motion with his hand for the Duke to go.

He had just before been talking of going to Ascot and then to Aix-la-Chapelle.

The King was perfectly satisfied with the proposed arrangement for the stamp.

253   He asked the news, was told Leopold was behaving very ill, and agreed.

As to Algiers he was told the note of the French Minister was unsatisfactory, and that it was under consideration whether a note should not be presented. He thought it right.

The Duke's opinion is that if the King should be seized with one of those attacks when no one was with him, he would die.

The opinion of Halford and the others is that the disorder is mortal; but he may live six weeks or two months.

The punctures are healed. They are afraid of opening them again for fear of mortification, and can only proceed by medicines.

The King's state seems distressing. He can neither remain quiet in his chair or in his bed. He is in a state of constant restlessness.

The Duke of Cumberland was there to-day, but the King had desired he might not see him.

Leopold has declined. He sent a note to that effect on Friday night at twelve o'clock very well written, not by himself. Aberdeen thinks Palmers ton wrote it. He takes popular ground, and cannot impose himself upon a reluctant people. The fact is Friday's bulletin wrote his letter.

The Duke thinks he will be shown up. The papers presented to-morrow will be no more than it was before intended to present; but Aberdeen will announce the evasion of the sovereign, and say that that circumstance will render necessary the production of other papers which will be presented as soon as they can be printed. The whole discussion will turn upon Leopold's conduct.

Aberdeen will be in the position of the manager of a country theatre who, just as the curtain is about to be drawn up, is obliged to come forward and announce that the amateur gentleman who had solicited the part of Macbeth, who had attended all the rehearsals, and whose only difficulty, which was about money, seemed to be in a fair way of adjustment, had unexpectedly intimated his intention to withdraw in a printed address to the galleries.

Forsooth there should have been an appeal to the people of Greece on the subject of their Government! An appeal to the people of Newgate on the subject of the new police! [1]

By a letter of C. Capo d'Istria's, dated 25 M., April 6, written immediately after his receipt of one from Leopold (after his acceptance), it appears that Leopold had intimated his intention to change his religion. He must have had about forty-eight hours to consider the point.

Lord Melville had heard that Leopold had consulted Lord Grey and Lord Lansdowne without acquainting one that he had seen the other.

[1 This sentiment, however severe, represents the feeling about the Greeks of many Englishmen at that time, and especially of those who, as in the case of naval officers employed in Greek waters, had seen much of them during the war. Their struggle for independence was undoubtedly disgraced, not only by cruelty, but by a treachery and disregard of faith which, though perhaps attributable to past subjection and oppression, was peculiarly odious to English observers. Lord Ellenborough adopted this view.]

Eode to the office at four to receive the manufacturers. Mr. Crawford was there, Finlay being ill. I told them of my plans as to the Indus. I directed their attention to the point of bringing out in evidence the effect the stoppage in China had upon the general trade of the East. I again desired them to show, if they could, why British manufactures did not go to China by the country trade.

Met Aberdeen. Told him I thought, on consideration, that a reply to Leopold would lead to an answer from him, to which the Plenipotentiaries could not reply without entering into an undignified discussion with Palmerston, who would be the real controversialist.

There should be an answer, but it should be addressed to the Eesidents, and what could not be addressed to them might be stated in Parliament, that is, all relating to letters, conversations, c.

I dare say Leopold will publish to-morrow. It is unlucky the French have troops in the Morea. If they had not, I should be disposed to leave the Greeks to settle their affairs as they pleased, giving them no money. They would soon become reasonable.

The bulletin had ' The King had a sleepless night."

House at five. The message and address. The Opposition made no objection to the address, which was carried nemine dissentiente. Lord Grey seems to expect a delegation of the royal authority. I told Lord Holland I thought he would be satisfied.

256   Then Aberdeen presented the Greek papers, and, having explained their contents, stated the change of circumstances since Friday night. He represented Leopold. as having made preliminary objections on other points, but none on any but money since February 20, when he accepted. Within these few days other grounds have been taken, and the abdication is on these other grounds.

There was much movement amongst the Opposition. Aberdeen was accused of unfairness. Lord Durham opened the fire, and I prevented Aberdeen from answering him. The others Darnley, Lord Londonderry, and Lord Winchelsea, all for Leopold. In short there is a general union of all those who prefer the rising to the setting sun. We shall have a personal debate.

We went into E. Eetford. I sat by the Chancellor, and worked the Bill for the King's relief.

In the House of Commons little was said upon these points. Aberdeen did well. He can make a biting speech as well as any one, and in a quiet way.

May 25   The King passed yesterday uncomfortably. He was a little relieved by medicines during the night. Water is forming again.

House. The Chancellor explained very well the objects and details of the King's Relief [1] Bill. The only objections made were to reading it to-morrow, and it was conceded that it should be read on Thursday to its duration, and it was conceded that should last a month. Lord Grey, I hear, says it is too complicated,[1 Believing him from the necessity of constant signatures.]

257   that it would have been better to appoint a Custos Regni. I hope he will say that on Thursday.

There is but little hope of the King's living till the Bill is passed.

May 26 Hardinge, whom I met in the Park, told me Sir J. Graham informed him there was to be an opposition a Voutrance. That Lord Anglesey was to be Minister Lord Grey would serve with him. Palmerston was to be made a great man of. Huskisson to have nothing but revenge. The Duke of Eichmond was to be had at all events. All this is childish.

House. I expected nothing but the Chancellor's Bill, and went at half-past five, expecting to find Eldon in the midst of his speech; but I found Lord Durham talking about Greece, and soon engaged in the talk myself. Lord Grey was decidedly in opposition. I called the attention of the House to this, that our conduct was to be judged of by the papers on the table the resignation of Leopold was not alleged to have taken place in consequence of any act of the Government. If noble Lords chose to put on one side the conduct of the Government, and to make this a mere personal question as to the conduct of Leopold we were prepared to enter into the discussion. In speaking of Leopold I said he ' was connected with this country by some of its dearest recollections

Cabinet dinner. The King's digestion is affected now; but otherwise he is well. He has had many attacks of embarrassed breathing; but none serious. The Duke of Clarence was in the room with him (the

VOL. II. S

258   Duke of W. being present) for a quarter of an hour today. The King talked of his own danger. He said, ' God's will be done. I have injured no man." This he often

repeated. He said, speaking of his own danger to the Duke of Clarence, ' it will all rest on you then." He was in very good humour, very angry, however, with Leopold his anger brought on a slight spasm.

He afterwards talked of going to Ascot, and told the Duke to manage that he might be able to go to Aix-la-Chapelle.

He is much pleased with the conduct of both Houses about his Signature Bill. After dinner Aberdeen read his proposed answer to Leopold to be addressed to the Eesidents with a copy of Leopold's letter. It was full of admissions, many of which Peel noticed. Aberdeen was going to meet Laval about it. I objected to sending a copy of the letter to Leopold, as that would as much lead to a reply as if they answered him directly. This the Cabinet seemed to feel; and if there is a letter to the Eesidents it will be printed with the other papers only, and not communicated.

May 27 Privy Council at one. The Archbishop of Canterbury ordered to frame a prayer for the King's recovery.

Cabinet. King's Signature Bill amended. Then Aberdeen read a letter from the Eesidents in Greece giving an account of all that took place from the notification of the protocol to the Senate to their adhesion. Unfortunately this letter was not sent to Leopold as it ought to have been, when he on the 15th sent Capo dtstria's letter to Aberdeen, and it is thought we cannot publish it. It shows that the adhesion was entire.

No answer to his letter is to be published. We are to wait till we can have a protocol. Laval would not sign any joint letter to the Eesidents. Being so near he prefers waiting for the orders of his Court.

House. King's Signature Bill passed, with some amendments. It is to last till the end of the Session.

The King's command is to be signified by word of mouth, a very inconvenient mode to a sick man.

East Eetford for a House.

All Columbia is at war again. The Mexicans are urging the Haytians to land 5,000 men in Cuba. Peel fears war will begin there by the Americans taking Texas.

Fitzgerald writes from Paris that he thinks the French will not retain Algiers. That an energetic demand on our part would have drawn from Polignac a distinct disavowal of the intention. That he does not think the channel (Lord Stuart) a good one.

I think Fitzgerald would not at all dislike being made Ambassador at Paris.

It seems there is a very sore feeling indeed excited by de Peyronnet's appointment. He thinks the only safety of the Government is in throwing themselves upon the ultra-Eoyalists.

The King is a little better. His stomach begins to bear a little light food again.

May 28 The account of the King not good.

Cabinet. Found them talking about Scotch boroughs. Aberdeen presented the papers relative to Leopold in the House. Some conversation as to the correctness in point of form of presenting them printed. The rule is to present papers written by the King's command, and to have them printed for the immediate use of the House.

The Commons passed the King's Signature Bill without a word.

I thought it necessary to determine at once who should be the new judge at Bombay, and upon full consideration thought Awdry the best man. The Chancellor had no objection, and I immediately wrote to Awdry to tell him I should advise the King to appoint him.

May 29 Before the Cabinet met Hardinge and walked some time up and down Downing Street with him. He told me the Duke had proposed an exchange between him and Lord F. Leveson. Hardinge declined; however, he was at last induced to acquiesce. There cannot be a better thing for him, for the Government, and for Ireland, than his going there. I have always told him so. We may now be satisfied things will go on well there. Lord F. Leveson is a mere boy, and quite, unequal to the situation. Hardinge will do admirably and be very popular. So will she. They will like an Irishwoman.

261 June 1.

The King had a quiet night. In other respects he is much the same.

June 2.

Employed all the morning on the Greek papers. Cabinet dinner at Peel's. The King rather better. They have opened punctures above the knees. 400 papers were stamped. Lord Farnborough was the stamper. The King was perfectly alive to all that was going on.

A steamboat has made the passage from Bombay to Suez in a month and two days, leaving Bombay on March 20 and reaching Suez on April 22. The letters arrived here on May 31. The steamboat was detained ten days for coals. There was no steam conveyance from Alexandria to Malta, so we may reckon upon gaining fourteen days at least upon this passage. Besides, the steam vessel was probably a bad one.

June 3.

House. Aberdeen, in reply to a question of Lord Londonderry's, promised all the protocols of Paris! A most voluminous mass of dull twaddle. The House postponed Miss Hickson's divorce case to Lord Salisbury and East Eetford. We had only 18 to 69! The Duke seemed very angry, and I heard him speaking to Lord Bathurst of some peer who went out without voting, whose conduct seemed to make him very indignant.

262 June 4.

House. All seems quiet again. Nothing more said about Leopold. There was to be a meeting to-day at Lord Lansdowne's which the Duke of Newcastle was expected to attend. Palmerston was at the last. [1] Ross-lyn does not know whether Lord Grey was.

The King not going on well by the bulletin; worse by the private account, which, however, I did not see. He has lost his appetite and grows weaker.

The Duke has not yet read my Nagpore letter; but he will to-morrow. He seems to agree with me in general views upon the subject of our policy towards the native States.

June 5.

Chairs at 11. They are dissatisfied with Malcolm for sending a steam vessel into the Eed Sea, because he had no important intelligence to communicate! I shall never make these people feel they are at the head of a State!

The bulletin to-day is very alarming. The Duke had not returned at half-past 4; but soon after he was seen coming into town looking very melancholy. The Duchess of Gloucester arrived an hour later. I thought the Duke had stayed to be there at the King's death. Knighton sent up to Goulburn to desire a warrant might be sent down to be stamped conveying the King's fines, c., belonging to the Privy Purse.

Goulburn very properly refused to send the warrant[1 The conjunction of these names indicated an alliance of Whigs, Can-ningites, and Tories irritated by the Roman Catholic Bill.]

263   till he had seen the Duke. This looks as if they did not expect 24 hours.

He was as ill as possible when Aberdeen saw him yesterday for a few minutes.

A Cabinet is summoned for half-past 3 to-morrow.

All is still again in the House of Commons, as well as with us. They have found the Leopold line will not do.

June 6.

Cabinet at half-past 3. They all say Scarlett did ill. He did not fight gallantly, arid he fought without judgment.

The Duke said he thought the King was really suffering yesterday; but from several circumstances he thought he would live three or four weeks. The physicians said eight days. He was better than when Aberdeen saw him on Friday. No stamping was done. Peel went down to-day. It was hoped some papers would be stamped. Peel had not returned when the Cabinet separated at 5.

Aberdeen brought forward the question of a Bill it is thought necessary to introduce in consequence of slave-dealing by Brazilian subjects having now become piracy.

Goulburn seems to be unable to fix any time for the conclusion of the Session in the event of a demise. I fear it will be necessary to sit a long time to get the necessary votes. There are no less than fifty subjects unvoted.

June 7.

House. In going down met Goulburn, who said the account of the King was very
264 bad. Halford had sug-gested it would be better for the Duke to go down; which he did. Peel thought the King very much changed indeed in the week which had elapsed since he last saw him.

June 8.

Cabinet at 3. The diplomatic expenses were carried only by 18, and the abolition of the punishment of death for forgery was carried by 13. This is a very serious state of things; with such a Parliament there is no depending upon the carrying of any measure, and Peel is quite disgusted. As to the Forgery Bill it will be difficult to find juries to convict when a majority has decided against the punishment of death. I am satisfied that the property of many will be exposed to much danger by the abolition of the punishment of death.

One Ashe who has libelled the Duke of Cumberland, or written a threatening letter, will be prosecuted as if he had done the same thing against any private individual.

The Fee Bill will be altered in the Committee (which out of delicacy is indefinitely postponed) and the commissioners continued by endorsement. This is a very ingenious device, saving all the difficulty of dealing with patent offices and of sharing the present fees.

Lord Combermere has written a letter to the Duke explaining and defending his conduct. This is a trouble brought upon us by Astell. He has written rather an impertinent answer to my letter respecting the 600. for the Eussian papers, or rather some one has written it for him and he has only signed it.

I find Mr. Archibald Campbell, who applied yester-

~~DINNER AT LORD ELLEKBOROUGH's.~~

265 day to me for an assistant-surgeoncy, is Campbell of Blytheswood, a good voter and a great friend of Lord Melville's, and others. I have given him the surgeoncy. I told Planta, who is much pleased.

The Duke was sent for because the physicians intended to acquaint the King with his danger.

He was restless yesterday. The bulletin says he passed a very distressing day. He walked across the room, however, and will probably last some days.

In the House, East Eetford till 8, when I came away.

June 9.

A better bulletin. Office before 12. Settled with Wortley the ' reasons' for abolishing the College. [1]   (Haileybury)

At 3 Sir F. Freeling came. Went with him and Wortley to Lord Melville's. There will be no difficulty in getting the steam vessel to Alexandria.

Eead Colonel Macdonald's Journal for January, February, and to March 10. It is not so interesting as the last portion, or rather not so entertaining. These make no doubt from the account of Khosroo Murza and of the others who went to Petersburg, that the conquest of India by the route of Khiva and Bokhara is the favourite object of the Prussians, and the whole people seem animated by hatred of England.

Cabinet dinner chez moi. The Duke did not see the King to-day; the Dukes of Clarence and Cumberland being there, whom he did not wish to see. The King is better. There is coagulated lymph in his legs, one thigh, Tierney thinks, is a little swelled. He has/had no embarrassment of breathing for thirty-six hours, and slept yesterday as soundly as a child.

The man who was with the Queen and the Duke of York when they died is with the King now. When the King was sleeping yesterday Knighton said to him, ' This is not the sleep of death!" The other answered, ' Lord, sir! he will not die!" They think the King has never thought himself in danger, not even when they told him he was. He seemed flurried, however, or they thought so, for a moment, and then they endeavoured to unsay; but the King, who was quite firm, said, ' No, no! I understand what you think. Call in the Bishop and let him read prayers."

Last night he was talking a great deal to Knighton, and was as amusing as ever. In constitution and in mind he is certainly a wonderful man. I have no doubt that the feeling that he is always in representation makes him behave in the face of death as a man would on the field of battle.

June 10.

The King passed a restless night. He is weaker than he has been yet.

East Eetford. Salisbury concluded his case.

June 11.

House. I expected to get away immediately; but Lord Londonderry made a motion for papers, which led to a discussion of an hour and a half. He was put down entirely by Aberdeen, who really, with a bad manner, said very good things. At last Lord

[267] Londonderry chose to say the Contents had it and did not divide, so that the motion was negatived nemine contra-dicente. Most scandalously many went out, not voting against the motion after Aberdeen had declared it would be injurious to the. public service to give the Papers.

The King rather better, but weaker.

June 12.

Chairs. They did not come till half-past 11. I began to think they had taken huff and did not mean to come at all, as I had taken no notice of Astell's letter. However, they came. They do not much like my Nagpore letter, which it seems is contrary to the line of policy laid down by the Court and approved of by Wynne. I told them I took the responsibility upon myself. They were ministerial only. My opinion was confirmed by that of Jenkins and of the Duke.

Met at dinner, at Hardinge's, Arbuthnot, with whom I had some conversation about the Eeport he is writing on the China Evidence. He is to show it to me. The Duke saw the King, who is much better. The King said he would defer taking the sacrament till he was well; but he takes it to-morrow as a convalescent.

June 13.

Cabinet at half-past 3. First considered the line to be adopted on the Forgery Bill, which seems to be to allow it to pass unaltered, throwing the whole responsibility on the House of Commons; but Peel is to see the bankers and merchants that he may [268] ascertain what their opinions are now the Bill has passed the Commons abolishing the punishment of death for forgery. Peel's idea is that no conviction would be obtained.

I believe the French and the Russians are so alarmed by the effect produced in France by the continued exhibition of democratic violence in Greece and successful rebellion, that they would be disposed to enter into our views with respect to the nomination of a prince rather than leave the question open; but that they will procrastinate if they find we will unite with them in giving money which may keep Greece in a state of tranquillity. As to Capo dtstria, he first wished to prevent the nomination of any prince and to keep the government to himself. When he found that would not do, he endeavoured to frighten Leopold into subserviency; but if he finds he can get money without having a prince, he will frighten other princes and remain there himself.

It is like paying money in consequence of a threatening letter. If it is done once there is no stopping.

I said I believed the dissolution of the Acarnanian army, happen as it might, would be better than its maintenance, and that the state of anarchy into which it was pretended Greece would fall if it had not money, would be a better foundation of improvement than the state of military thraldom in which it is now held.

Peel proposed that Dawkins should be instructed under circumstances of imminent danger to advance money not exceeding 20,000., and this would be the best way of doing it. The Duke has great repugnance to giving anything, and objects to doing [269] what might be considered an unconstitutional act. He hopes Aberdeen will be able to persuade the other Powers to give 30,000. each, leaving us out of the subscription.

The thing was left undetermined. I suggested that it was by no means impossible a question might be asked by some c friend of Greece' whether we intended to give or had given money in consequence of Capo d'Istria's representations, and then what we had done would come out. In fact if the King was well the matter would be brought before Parliament.

His illness creates great embarrassment. It is doubtful whether the Government can command majorities on questions on which a defeat under ordinary circumstances would lead them to resign; but it is known that now they cannot resign and cannot dissolve, and the Opposition has no other effect than that of interfering with the conduct of public business.

A powerful man would place this strongly before the country and bring the House to a sense of its duty.

The Duke showed me the letter he had written to Lord Combermere in reply to his, upon my Memorandum. It is excellent.

There is to be a great fight upon sugar. Charles Grant makes a proposition, and Goulburn proposes to modify his original proposition by suggesting the addition of 6d. a gallon to Scotch and Irish spirits and to rum, thus leaving the proportional burthen nearly the same. In addition to this he proposes lowering the duty on the inferior kinds of sugar.

The. French Expedition was in Palma Bay on May 31, awaiting the arrival of the last division, which was expected the next day.

June 15.

The King much better. He has been in good spirits about himself, and has expectorated, which is thought a good sign.

In the House of Commons Goulburn's altered plans seem to have succeeded with all parties as far as first impression goes.

June 16.

At the Cabinet dinner spoke to Lord Melville and Goulburn about the embarrassments of the civil servants. Both are very much indisposed to grant the papers asked for by Hume on the subject. I shall write to Arbuthnot to do what he can to prevent their being given.

The Duke got a number of papers stamped indeed all the arrears, about 400. The King paid more attention to them than he ever did while he was well. He recollected everything.

The Duke did not think him so well as when he last saw him. The physicians do not like this catarrh. The Duke thought his hand was hotter than usual, that he was larger, and that altogether he was not so well. His judgment has hitherto been so correct that I attach much importance to it.

Peel spoke after dinner with much ennui of his position in the House of Commons. He complained that it really was not worth a man's while to be there for so many hours every night. The sacrifice was too great. He said the Eadicals had brought the House into such a state that no man could do business but themselves. He seemed not well, and thoroughly out of humour.

We had some discussion about the Forgery Bill. We are to see the Governor and deputy-governor of the Bank, c. The Duke is much indisposed to acquiesce in the Commons' amendment.

Peel thinks that after the vote of the House of Commons no verdicts will be obtained; but may not a contrary vote of the House of Lords turn public opinion into its former course? I think it may.

June 17.

In French newspaper a bad report of the French fleet, which is very much dispersed. One division was in sight of the shore on May 30 when it came on to blow, and they ran to Majorca. The other divisions will have gone to the rendezvous on the African shore, where they will have met no men-of-war and much bad weather. The star of Napoleon is set.

Lord Combermere has written another letter to the Duke, in which he acknowledges his error as to the compact in 1796 and 1801, and says he was led into it by Col. Fagan. He restates all he before said on the other points, and still wishes his letter to go to the King.

The King seems to have had a good night. I did not hear the private account.

June 18.

Eeceived last night from Astell a letter in which he speaks of an intended address of his respecting the Nag-pore letter. I have told him he has already privately told me his opinion that the Act of Parliament has made no provision for a representation on the part of the Secret Committee if they disagree with the Board, and I cannot receive any such representation officially. I have further told him that I think any more delay will be injurious to the public service.

Wrote a letter to Runjeet Singh to go with the horses. Showed it to Lord Amherst, Clare, and Auckland. Lord Amherst and Clare were delighted with it. Showed it to the Duke, who approved. Saw the

Duke.

The King alarmed the princesses yesterday, but the

Duke of Clarence did not think him so ill. I saw the Duke of Clarence's letter to the Duke of W. Halford thinks the expectoration is an additional evil.

June 19.

At 11 Privy Council to hear the appeal of Elphin-stone (that is, East India Company) against Ameerchund Bidruchund, a case of booty. Eemained till half-past two, when I was obliged to come away, having a dinner at Eoehampton. Indeed I do not think that upon a point affecting the revenues of India I ought to vote as a, judge.

Brougham ridiculed the Directors who sat there in a mass, nine of them. Fergusson spoke of 6 the Court Brougham said he was not surprised he should make that mistake seeing such an array of directors. Brougham put it ad verecundiam to the directors whether they would vote upon a question in which they were directly interested, and in which they had already appeared by Counsel.

They were and will be very sulky. They will stay away and decline supporting Government.

The bulletin is bad.

Two most impertinent letters from Lord Arbuthnot and Mr. Arbuthnot asking for, or rather demanding, cadetships. They will find I am not to be bullied.

June 21.

The King expectorated blood yesterday. He is failing in strength, and now certainly dying.

Read a memorandum of Wilson's on a proposed remodelling of the army. It is founded on my idea of bringing it into the form it formerly had, with fewer European officers and more native officers, in higher ranks. He proposes having two more European Non-Commissioned officers, a Subadar Major, and another Subadar, and several minor things.

June 22.

Cabinet. The Duke thought the character of the Government would be affected if we gave up the Forgery Bill in the Lords, not in consequence of any change of opinion, but of a majority of 13 in the House of Commons. I am satisfied the law, as it is, ought to be maintained. In the House Lord Lansdowne made a speech on moving the second reading, and Lord Win-chelsea and the Duke of Eichmond said they should vote for the Bill as it was none, however, taking reli-

274   VOL. II. T gious objections, Lord Lansdowne throwing out that lie would consent to make the bill temporary. The Chancellor made a very good speech, expressing his general objections to the Bill as it stands, and reserving his reasons for the Committee.

The King is rather worse and weaker.

In the House of Commons last night a mine was sprung and all parties, Whigs and Tories, East and West Indians, united by a trick on the sugar duties. However, we had a majority

June 23.

It seems Peel and Herries and even Goulburn himself rather doubts whether the sugar arrangement will work, and Peel has some doubt as to his majority. Altogether he is very much out of humour, or rather ennuye, and a very little would induce him to give up.

Cabinet dinner. The Duke saw the King and some stamping took place. The King was much worse than on Saturday. The expectoration is matter from the lungs. Knighton 'says that if they can keep the bowels right he may live a month. Halford says if he was an ordinary man he should think he would not live three days. Tierney says his pulse almost failed while he was asleep this morning, and he thought he would have died. The Duke says he thinks more with Knighton than the others.

The King was perfectly alive to all the business done. He talks of going to the Cottage still.

275   Much talk at the Cabinet dinner as to what should be done as to dissolution; but all depends on the time of the King's death, and the state of public business then.

Peel, Herries, and all seem to think the Low Party gains, and will gain strength. Hume, on Whitbread's retirement, is to come in for Middlesex.

June 24.

House. Galway Franchise Bill read second time Counsel were to have been heard; but the petitioners declined having them. I fear we shall have a sharp debate about it to-morrow, and Lord Grey be directly opposed to the Duke, and the worst of it is I do not believe our case is very good:

Hardinge and Wortley both say we are in a great scrape with these sugar duties, and Ireland, which was all with us, is hostile again on account of the spirit and stamp duties.

Walked as far as Mrs. Arbuthnot's with the Duke He told me his view of the Galway Franchise Bill, and is very certain of his case. He feels Goulburn has satisfied no one with his sugar duties.

The King seems much worse by the bulletin; but the private account was not much so. He was said to be worse when Lord Hill left Windsor. I really believe that we are so bothered with sugar duties and other things that an immediate demise and immediate dissolution would be best for us, and for the country

276   June 25.

Went to the Duke about the Galway Bill before the House met. The Duke spoke very well and made a very good case. Lord Grey well, but the Chancellor demolished his speech, and placed the question on such good grounds that it was useless to speak afterwards; nor was there much subsequent debate. The Duke of Buckingham made a speech against us, in which he mistook every point, and gave me a great disposition to follow him; but I knew if I did I should have a whole hornet's nest upon me, and I wished to keep Durham and Eadnor in check, or answer them. Had I spoken the debate would have lasted three hours more. As it was we got away by nine. On the division we had 62 to 47. Not brilliant. Our case was excellent. I had feared it would be indifferent. The Chancellor had got it up admirably. Lord Londonderry, the Dukes of Newcastle and Eichmond, Calthorpe, all the Canningites, of course voted against us. Dudley was in the House at one time, but he did not vote against us, nor has he once since he went out.

The King much weaker.

June 26.

At half-past eight this morning I received a Cabinet box containing the bulletin signed by Halford and Tierney of the King's death, and Halford's private letter to the Duke of Wellington. The letter stated that the King had slept for about two hours and

[277 woke a little before three. Soon afterwards, Sir W. Waller only being in the room, he suddenly put his hand to his breast, and said, ' Good God, what is the matter? This is death?" He then sent for Halford. He and the others came, and so soon afterwards as I have said, he expired without the least struggle or pain.

Peel summoned a Cabinet at half-past ten. We met and talked of very little but in what dress we should go to the Council, which was to be at twelve. It was agreed we should go in black, shoes and stockings, but not full dress. However, after I left the room the Duke arrived, and said the King intended to appear in uniform, so the Duke, Lord Bathurst, Eosslyn, and Sir J. Murray, who were there, put on their uniforms. The group at the Council was most motley. Lords Grey, Lansdowne, Spencer, Tankerville, Sir J. Warrender, and some others being in black full dress. Lord Cam-den and some more in uniform, which several sent for after they arrived, as Salisbury and Hardinge. The mass, however, in plain black, some in colours. The Eoyal Dukes came in full dress.

We waited a long time before the Council, almost two hours, a time occupied in audiences.

The Duke of Cumberland got the King to send for Lord Eldon, who went in for a minute only. The Duke of Cumberland received his gold stick, and seemed very active. The Duke of Wellington, Lord Bathurst, Eosslyn, the Chancellor, and Sir R. Peel went in together, and personally acquainted the King with the late King's death. The King said he might not have an opportunity of seeing that day the rest of his late Majesty's confidential servants; but he told those present that all had his confidence, and that they would receive his entire, cordial, and determined support. He told the Chancellor in a private audience not only the same thing, but that if at any time he should hear reports of his ceasing to place confidence in his Government, they were not to be believed. If he had any fault to find he would at once tell them.

When the Duke and the others came out from the King we all went to the ball-room, where we began to sign the proclamation, and a few, the Eoyal Dukes and others, had signed, when we were called to the Privy Council Eoom, where the King soon arrived, attended by the household of the late King. He took his seat, and read his declaration. He read it with much feeling, and it was well imagined, and will have a good effect. The Lord President entreated it might be printed.

I should have mentioned that before the King came in the Council made the usual orders, with the addition of an order for defacing the late King's stamps, which was accordingly done by the clerk of the Council.

When the declaration had been read the King took the Scotch oath in the usual form, the Lord-President reading it to him, and the King holding up his right hand.

He then said it was a satisfaction to him to find such a Privy Council, and requested them all to take the oath.

This the Royal Dukes did first, then the Speaker, that he might go to the House of Commons. Then the Archbishop and the Chancellor together, then the Dukes, with the Lord President and Privy Seal, then the Marquises, then others according to their rank. When all had taken the Privy Councillor's oath the Lord Chancellor took his, and the Clerk of the Council was sworn by the Lord President. The King then retired, and the Council ordered as usual respecting the disposal of the late King's body.

After the swearing in we signed the Proclamation. Some remained to alter the Liturgy. Queen Adelaide is to be prayed for, and the rest of the Eoyal family.

The Duke of Norfolk was there as Earl Marshal. He observed he was the only person there who was not a Privy Councillor, and expressed a wish to be one. The Duke mentioned it to the King, who readily assented. He observed there had been no Duke of Norfolk a member of the Privy Council since the time of James II., and that that Duke of Norfolk was a Protestant. The Duke of Norfolk, however, will consider the oath before he takes it. He would have taken the Earl Marshal's oath to-day, but it was not there. We met in Cabinet at 4.

The only innovations I yet hear of are in the dress of regiments. The King intends, as he told Lord Farn-borough, to live at Windsor. He intends to have a battalion of the Guards at Edinburgh, and a regiment of the Line at Windsor.

I went in, by some misdirection, the wrong way, and found Wood and Sir Ch. Pole waiting for the King. Wood, whom I met near the Horse Guards, as I was riding down to the Cabinet, told me the King had rehearsed his declaration to him, Sir Ch. Pole, and Lord Errol, before he went into the Privy Council.

There was no grief in the room in which we waited. It was like an ordinary levee.

The Chancellor went down to the House between the Cabinet and the Council, and took the oaths.

The Lord Steward was sent for by Peel, and only arrived a quarter before four at the House of Commons.

Lord Holland, Grey, and others seemed to think the Proclamation ought to have been made to-day, and I think it might have been just as well.

The Duke of Wellington was much cheered by the people.

The Duke was called out of the Cabinet to see Halford, but we had a long conversation as to the course to be pursued with respect to the Parliament, and especially with respect to the Eegency question.

The House must sit next week, as the sugar duties expire on Saturday next, and Goulburn seems disposed to propose a Bill for the continuance of the present duties for a time; to take money on account for miscellaneous services; to throw over the judicial Bills and end the session at once.

The stumbling block is the Eegency question whether it should be brought forward now, and if brought forward, who shall be Eegent.

Peel seems to think we can hardly avoid bringing it on; as the session would have lasted two months in the event of the late King's living, why should it not now, when the reason for Parliament sitting is so much greater? And what would be the situation of the country if the King should die, leaving a minor Queen?

Peel suggested appointing the Queen Eegent for a year. I said, depend upon it, when the King once has her as Eegent he will never consent to change her, and if you appoint her for a year you appoint her for the whole time.

He afterwards suggested her appointment for a year after the King's death on account of the probability of her pregnancy. To this I objected, the state of distraction in which the country would be placed during that year. It is impossible consistently with the constitution to have an Executive, of which the existence shall be dependent on the good pleasure of Parliament.

Peel then suggested the giving to the King the power of naming either the Queen, the Duchess of Kent, or any member of the Koyal family. The objection to this is that he ought to name one of the two first that we got no security against a bad nomination, which we ought to do.

The views we ought to have are these: to give all possible strength to the monarchy. This we do not, if we permit a frequent change of the Executive; if we diminish the power of the Crown while in the hands of a Eegency. We want to give stability to the Government, and this can only be given by making the Queen Eegent. If we do that we provide, as far as human wisdom can, for a stable Government of seven years.

We can in no case name any other person than the Queen, because she may become pregnant, and in that event it would be monstrous to make the Duchess of Kent Eegent. All we can do, then, is to give the King the option of choosing the Queen or the Duchess of Kent. He will name the Queen, and she will be the best.

It has been observed that all Kings of England die either on Saturdays or Sundays.

June 27.

Came up to a Cabinet at half-past three. We had a great deal of conversation as to the course to be pursued. The Chancellor said that in the event of a minor succeeding to the throne, all the minor's acts would be valid, and under the responsibility of ministers the Great Seal might be put in the minor's name by the minor's sign manual to an Act creating a Eegency.

It was determined to take the opinion of the Attorney- and Solicitor-General upon this point.

On the supposition that the law is as the Chancellor states, we considered what should be done. All turns upon our being able to get a temporary Act for the sugar duties, and if we cannot get that we are really no longer a Government. It was determined to carry through the Beer Bill and Beer Duty Bill, to throw over Stamps in Ireland, and carry Spirits. To take a sum of 800, OOOZ. on account of miscellaneous estimates, and 250,000. on account of the civil list.

These last points were decided at a Cabinet at Sir R.. Peel's, which assembled at eleven, and sat till near one; at which the Attorney- and Solicitor-General delivered their opinion, in conformity with that of the Chancellor as to the legal competency of a minor sovereign.

The Attorney-General reminded us that if the King died before the new Parliament assembled, the old Parliament would revive.

Peel talked a good deal of the Eegency. He is much in favour of making the Queen Kegent for a year after the King's death, to provide for the possible pregnancy. It seems the principle of all Eegencies has been to make the guardian of the person Eegent. It is curious that the case should never have been provided for of a Queen being left pregnant of an heir apparent, and that it should never have occurred. The difficulty would be infinite.

I consider the death of the King to have been one of the fortunate events which have often saved the Duke of Wellington. I really do not know how we could have gone on, had he lived two months.

The King wishes to make Lord Combermere a Privy Councillor, thinking all gold sticks have been so. We find he is misinformed, and the Duke means to show him the list of gold-sticks not Privy Councillors, and at the same time to tell him how Lord Combermere stands, having within these few months been censured by the Government. The Duke will show the King the correspondence which passed lately, and leave it to him to decide. There would be no objection to making him a Privy Councillor some months or a year hence.

Brougham made a violent speech against Lord Conyngham for not being in readiness to swear in the House of Commons.

June 28.

Went to St. James's at eleven. The Household, the Eoyal family, and the Ministers only were there. The King was dressed in plain black. He went to a large window looking into the courtyard, and stood forward. There were but few people there at first, the Horse Guards and the Heralds. The King's band played God Save the King, and those who were there cheered, upon which numbers of people came round from before the Palace and filled the courtyard. They then cheered well.

As the King passed through the line we formed for him to go to the window he came up to me and said he must begin by chiding me for not coming to him yesterday. In fact he had forgot I was a Cabinet Minister, and he therefore would see me to-day. I said ' it was my first and I hoped it would be my last fault." After the Proclamation he sent for the Duke of Wellington, and when the Duke left him, for me. He asked about China. I told him how we stood there. That there was an interruption which would probably prevent the arrival of any ships this year; that orders had been given for a double investment next year. I said the state of affairs generally was by no means satisfactory. The King said he was afraid Lord W. Bentinck had not been doing well. I said I feared he had let down the dignity of his office, and had when he first went there run after popularity too much, and allowed the press to get ahead. It would now be very difficult to check it. I added that he went to make great reductions and had made some. That that had rendered him unpopular. He was honest and well-meaning. The King said he should go down to Bushey soon, and as I was living near he would have me over at eleven o'clock some morning, and give me some hours to make him acquainted with the state of India. I told him of the secret letter to the Bengal Government about the Nag-pore Treaty, and the principles laid down, of which he highly approved. He then expressed apprehension of Eussia. I told him all that had been done upon that subject, and of the present to Eunjeet Singh, and the navigation of the Indus, with all which he seemed much pleased. I said I would send him the secret letters, and get together information that would bring the whole state of India before him as concisely as possible. As I was led to mention Sir J. Macdonald, I asked a coat for him, and the King granted it, thinking it very proper.

The Duke attends the opening of the King's will at 12.

The late King died, as was thought, of fatness about the heart. The dropsy was gone.

Cabinet. We had none at St. James's, but there was a council. The Duke of Norfolk attended to be sworn in as a Privy Councillor. We found, on reference to the Act of last session, that he must have taken the oath within three months before his receiving any office of trust or profit. So, on my proposal, the Petty Bag was sent for, and the Chancellor held a court of Chancery in the ball-room, where the Duke took the oath. He was afterwards sworn in, as were the Duke of Bedford, Sir S. Canning, Sir J. Mackintosh, Lord Bexley, and two or three others who were not in time yesterday. There were a good many orders in council, but of no moment.

There was the usual proclamation against vice and immorality.

The King did very well. He was very gracious to all who approached him, and had something to say to every one. He took little notice of Sir. J. Mackintosh.

Lord Bathurst had to change a sheriff. The King, when he heard the name of the new one (sheriff of Suffolk, I think), said,; He is a Whig' Lord Bathurst said, 'He is a very good man, I believe, Sir, and is recommended by the Duke of Grafton." ' Oh!" said the King," I do not mean to say it is wrong; only remember, he is a Whig."

After the council we went to Peel's, but we remained but a short time, the Duke going to the House and Peel too before 4. In our House not a word was said.

In the Commons Brougham, who seems, as Frankland Lewis told me, half frantic, made rather an apologetic speech for his attack upon the Lord Steward, but again hinted at intentional disrespect towards the House of Commons, not on the part of Ministers in that House, but of persons elsewhere. He reminded Peel that whatever accession of strength Ministers might have recently obtained, they could not carry on the Government without the confidence of the House of Commons.

His speech was very mysterious, and hardly any one understood it. Some thought he alluded to the accession of Lord Grey to the Government; that must have rested upon foolish rumour. He alluded, I conclude, to the King's support, now well known. What symptoms of disrespect for the House of Commons he may have discovered I know not. Probably he chooses to imagine them, to produce an effect.

He is evidently mad with disappointment. He could not well be wooed in such a temper, even if he were to be wooed at all.

After the House I rode to leave my name at the Princess Augusta's, and forgot the Duke of Cumberland, who lives close by; then I went to the Duke of Gloucester's, where I met F. Lewis, who told me of Brougham's speech and so on. I went with Wood to the Princess Sophia of Gloucester's. He told me all the King said of the late King's error in not frankly supporting his Government, and of his own determination to do so. He had been long in the habit of saying, the Queen is not with child." There had been a report to that effect. Eode to the Duchess of Kent's and Duke of Sussex's. Met Lord Graham, Mr. and Mrs. Arbuthnot, and the Chancellor. Eode on with the Chancellor to Kensington. As we were coming away from the Palace we heard the trampling of horses behind us, and turning round, saw the King coming full tilt with his lancers; we had but just time to wheel round and salute His Majesty, who seemed much amused at seeing two of his Ministers amongst all the little children who were running by his carriage, and the Chancellor, so lately in all the gravity of his official robes, mounted on a little white New Forest pony of Lady Lyndhurst's. I rode on to Koehampton, dined there, and rode back.

At 10 a Cabinet at Peel's. We framed the message. Peel was very flat. The measure of immediate dissolution is one he does not half approve. He wished to settle the Eegency question. He has been put out of humour by having his opinions upon that point not at once acquiesced in. He sees all the difficulties of our position, and does not meet them with energy and elan. He certainly is not an agreeable person to transact business with, but he is a very able man.

The accounts from Ireland are very bad. The potatoes are exhausted at Limerick, Tralee, and other places, and the new crop will not come in till August. At Limerick some stores have been forced, and the troops attacked with stones.

At Tralee there was a subscription of 450. for the purchase of potatoes; 3QO. was expended, and the Mayor of Tralee and other gentlemen bought some of these potatoes, which were offered at a reduced price to the people, for seed Can any country be tranquil in which resident gentlemen can do such things?- A discretionary power has been given to the Lord Lieutenant to expend 3000. in food, should it become necessary, without further reference.

About 180 peers have taken the oaths. I fear we shall be beaten upon the Forgery Bill; we have a very narrow margin indeed, not above six or eight without bishops.

It is supposed the bishops will stay away. I fear those will stay away who would, if
present, vote⌋with us, and all who are against will come. If this should be the case we
must be defeated.

The King was perfectly reasonable about Lord Combermere. The Duke showed
His Majesty the letters which had passed, and the King said he should not think of it.
He told Peel and Lord Melville he wished the Eoyal Academy to remain open till after
the King's funeral, that he might see the exhibition, and said Peel should attend him
when he went. This Peel thinks very foolish, and his disposition seems to be to turn
the King into ridicule, and to throw the suspicion of insanity upon all his acts. This is
the tactique of the Whigs. The King takes the Sacrament on Sunday, and has desired
the two English and one Irish archbishop to attend. This they call 4 an indication."

June 29.

At half-past ten went to Lord Eosslyn's, to arrange with him the Lords' Address.
Went with him to Peel's, to show it to him. He was reading when we went in, and
hardly looked up. He heard the Address which I read, and approved of it; but he
hardly took any notice of us or of it. He seemed really ill, and quite broken down.

Called on Hardinge. We had some conversation respecting the state of the Government. His idea is that the strength of the Government in the House of Commons
is much injured by Peel's being in a subordinate situation to the Duke. That if he was
Chancellor of the Exchequer and First Lord of the Treasury, things would go on better,
the Duke taking a secretaryship of

VOL. II. U

State. This would do very well in the House of Commons, but very ill in the
Cabinet. He is for getting Mr. Stanley, and suggests (or Eosslyn did, or both, for
having talked to both on the same subject I may confound them) that Lord F. Leveson
should be made a peer. I think that a good idea. He is of no use in the Commons, and
his peerage would open a place which Mr. Stanley could fill.

Eosslyn thinks Aberdeen's notions upon foreign politics have, together with his
assumption of independence which is of recent date, made the Duke rather sore, and
that he would not be sorry to have another Secretary of State for Foreign Affairs. Lord
Eosslyn wants to have Lord Grey in, and says he would as soon be First Lord of the
Admiralty as Foreign Secretary. Eosslyn would, I think, like to go to Ireland as Lord
Lieutenant. He would willingly give up the Privy Seal to Aberdeen. He thinks Sir G.
Murray would make an excellent Governor General. I fear he would be too indolent.
He said he knew, if there was a vacancy, the Duke would be glad to make him Master
General.

I had said I believed Lord Beresford would go to Portugal as Minister, if Miguel
would be on good terms with us. It seems Goulburn would be glad to be Speaker.
That would open a proper office for Herries, and his offices might be divided, Lord
Althorpe having the Board of Trade.

I really think some arrangement must be made to give us strength in the House of
Commons. Saw the Duke at two. He approved of the address. Eosslyn⌋was with him.
I told him how ill Peel seemed. He said he would go to see him.

House. The Duke moved the Address. He gave a character of the late King as
one of the most accomplished, able, and remarkable men of the age. I saw Lord Grey

smile a little, but the House generally was grave and formal. Lord Grey assented to the Address, but laissait entrevoir that he should be hostile to the Address to-morrow, hinting at the Eegency. The same thing was done in the Commons.

The Duke told me the late King had three disorders which must have proved fatal, and he died of bursting a blood-vessel in the stomach. He had a concretion as large as an orange in his bladder, his liver was diseased, and his heart was ossified. Water there was not much, and all proceeding from the interruption of circulation about the heart. I read the report, signed by Halford, Tierney, Brodie, and A. Cooper.

We had East Eetford again. Lord Londonderry, whom Lord Durham puts forward as his tool, moved an adjournment. The question was postponed till Friday. Afterwards the Duke of Buckingham, when most peers had gone away, moved the same thing, and then Lord Londonderry twice. We had majorities but gave it up at last. The Chancellor is heartily tired of the whole thing. The Duke went away while Lord Londonderry was explaining in answer to his speech, to the noble Lord's great annoyance.

I rode home with the Duke, who spoke of Lord ndonderry as a madman. He said Peel had not taken a sufficiently high line. He did not like the position he stood in in the House of Commons. The Duke said no Government was ever beaten by its enemies, but many have been by their friends.

The King was very amenable and good-natured to-day.

June 30.

Occupied all the morning in looking at the precedents in the case of regency. There are two modern contradictory precedents, 24 Geo. II. and 5 Geo. III., and no experience of either, nor has there been a minority since Edward VI. in 1547.

It is clear the sovereign is sovereign whatever be his age, and the Act appointing a regent must have his assent. Whatever has at any time been done, has been done or sanctioned by Parliament. Parliament cannot supersede the Eoyal authority.

It is remarkable that Parliament in 1811 made provision for the care of the King's person in case of his death; but none for the care of the kingdom in the event of the Eegent's death, although the Princess Charlotte was but fifteen.

House at 5. The Duke moved the Address in a very short speech, not adverting to the regency. Lord Grey followed and declared his opinion of the incapacity of Government as exhibited in their measures during the last five months. Goderich said ' nothing had been done," and was for going on with the business. Lord Harrowby wished a short Regency Bill to be passed, giving the regency to the Queen for six weeks, to provide for the case of pregnancy. The Chancellor made a speech, not long, admitting the law to be as stated, that is, that the sovereign immediately on accession possessed all Eoyal power. Eldon spoke against us, and treated the question of a King en ventre sa mere with jocularity. I followed, and observed gravely upon his jocularity on such a subject; then stated my view of the question, and expressed my regret and surprise at Lord Grey's declaration, added I was happy to know at last where we were, who were our friends and who were our enemies.

Then got up the Duke of Eichmond, totally misrepresenting what I had said as to Lord Eldon and Lord Grey, and endeavouring to make them appear as personal attacks to which no gentleman could submit. Lord Londonderry followed in the same tone. (After the Duke of Eichmond I explained that I had not attributed improper motives to

Lord Grey, nor attacked Lord Eldon's character.) We had afterwards Lord Lansdowne, Lord Harewood giving his first vote for the Government after the Catholic Question, and that because it was the first measure of the new King. A foolish reason, but I dare say many voted on the same ground. Lord Wharncliffe spoke against us, Lords Bute and Wicklow and the Duke of Buckingham for us, Lord Eadnor shortly against. The Duke replied. Then Lord Grey spoke, and observed, of course, upon what I had said, but not angrily, and I made an explanation which was satisfactory, and set us quite right again. He had imagined me to say he owed a debt of gratitude to the Government for the measure of last session. I said he had expressed gratitude, but we had not claimed it, because we only did our duty. In the lobby during the debate Lord Jersey told me lie was afraid Lord Grey might have misunderstood the meaning of what I said about gratitude, and begged me to set him right immediately if it was so.

We had 100 to 54. A very good division. We went, at ten, to Goulburn's to dinner, and expected soon to see the members of the House of Commons, and to hear of as good a division there as in the Lords, but after an hour we heard the division had only been 185 to 139. This made us a little flat, and Lord Bathurst drank no more champagne.

I intentionally committed the Government thoroughly with the Whigs, for after Lord Grey's declaration it was idle to expect a vote from them, and our people were pleased, as I knew they would be. The Duke of Bedford and Lord Jersey voted with us. So did Dudley.

I shall have work enough now, as they have ten or twelve speakers, and we but three.

July 1.

Looked over the debates on the Forgery Bill this morning. Committee at one. Examined a manufacturer of camlets and bombazines from Norwich. House. Forgery Bill. The Chancellor made an admirable speech, Lord Lansdowne followed him, then Lords Wynford, Tenterden, and Eldon all against the bill. We divided 77 to 20. The Duke was delighted, he said, ' How very right we were' So said the Chancellor. Peel would have given it up. Now, I think one large majority will set public opinion right again. The

Chancellor said all that was contained in Peel's two speeches and much more. Peel and Brougham were under the throne.

. Lord Bathurst, with whom I walked home from the House at three, when we talked of Goulburn's becoming Speaker, suggested Hardinge as Chancellor of the Exchequer. He would be an excellent one.

I met Goulburn in the Park this morning. He did not seem much pleased with the House last night. I see there were strong words indeed in the second debate, Brougham talking of the parasites of the Duke of Wellington. Peel asked whether he presumed to call him a parasite? There was great confusion, and it ended by Peel's making an explanation for Brougham, in which Brougham acquiesced. Several members, amongst the rest, I hear, Castlereagh, were going to call Brougham out.

In the House Lord Bathurst told me Wortley had stayed away from the division last night, and had sent in his resignation. Soon after I received a note from Wortley telling me so, expressing great regret that he could not vote for a course of measures which excluded a Eegency Bill. His regret was increased by my kindness and encouragement. I have sent his letter to the Duke, having shown it to Lord Bathurst in the House. I wrote an answer to say I felt great regret at his not being able to adopt our line, and expressing my personal regret at losing him, and my acknowledgments for the assistance I had derived from him.

[296] His father and father-in-law both voted against us last night. He says in his note he has taken his line entirely on his own view.

I had some talk with Dudley in the lobby of the House. I began by saying he had acted very handsomely by us. He said he was friendly to the Government, and above all things unfriendly to Lord Grey and the Duke of Newcastle. The motion of last night he called pure faction.

Salisbury told me he stayed away to-night not liking to vote against us, on account of yesterday's declaration of war. The Duke of Gordon told me he was much pleased with me last night. I do not, however, think I spoke as well as usual.

Bankes I had some talk with. He said the Duke of Cumberland was hostile to the Duchess of Kent and Leopold. He would prefer the Queen as Eegent. He had been much with the King for the last six weeks, and there was a good understanding between them. Bankes asked if I had left my name with him. I told him I had, and I believed all the rest had. By some mistake of a servant the summons to the Privy Council did not reach the Duke of Cumberland till the day after the accession, and he was very angry. It had been sent to Kew. He is satisfied now. Goulburn has hit upon a mezzo termine which answers for the present session. He has reduced the duty on West Indian sugar to 24s., and on East Indian sugar to 32s. The duty on other sugar to be 63s. I did not fail to tell Dudley and Bankes in what strong terms the King had expressed his determination to support the Govern-. ment. They were both ' colpiti."

[297] Dudley had had no idea terms so strong had been used. He comes to the Council to be sworn in on Saturday.

July 2.

Chairs at eleven. They have sent a representation on the subject of the Kattywar draft, impugning, as I understand, for I have not yet read it, the power of the Board to give orders in the Secret Department which do not require secrecy.

I told the Chairs distinctly that I intended to take upon the King's Government the whole responsibility of the foreign policy of India.

I saw Wortley, who thanked me very much indeed for my note of yesterday evening. He was much distressed, and evidently regrets extremely that he has tendered his resignation. He adheres, however, to his opinion that the Eegency question should have been settled at least provisionally before Parliament separated. He was going to see Peel and afterwards the Duke.

He told me the Government could not be conducted in the House of Commons unless some more Ministers would speak that there must be a change.

I called at Hardinge's. He told me the same thing, and that he had talked about it to the Duke yesterday and made him promise to place the ministerial seats in the House of Commons at Peel's disposal. Hardinge is for having Edward Stanley. He spoke of Wilmot Horton, but he is not of Cabinet calibre. I think Hardinge is disposed to displace Murray rather than either of the others. He talked again of making Peel

298   First Lord of the Treasury and Chancellor of the Exchequer, and the Duke Secretary of State for Foreign Affairs Aberdeen going to Ireland. Aberdeen would not go there, I think. I told Hardinge Lord Bathurst had suggested him as Chancellor of the Exchequer. He would not hear of it.

It seems Brougham was almost drunk the other night. Hardinge and several others were getting up to question him when Peel stopped them. He pulled Hardinge down by the coat. Hardinge says Peel managed admirably.

In the House spoke to the Chancellor and Lord Bathurst, and told them I had heard we must have an addition of strength to the Treasury Bench. They both said they believed so too. Lord Bathurst again mentioned Hardinge.

Spoke to the Duke about Wortley. He said he had written a kind note to him, and told him he had been too hasty. He should have spoken to some of the Ministers first. The Duke evidently intends the thing to blow over.

Spoke to Lord Wharncliffe about the same thing. He said he would neither have voted nor have spoken against Government on Wednesday if he had had, an idea of Wortley's resigning, because it gave the appearance of concert, and there really was none. He did not know of the letters till after they had been written. I said Lord Harrowby's taking the same line, both voting and speaking, gave the appearance of concert. He said he thought Wortley altogether wrong. That a young man, having
299 joined a Government, had no right, for a difference on a single point, to resign. If he differed upon a system of policy it was another thing. I said I thought it would be allowed to blow over. He afterwards talked to the Duke, and I have no doubt Wortley will remain.

Lord Bathurst says W. Horton is a gentleman. I doubted it. He rather wishes to have Wilmot in office. But the person to be got is Mr. Stanley.

We had a discussion on a motion of Lord Londonderry's whether we should proceed with East Eetford or not. I followed Lord Grey and spoke very quietly but, I think, reasonably, for going on. I said if we were obliged to postpone any measure, the last we should postpone should be one deeply interesting to the House of Commons and affecting their privileges.

I think we did all Peel could require. We had 45 to 13. I remained till eight, but I could stay no longer.

Lord Londonderry attacked me again, and said instead of planting a dagger in the side of Lord Grey I should have applied a healing plaster! His comparative civility to the Government to-day was to conciliate their support to Sir E. Gresley for Durham.

The Duke told Hardinge yesterday I was always ready. I was a little too lively, but I was of great use.

July 3.

The King has done two popular things. He has allowed a passage to be made from Waterloo Place into the Park, and he has dismissed all the late King's French cooks! He will have no foreigners about him.

300   The foreign Ministers were all introduced to him to-day. He was very gracious, Aberdeen said, but he did not choose his topics quite so well as the late King, who had much tact and grace, neither does the King speak French well.

Lord Combermere came and had an audience to present a picture of the King of Delhi, painted by an Indian artist. It seemed not ill done, and had the appearance of an ordinary picture, but when placed against the light was a transparency. Lord Combermere did not remain long with the King, and when he came out he seemed annoyed. He remained some time, and the Duke was afraid he remained to be sworn in, in consequence of some incautious promise of the King. It was arranged that Buller, who had a list of the Privy Councillors, should turn him out with the rest who were not so, when the Council began. However, he went away a little before.

The Duke of Montrose has resigned, and the King has placed the office at the disposal of the Duke of Wellington.

Peel seems to think Lord Graham is dissatisfied and unfriendly. It seems he has been heard complaining of vacillation, c., on the part of the Government, and does not attend well.

The Queen has named Lady Wellesley and Mrs. Berkeley Paget as two Ladies of the Bed-chamber. Valletort is to be in some high situation about the Queen. Lord Errol, her Master of the Horse.

I conclude Lord Conyngham will resign, but it is not known.

The Duke goes to Windsor to-morrow respecting the late King's papers, the Duke of Cumberland having meditated an enlevement.

Peel thinks Brougham really rather mad, and would not be surprised to hear he was confined. Last year he was melancholy, and his friends and he himself feared he might commit suicide. Now he is in an excited state. Peel speaks of him as a most wonderful man in ability.

It seems that last night the leaders came down to make an attack, but the followers, not having been consulted, would not support. E. Gordon came over to Herries and said he should vote with Government. Hume, who in the morning had sent to ask Planta whether Government intended to oppose him for Middlesex (a question Planta was desired not to answer till the end of next week), was very civil, and disposed to let business pass. It is not impossible that the House of Commons may have done their business by this day week.

I am to look at the Beer Bill, and have already begun to read the Commons' debates upon it.

July 4.

Eead all the debates on the Beer Bill, made notes, and considered the subject. The Queen seems to have selected her maids of honour from the neighbourhood of Bushey. This is amiable and very right.

July 5.

I proposed to Wortley, as Edward Stanley was an acquaintance of his, to give him a hint not to commit himself against the Government just now; but he says he does not know Stanley intimately enough.

I asked him whether he did not find the Duke of Wellington very kind. He really had the kindest heart of any man I ever knew. When I looked up I saw the tears in his eyes.

Clare told me he heard all the Whigs in our House, except Lord Lansdowne, were determined to push us a Voutrance; but Lord Lansdowne thought the Duke must endeavour to strengthen himself during the vacation. He could not do it now, as it would be a confession of weakness; but he thought he would do it before Parliament met. However, the others would not hear him.

There was a meeting at Lord Althorpe's yesterday, but I have not heard the result.

Talked to Clare about the affairs of Kattywar, and promised to give him precise instructions before he left England.

He will remain at Bombay, I think. He tells his mother three years, but he will remain till he has made some money and done something worth going there to do. He has got Elphinstone to make a list of the civil servants with their characters.

The King took the sacrament yesterday with the Koyal Family, and afterwards received the bishops and the judges. He made long speeches to both. Thirty minutes to the first, and twenty to the second.

Polignac seems quite firm, although certain he shall be in a minority of 1 to 2 or 3. It is expected he will evade, and that Villele may be able to go on with the new Chamber.

No news from Algiers. 15,000 men are assembled at Toulon as a reserve.

July 6.

Cabinet. Peel said the Lord Advocate would resign if we did not pass the Scotch Judicature Bill, so we must struggle through with it. The Welsh Judicature Bill is to be passed too. This will keep us sitting some time. The Commons will have finished on Friday.

House. We had the second reading of the Beer Bill. I said a few words to show the inaccuracy of one of Lord Malmesbury's conclusions; but I must, speak in detail in the Committee.

July 7.

Last night we had 247 to 93, a great division. The Tories in general voting with us.

Looked over again all the papers relative to the Beer Bill.

In my way back from Eoehampton met Lord Eavensworth, who told me the King had the gout, and that he had given the ' Guelphic ribbon to his three sons-in-law. He likewise told me what I knew before, that the Duke of Montrose had resigned.

I told him of the dismissal of the French cooks, which horrified him.

Cabinet dinner at Herries's. All the House of Commons pleased with their division. They got three county members to speak for others. The Whigs did not like the motion, and were unwilling to divide.

Robert Grant divided the House. The King was delighted with the division.

He came to town to-day, almost for nothing, and received the Duke and others. He sent for Lord Eosslyn and told him he had made his regiment the Queen's Own.

He has changed the uniform of the navy, which is to be blue with red cuffs and facings. He wore the uniform so to-day.

Aberdeen introduced Prince William of Prussia. The King desired him to stay, and said he should never receive foreigners except in his presence, and never but in his naval uniform. He should wear the military uniform now and then, but as little as possible.

All the cavalry are to be in red.

No news from Algiers. The Duke thinks they must be rather in want of provisions. The French are all in a state of sentiment, as Bourmont's second son has been dangerously wounded. Certainly the way in which it is mentioned in the dispatch is good, and indeed Bourmont, a very clever man, and first under fire with his four sons, will soon be popular with an army.

Polignac seems to be insensible rather than bold. He thinks all will go on well still.

The present intention is that we should all be in gala at the funeral, with black scarfs, c.

I have asked several to dine at Eoehampton and go from thence.

The Queen is to be present, I suppose, in the King's pew. The King is certainly to be chief mourner.

305   ⁸We had a great deal of talk after dinner about elections. I fear they have not been attended to in time. It is hoped Seaford will be conquered from Lord Seaford, and that the two Grants will be thrown out. We have nobody for Surrey and nobody for Middlesex.

July 8.

House. Answered the Duke of Eichmond on the sale of Beer Bill. The Duke seemed very well satisfied, and the House was very attentive and cheered frequently. We had on a division 60 to 15.

July 9.

Lord Eadnor made some observations upon the continuing of the Irish Arms Bill without explaining the reason, the Bill having been introduced in troublesome times and expiring at the end of this Session. Lord Grey supported him. It is clear Lord Durham and Lord Eadnor evidently intend to make us look about us and not do work in a slovenly manner. I cannot find fault with them.

Lord Durham moved the printing of the Appropriation List, which was negatived without a division, as unusual; but I dare say he will ask questions as to some of the items.

July 10.

As I was coming home from the office I called on ardinge. He considers the division to have been ivaluable to us here and even to France. Certainly ie French funds rose when it was known the present Ing held the same course as his predecessor. Har-

306   ~~VOL. II. X~~dinge thinks many men are disposed to support the Duke's Government under the idea that all sorts of calamities would attend the weak Governnient which must succeed it. He thinks Palmers ton the best man to have in Goulburn's place, Goulburn going to the Speakership. He thinks W. Horton would be better than Frankland Lewis as his successor at the War Office, it being necessary in either case to get Lord F. Leveson into the House of Lords. Fitzgerald has written to Hardinge, and seems eager about politics. I wish he was well and could come into office again.

I do not know that the Duke or anybody would have any objection to Palmerston coming in by himself; but I doubt Huskisson's ever being in office again while the Duke lives. Neither will the Grants come in indeed it is to be hoped they will both be turned out of their seats.

July 12.

Office. Backhouse brought the account of Sir J. Mac-donald's expected death; the date, May 12. Sir Henry Willock will take charge of the mission ad interim. He may be a sensible man, but the loss of Macdonald is severe. I do not know how we shall replace him.

Cabinet at 2. The business was the eternal slave question what answer should be given to Brougham to-morrow. He is expected to propose some pledge of proceeding legislatively in the next session as to the admission of slave evidence and other points. A Bill has been prepared making slave evidence admissible, and it would probably have been introduced but for the early termination of the session. However, there seems to be great reluctance to embark in a contest with the Colonial legislatures. The foolish resolutions moved by Canning are deeply regretted. I was the only man who objected to them, when, two years after they had been found of no avail, it was proposed that the Lords should concur in them. Peel objects to any pledge on the part of Parliament, more particularly on the eve of a dissolution. It is thought that by paying from our funds for an improved judicature in the West Indies we may induce the colonies to acquiesce in the admission of slave evidence, although imposed by the interposition of Parliament. I doubt it, and if we pass a law to which the colonies are adverse, which they will regard as being no law how are we to execute it? We may make judges and pay them, but we must procure submission to those judges, and further, we must make jurymen.

All these difficulties I foresaw when the Lords adopted the Commons' resolution; but I suppose Canning forced it upon Lord Bathurst and the Cabinet.

House at 5. Debate on the Scotch Judicature Bill. Lord Wynford made a miserable speech, which proved he knew nothing about the subject. The Chancellor was very angry with him, and once interrupted him improperly. The debate was dull, and there was no division.

July 13.

Went to St. James's at half-past one. A few Privy Councillors were there to be sworn in, amongst the rest the Duke of Hamilton.

The Duke of Wellington had to talk over the King about giving a lodge in Bushey Park to one of the Fitz-Clarences for his life, and about gazetting the Queen's household. He found the King very reasonable indeed.

The King means to give his Ministers a grand dinner. He intends asking the Speaker and the two Gold Sticks, but not the third, the Duke of Cumberland.

The Duke of Buckingham is Lord Steward. A bad appointment. The office of Lord Chamberlain was offered by the Duke of Wellington to the Duke of Bedford, Lord Eosslyn going to make the offer. The Duke of Bedford was much gratified, but declined on the ground of his health. The office was then offered to Lord Jersey, who accepted willingly.

House. The Chancellor made an excellent speech on the Welsh Judicature Bill, and it was read a second time without a further word. The Forgery Bill passed with a motion of Lord Holland's pro formd that he might protest.

We had Sir Jonah Barrington for a short time. He is very roguish and sly.

There are no particulars yet of the capture of Algiers, except that the fleet co-operated.

The French seem to have been highly delighted.

July 15.

Sir G. Murray, Goulburn, and Herries came down to Eoehampton at four to dinner. At five we set off for Windsor. The day was beautiful, and all the world made it a holiday. Carriages of all sorts and hackney coaches were on the road all the morning to Richmond.

I never saw so many persons there, and chiefly of the class of shopkeepers. London was quite empty, but the Park quite covered with the people. It seemed to be a day of general recreation.

Arrived at Windsor at a quarter after seven. There were a few Lancers along the road from Frogmore, where the King and Queen were, but no crowd. Near the town there were a great many waggons. We turned to the right at the end of the Long Walk and drove through the park to the great gate of the Castle. Within the court were Horse and Foot Guards. We entered at the visitors' entrance, and went to St. George's Hall, where we all assembled. A great many were already come. They began forming the procession at half-past seven, and it was all formed so as to move before nine. I walked with Lord Hill. There were ten or twelve barons, a number of judges, six or eight bishops, and upon the whole a fair representation of the peerage and the Privy Council. There was a double line of Life Guardsmen within the castle, without Foot Guards, and the Blues in the chapel. We did not see the body as we passed. A screen of black concealed the room in which it lay in state. I imagine the King was in the room. As we returned it was open.

It struck nine as we came to the Eound Tower. A rocket was fired as soon as the body moved, to give notice to Linden for the firing of the minute guns. The bands of the several regiments played the Dead March in Saul, c., as the procession passed. The Foot Guards stood close together with arms reversed, every fifth man having a flambeau. The platform was, in most places, open on both sides. There was a good deal of air, but the night was warm. Had there been rain, or had it been cold, some must have died. There were but few people on the right of the platform in the inner court, but in the outer court there was a dense mass of people, and all the roofs were covered. There was hardly a whisper. All the people seemed very decent in their dress, and their conduct was perfect. The procession entered at the great door of the chapel and turned to the left, went down to the end of the aisle and then turned, facing the door of the inner chapel. In the space we thus went round were the Eton boys. In the chapel there were some persons on the right of the altar. I could not well see who they were, as there was a sort of haze, but they were all in uniform. With this exception the chapel was empty. We were all placed as we entered in the seats and stalls. The body was drawn upon a carriage. It was too heavy to be carried. The King had a vast number of attendants, such as equerries, c. Half of them captains in the navy. The attendants pressed rather too close upon him. He was in black with the collars of all the orders. He nodded occasionally as he recognised people; but when his countenance was still he looked very grave. He is become very like his father. The assistant mourners, who were Lords Goderich, Sid-mouth, Granville, Grantham, Carlisle, and some others, had no seats and stood during the service. The last who entered were the Guard, the colours preceding. These came half way into the aisle,

311   the colours de-pressed. The colonels of the battalions and the general, Sir H. Vivian, came in with their caps on and swords drawn, and stood to the right and left of the King, but not near him. The banners were depressed on the two sides of the grave. Over the grave was a black canopy, on the top of which was an enormous crown. The music was good. The service was very ill-read by the Dean Hobart, and the Garter could not make himself heard when he recited the King's titles. Lord Jersey walked as Lord Chamberlain, Lord Conyngham as Steward. He broke his staff into the grave. Lord Cholmondeley was there as Lord Great Chamberlain, and sat on the left of the aisle in a stall opposite the passage. On the other side was the Earl Marshal. When all was over the King went out by the small door on the left near the King's closet, and so by the cloister to the platform. As soon as he appeared the Guard received him with presented arms and God Save the King. We all returned by the way we came. There was tea in St. George's Hall but we went on, and finding Goulburn's servant, followed him to the carriage, which was on the other side of, the entrance gate, and so got away even before the King. We were at Eoehampton by half-past one. The whole procession lasted about two hours and a half or rather less that is, from the first move to the end.

It was very well arranged. Pohlman, our Deputy Black Eod, who is a Herald, was the acting person, and did his duty admirably. There was no interruption, no confusion, but everything managed as if we had been drilled and did the same thing every day. And so

312   King George IV. is gone to his grave with all the pomp of royalty, and splendid the pageant was; but it was considered a mere pageant even by his household, who had lived so intimately with him for years. There was no regret. A coronation could hardly be gayer; but the procession was gravely done and decently.

The magnificence of the castle aided the spectacle and made royalty appear almost as imposing in death as at the moment when the Crown was assumed in the Abbey.

We had supper and they all went to London.

Huskisson and Palmerston were there. Huskisson very sulky and sour. Palmerston very cordial, as if he thought he might come in. I should be glad if he did.

It seems the Duke of Buckingham hints that he must have something more than the stewardship for his seven votes. No one likes his appointment, and we all feel as if an alliance with the Grenville party would bring us ill-luck.

July 16.

House. Administration of Justice Bill. A great many amendments made by Lord Tenterden. We struck out a clause by which Le Blanc would have been obliged to sit to tax costs every day in the year. Lord Eldon said the Bill as it was originally drawn was more like a string of resolutions at the London Tavern than an Act of Parliament.

The Attorney-General was very angry indeed at the alterations made in the Bill, and threatened to throw it over in the House of Commons.

313   Nothing said about the Libel law; but Lord Holland is to say something on the third reading. Sir Jonah's case. W. Goady spoke. He spoke so slow, it was like a banker paying in sixpences to gain time. He was so dull I went away for fear of falling asleep. The Duke stayed and slept.

The Duke remained at Windsor all night. I met him as he was coming down to the office to-day. He said he had remained to see the King and give up to him the late King's snuff-boxes, c., which were all in a great box.

Lord Wharncliffe told me he thought Duncombe, Bethel, Lord Morpeth, and Eamsden would come in for Yorkshire. Afterwards we heard Brougham was to stand. It will have a very bad effect if Hume and Brougham come in for great counties. Yet I dare say they will.

Wortley goes down to stand for some Scotch boroughs, which will lead to the County of Forfar.

Long Wellesley has been arrested by Gosling the Banker for 4,000., on which it was found that he had but 3,000. in the books in the Bank, so he remained in durance for the other 1,000. till he found five people, each willing to be bound for 200. This disposes of him for Essex. He had given out that he had 30,000. An express has been sent off to a Mr. Lloyd, the son-in-law of the old Eliab Harvey, to stand for Essex. I' know the man. He was at Kyde in 1813, and at Cowes 1826. His daughters are rather pretty girls. I suggested Tower, who w6uld have done very well for Essex.

314   July 17.

St. James's at 2. The Lord Mayor and Aldermen first came up with their address, then the same with the Common Council. The King received the addresses, which were very loyal, on the throne. He read the answers very well. The Ministers stood on his left and the household on his right. About seven gentlemen pensioners were on each side from the door to the foot of the throne. The Lord Mayor, c., were introduced by the Lord Chamberlain. It was well done, and is rather an imposing ceremony.

Cabinet. First a question as to what should be done about Ashe, the man who wrote a libel on the Duke of Cumberland, which he sent to him and now reclaims. He has written many letters indicative of an intention to assassinate, and is now come up from Carlisle on foot, and has been walking opposite the Duke's house for three hours, having first written another letter of a threatening nature.

Lord Wynford wrote to Peel on the Duke of Cumberland's part; but the Duke will not exhibit articles of the peace. Colonel Peter gave Ashe 5s. and he went away.

The question was what could be done with him? I suggested that, as in the case of an expected duel, a magistrate on mere information that a breach of the peace was apprehended would take persons into custody and hold them to bail; so here the same thing might be done, one of the letters distinctly threatening a breach of the peace. This would secure the man till it could be discovered whether there was legal ground to indict him for the letters. This will be done.

315   We then came to the consideration of the East Eetford question. All the press were for giving up the Bill. I took some part in the discussion. However, Peel was so strongly for the Lords going as the Commons had done, and for preventing the appearance of disunion in the Cabinet, that his wishes were acceded to, and we support the Bill. The Duke thinks it will be thrown out, and I hope it will. It will, be very difficult to make a speech in favour of the Bill which will not commit us to a bad precedent. However, I shall try. Peel was very obstinate and disagreeable. In fact the interfering with the existing franchise never was made a Cabinet question. The giving the franchise to Bassetlaw [1] rather than to Birmingham was, and it was because after

an agreement that we should all vote for Bassetlaw, Huskisson voted for Birmingham and then resigned, that the separation took place.

These questions never were made Government questions before, and it is much better they should not be.

. Peel thinks he will not be able to oppose reform in general if we do not show a disposition to punish individual cases of corruption.

I did not get away till seven, and then went to Har-dinge's to bring him down to Wilderness. [2] He told me the Speaker had been with the Duke and did not resign [1 The Hundred of Bassetlaw, forming the existing "borough of East Eetford.

2 Seat of Lord Camden, near Sevenoaks.]

316   just now. There had been a question whether he should not; but it was thought we might be damaged at the elections if we made any change now. The Duke asked Hardinge what he thought as to taking Huskisson and Palmerston back again? Hardinge declared against having Huskisson, but recommended Palmerston. I dare say as soon as the elections are over something will be done, and that Palmerston will be offered the Chancellorship of the Exchequer.

Peel once wanted Edward Stanley, but it seems he has wavered a good deal. Unless his manner should change it would be impossible to go on with him as Minister; but I trust in God we shall never lose the Duke.

July 19.

Eeceived at nine a card from Lord Bathurst informing me that the Queen would be in Downing Street at ten. Went in plain clothes as I was desired. Found the Queen was to be there to see the Guards, whom the King was to inspect. The Ministers were invited and the connections of the Bathursts. We were presented to the Queen, and kissed her hand. After the parade, which the King attended on foot, he joined the party, and they had breakfast. However, before that I went away. At one again at St. James's. The two Universities came up with addresses to the King and Queen. Oxford first. They very properly put their doctors first. The address was read by the Vice-Chancellor, and then, after the Queen's reply, the doctors and proctors, and a few others who formed the deputation, kissed the King's hand. As the Queen has 317   no separate apartment the King retired, the Queen entered with her household and ladies, and then the same ceremony was gone through, the Ministers remaining on the left behind the ladies. The Queen read pretty well. She was obliged to rise each time to give her hand to be kissed. Cambridge came afterwards with the Duke of Gloucester and all the Peers, who belonged to the University, in their gowns at the head. This destroyed the character of the collegiate body. However, those only were presented who were presented of the Oxford deputation. The King went beyond his written speech to the men of Cambridge, and put us in a fright. However, it was good-humoured, and of no great harm a sort of joke.

I came away as I had business. Afterwards there was a Council, and the Lords Lieutenant were admitted to take the oaths.

House. East Eetford. The Chancellor made a capital speech, and we had a better division than case, 29 to 7. Lord Durham spoke temperately and well. Lord Grey well too. We had Wynford with us. There is no explaining that man. The Duke of Cumberland voted against us, and Eldon spoke.

At St. James's. Lord Westmoreland told me that yesterday at a great dinner the King gave his household he gave as a toast, ' The land we live in, and let those who don't like it leave it."

This and many other things show his feelings towards the Duke of Cumberland.

The King reviews a regiment every morning this week. He has been on horseback within these six weeks, but lie has a rupture, and is now rather afraid of riding. He is going to change the uniforms of the Lords Lieutenant.

We expect to prorogue on Friday and dissolve on Saturday.

July 20.

Then East Eetford. Lord Wharncliffe moved a resolution with the view of giving the franchise to Birmingham instead of the Hundred. Dudley spoke for Birmingham and well. I spoke shortly. I guarded myself against being considered as pledged to any other measure, intending to decide all measures according to the special circumstances of the case.

The Duke was not so cautious as I was, and spoke strongly against giving the franchise to great towns. [1]Lord Holland said to the Chancellor, 'He will live to see it done." I think I may, and therefore was cautious.

So ends the business of this Session.

July 21.

Went at ten to the Duke of Wellington's, where the King and Queen were to breakfast after an inspection of the 2nd Life Guards. The day was beautiful and the people in excellent humour. The King first went with the Queen to the Eegent's Park barracks, and then to the Knightsbridge barracks. When they came to the Duke's the King went to the window and [1 No one expected it to occur in two years' time.] was well cheered. They then called for the Queen, who went to the window and was very well received indeed.

Yesterday evening the King walked out alone into St. James's Street. He found Watson Taylor and took his arm. The mob pressed upon him so much that "Watson Taylor's shoes were trodden down at heel. While the King was alone an Irish woman came out of an alley and kissed him. This and a lecture from the Duke have cured him of walking out alone. At least he has promised not to do so again.

House at 2. Aberdeen says the King spoke very well to the foreign Ministers to-day. There was an extraordinary number of naval officers, and the fullest levee I ever saw. The King recognised very cordially all his old friends. He was very gracious indeed to Elphinstone, whom he saw for the first time. He was imprudent enough to make a sort of speech to the West Indian deputation, and pledged himself warmly to support their interests. This I saw. After I was gone I hear Astell and Campbell came up with the address of the East India Company, and that he spoke in similar terms to them. This the foolish Astell will publish everywhere.

The Duke says he goes away when the King begins to speak. I really covered my face when he began to speak about the Catholics to the deputation from Cambridge. What he said to them, which was no more than an indifferent joke, has been variously misrepresented and not at all understood. It must have been imperfectly heard.

The King is angry with the Duke of Gloucester for slurring over a part of the address from Cambridge, which was very loyal, and for not kissing his hand. He has reason to complain of this. The Duke of Gloucester kissed the Queen's hand with marked devotion.

The Duke of Sussex has been already infusing poison into the King's ear and talking of invasions of the property of the Church. This the King told Peel. Those who observed the Duke of Sussex at the levee thought he seemed very triumphant, and received his Whig friends with a smile which said, ' We shall do them yet."

He was invested with the Thistle to-day. The King asked all the knights presented to drink a bottle of claret with him in October.

Blomberg was up with an address. The King said, ' You and I know each other of old. You need not be presented. By-the-bye, you may as well dine with me to-day."

The King made an extemporaneous reply to the address of the Canons of Windsor the day after the funeral. They begged to have a copy. He endeavoured to recollect it for them, and sent it to Peel. Peel found some curious historical inaccuracies.

The Duke of Wellington thinks we shall gradually bring the King round, and induce him to move more quietly. To thwart him directly would have a bad effect; but he may be led. In the meantime he is very well in health.

[32 The King has promised to dine with Leopold, who has asked the Duke, but not Aberdeen. The Duke thinks the King should not dine with him now. The two other Powers having manifested the greatest dissatisfaction with Leopold's conduct, and we having intimated it in the House, it would be incongruous and injurious for the King to dine with him. Leopold has written one if not two letters complaining of the conduct of the Allied Powers.

We went to the House for fear Lord Durham should play us a trick, and it is perhaps fortunate we did, for he was there and made a protesting speech, which was followed by one from Westmoreland on the East Eetford Bill. However, we had a majority in the House, and there was no division.

July 22.

Eode to town. Cabinet. Considered the King's Speech. Peel had introduced a plagiarism from the first speech of the old King, 4 Born and educated in this country, I glory in the name of Briton." However, the whole sentence would not do, and it was omitted. I assisted in working the sentences into form, and breaking them up into short ones. Went away to dress for the Council, thinking the whole settled. Council at three. First the deputies of the two Houses carried up the joint address respecting Sir Jonah Barrington. Then the King being alone, and saying he was ready for his Ministers none being there but me I went in, and first asked him to allow Clare to wear the uniform the late King gave him. This led to a long talk about uniforms for Indian Governors, and I had some little difficulty to carry my coat without having a general

322 ~~VOL. II. Y~~ consideration of the whole question of Governor's uniforms. I then told the King of the approaching death of Sir J. Macdonald. He asked whom we proposed sending in his place? I told him it did not entirely depend upon the King's Ministers, but that I thought, if we recommended a very fit man, we should get the Chairs to name him.

The King said, ' You heard what I said to the East India Company yesterday?" I had not, but I bowed, and he added, ' I told them they should not be unfairly dealt with. There is a run on them, and the notions of people are very much exaggerated with regard to the question."

I said the question would require and receive the most mature consideration from his Ministers before they ventured to offer any advice to his Majesty upon the course to be pursued.

The King said in about ten or twelve days he should be able to give me a day or two for Indian matters.

I thought I had given time to the others to arrive, and rose. I should mention that he spoke of Algiers, and said he suspected there was an understanding about it between the Eussians and the French.

I said I did not entertain much fear of the French having Algiers. With a little money we could raise Morocco on one side and Tunis on the other, and harass them from the interior, and while we took care they had not Tunis, Algiers was comparatively unimportant. With Tunis, Malta, and Corfu we should hold our hands across the Mediterranean.

I went out and found them come. The Duke went in.

323   The King gives up dining with Leopold. He gave it up the moment the objections to it were mentioned to him.

The speech was, I found, much improved after I went away. The King said he thought nothing could be better, and indeed it is a very good speech. He said he thought the reference to the Catholic question was unavoidable, as it was the great measure of the Parliament; and it was particularly proper that he should refer to it as he had voted for it, really thinking that the Church would be more secure by means of Catholic admission than by their exclusion.

I thought the King seemed a little tired. Well he might be. He had been at an inspection of troops, the Grenadier Guards and the Lancers, from ten to one, and the day was very hot. He inspected the troops on foot.

The Duke of Wellington passed the King at the head of his regiment, and Lord Eosslyn at the head of his. Lord Eosslyn is delighted with the opportunities of wearing his uniform, and playing the general officer again.

July 24.

Council at 11. Parliament dissolved. The seals were delivered to the Secretaries and to Goulburn. Herries kissed hands.

Sir G. Clark becomes Under-Secretary to the Home Department. W. Peel goes to the Treasury. Charles Boss comes into Clark's place. Macnaughten goes out.

July 26.

Dined at St. James's. The King of Wurtemburg, the Ministers, Foreign Ministers, 324   Household, and Knights of the Garter there, in all 80. After dinner the King made a speech which made his Ministers' hearts fail within them. However, we were quitte pour la peur. He only spoke of his love of peace. The only tiling painful was that he should speak at all, and before his servants, like a chairman of a public meeting.

At the Duke of Wellington's on Sunday he made a speech, praising very much the Duke, and declaring his entire confidence in him. This was before the Foreign Ministers. The speech was a little warlike, I believe. The Duke's reply very short indeed, and peaceful. The King should recollect that what he speaks is as important as what is written in a State Paper.

July 28.

Levee. Before it a Council, standing, in the King's closet, for swearing in Privy Councillors. Sir E. Wilson was presented on his restoration to the army, and holding the King's hand in his expressed his gratitude.

The King made an energetic reply, and then there was a short rejoinder from Sir E. Wilson. I could not hear what was said. We afterwards shook hands cordially with Sir E. Wilson, whose restoration pleases everybody.

The French Government have dissolved the Chamber without allowing it to assemble; have placed the press under restriction, and altered the mode of electing deputies, so as, as far as I can understand, to give to les plus imposis the power of electing a majority.

No letter has been received by any Foreign Minister or by us. The whole was kept a profound secret. The report to the King respecting the press, which is made the foundation of the Ordonnance, is a long violent declamation, very weakly written indeed. [1]

July 28.

Cabinet at half-past three. I was rather late, and found them considering what should be said by Lord Stuart at Paris, respecting the late violent measures of the French Government. They had decided that Lord Stuart, if Prince Polignac endeavoured to draw from him in conversation his opinion, should say he was directed to offer none. They seemed inclined to tell him, if Prince Polignac required his opinion by offering an explanation, to say we considered the measure adopted was in violation of the Charter. At my suggestion, if Polignac asked his opinion more formally and offered no explanation, he was directed to request the explanation might be in writing, and he would transmit it to his Court, or it might be made through the French Ambassador here. The French Ambassador, however, knowing nothing of what was doing, left England on Monday, and would meet the news on his road to Paris.

At six o'clock on Tuesday evening a row was going on, and a Guardsman had been killed. This was resistance when the police broke the types, c., of a press which would go on. The idea is, that the Chamber of Deputies will meet, considering the dissolution to be illegal.

[1 These were the celebrated Ordinances which cost Charles X. his crown.]

Matuschevitz openly inveighs against the measure. It is doubtful whether Metternich did not advise it. He sent a long paper from Johannisberg, giving his views on the present position of the French Government.

The King of Wurtemburg had an interview of two hours with the Duke of Wellington yesterday. He is very anxious on the subject of France. He says the people of Wurtemburg will cry out that a similar measure is intended against them that everywhere the two extreme parties will be placed in collision. Bulow thinks the same. The Duke advised the King of Wurtemburg to avoid Paris on his return; but the King has some emplettes to make, and goes there. The Duke advised him then, if he must go for his emplettes to stay only a day. He said he would not stay above five or six!

Thus is every consideration of real importance sacrificed to motives of private fancy and convenience!

Lea informed Aberdeen that a vessel was fitting out in the Thames with Spanish refugees and arms to endeavour to raise an insurrection in Spain. After some time they found the vessel, and to-day she was detained. She had sixty-nine men, and about 150 stand of arms on board. They sank the printed proclamations which were picked up. Torrijos and Valdes were to be the leaders. Torrijos was to join below the revenue vessels. Some of the men had 10. each, given to them by the Spanish Committee, to aid their voyage to Bio. There is some doubt under what law they are to be indicted, and the Attorney and Solicitor-General are out of town.

⌊327 Received a letter from Lord Heytesbury, enclosing one he had received from Captain Campbell, announcing the death of Sir J. Macdonald.

July 29.

The Duke told me he had seen Rothschild that morning, who had recent intelligence from Paris. The Guards were faithful, but the 53rd Eegiment, which was at the Hotel de Yille, had joined the people, and so had individual soldiers of other regiments. The people and the National Guards were arming. The Chambers had assembled. The King was not at Paris. He was nought to be at Compiegne.

The Duke thought Henry had better not go to Paris, that one party or the other would soon attack the English.

Called on Elphinstone. Offered him Persia. He was much obliged, but said nothing would induce him ever to go to Asia again.

Spoke to him of Monteith. He knows him, and a little doubted his discretion. He promised to find him, and send him to the Duke if he was in town; but he thought he was at Algiers. Spoke to him of Jenkins and Briggs. He says Jenkins is the abler man.

Saw Lord Essex and Lord Clinton. They had heard the Duke of Orleans was proclaimed Regent.

July 31.

Went to town early. Called at the Duke's to hear the news. None had arrived since yesterday morning. The Duke said he considered the King dethroned, and we ⌊328 should soon have to consider whether we should acknowledge the new Government. I observed that our course must depend very much upon the manner in which the French effected their Eevolution. The King had put himself decidedly in the wrong, and if they make their Eevolution as we made ours in 1688, there was no reason why we should not acknowledge the new Government, be it what it might. The Duke said the foreigners were already coming to know what we thought and meant to do. We should have them all in our train, and provided we took a reasonable course on the question of Algiers, and others which might arise, we should do very well. The mischief was that this event would place the two parties in presence on every occasion, and every trifling difference would resolve itself into one of Liberal and anti-Liberal. I said I feared whatever party predominated, even if the King regained his power, France would be precipitated into a war, for no party would be able to maintain itself in quiet times. The Duke said the King's Government was becoming very dangerous. It had, as was shown in the case of Algiers, and their discussions with us, no more morality than that of Buonaparte, and it had the favour of European Powers as an ancient dynasty, while it was prepared to act upon the principles of a new one. Now, under a Government of Eevolutionary origin, all their Acts would be viewed with disfavour and suspicion.

The Duke spoke very strongly against Canning's policy, in admitting France to the Triple Alliance[1] and thus bringing her into a prominent station in Europe [1 By the Treaty of London with reference to Greece)

329   again. She would naturally have risen again in good time. The time should not have been anticipated by us.

The Duke agreed with me in thinking the Government here would be strengthened by what was occurring in France.

I lamented Brougham's success in Yorkshire, and viewed with some apprehension the increased power it would give him. He said Yorkshire was quite radicalised by having four members. No gentleman could bear the expense the middle classes had it all to themselves.

At a quarter to four I called at the Treasury and found Kothschild had received intelligence down to the 29th, at 4 P. M. Drummond showed me the Duke's letter to Peel which contained this account: That there was fighting all Wednesday, the 28th, and Thursday, till 3 P. M. There had been a terrible massacre, but the troops got the worst of it. The people were led by the students of the Ecole de Droit, and of the Ecole Poly technique. The 53rdeegiment, which it was said yesterday had joined the people, had in fact surrendered. The people had armed themselves at the Arsenal. On the night of the 28th the Guards retook the Hotel de Yille, but were driven out again, and retired to the Louvre. The firing did not cease at the Tuileries till past 3 P. M. The people pillaged it when the troops retreated, and the tri-coloured flag was hoisted there, and on the column in the Place Vendome. The Ministers escaped by subterraneous passages from the Tuileries, and were with the King, who had a great

330   many troops about him at St. Cloud. La Fayette commanded the National Guard, and was a member of the Provisional Government. Generals Gerard, Lafitte, and Casimir Perrier were the others. C. Perrier was deputed to the King at St. Cloud.

No couriers were allowed to leave Paris. These letters were sent by private servants to the first stage.

I told all this to Henry, but he goes. So do many others. There were thirty people applying for passports when he went for his. On the other hand many

English come away.

August 2.

There is a great deal of information in the ' Times The result is, that the King's offer to change his Ministers and to recall the Ordonnances was not accepted, and the Duke of Orleans accepted the office of Lieu-tenant-General of the kingdom. His address is quite in the spirit of the Eevolution.

The Guards are disorganised and desert.

The Swiss only are said to remain with the King, who it is thought is gone to Nantes.

Lord Stuart says if the Eoyalists do not resist, the French will invade Belgium in three months. The Deputies, at first in very small numbers, not more than thirty, nor at any time much above sixty, seem to have been irresolute. They were decided by others, and indeed the whole seems to have been done by the people. There is no appearance of previous concert. If there were leaders, they were the boys of the Ecole de Droit and the Ecole Poly technique. Polignac seems to have been firm after the beginning of the fight, and when Lafitte and others went to Marmont at the Tuile-ries, in the middle of the tumult, he declared concession impossible.

The Guards at St. Cloud told the King they would protect him, but would not advance again to Paris. General seems to have had 6,000 men at Versailles, but the people would not admit him. At Eouen there was great ferment, and forty pieces of cannon were sent by the people to the assistance of Paris. The troops seem to have been ordered upon Paris from all quarters. The total loss of life is estimated at 5,000.

The people were becoming impatient, and cried Vive la Republique! Vive Napoleon II.! This, it is said, determined the Duke of Orleans to accept: and the Deputies offered, because they feared the establishment of a Ee-public would be the signal of general war.

I do not hear of the pillage of private houses. The churches have been pillaged and the palaces ransacked. The priests thought fit to fire from the Archbishop's palace, which led to the death of many and to the pillage of the palace.

The Duke said they had done everything in the most offensive way, re-establishing the tri-coloured flag, c. They seem determined to force the Eevolution down the throat of Europe. He spoke of the Duke of Orleans' address. I said I supposed he was obliged for his own safety to throw himself at once into the Eevolution. The more natural thing would have been for the French to have sent for young Napoleon. The Duke said he heard young Napoleon was getting hold of French pamphlets, c.

The Duke of Orleans asked Lord Stuart's advice as to accepting the Crown. Lord Stuart reminded him of his oath, and told him the Powers of Europe which restored the Bourbons could never recognise him.

On consideration I think we should endeavour to induce the Powers which signed the Treaty of Vienna to declare that they are determined to maintain the territorial arrangements made by that treaty; but that they will not interfere with the internal Government of France.

I think this declaration, made at once, would perhaps prevent any attempt on the part of the French to make war for the frontier of the Ehine.

The elections go well for us, except Canterbury, where Lord Fordwich has beat our man, Henry B. Baring, the husband of Lady Augusta.

August 3.

The accounts from Paris state that the Due de Mor-temar, who had been appointed Minister by Charles X. himself, saw it was too late, and that the only chance for the House of Bourbon was in the placing the Duke of Orleans in the office of Lieut.-General.

This he proposed himself to the Duke of Orleans, who wrote to the King, and in accepting the office said his conduct would show with what views he did it. Then he issued a tri-colour proclamation! Lord Stuart says this was done at the last possible moment. The proclamation was received with cries of Vive la Republique! Vive Napoleon II.! However, these cries ceased, and it was hoped things would go on quietly. Sebastiani and

333

B. Constant expressed hopes that in a few months men's minds would be tranquil-lised, and things placed on a regular footing It seems that the King is at Trianon, with about 4,000 guards. He talked of resigning to the Dauphin, if he had not already done so. It will probably be too late, and the Dauphin is supposed, I believe very justly, to be implicated in all that has passed.

Lord Stuart states the loss of the troops at 3,000. That of the people at 6,000. Of course these calculations are very vague, and probably exaggerated. It would appear as if there had been more preparation on the part of the insurgents than was imagined. The decisive measure, that of the Bank refusing discounts, was of course suggested by Lafitte. The Eoyalists are much in want of money. They left forty-two millions in their caisses, and 150 millions at the Bank! Bourmont was to leave Algiers on the 25th. Probably he was called home to be present at the crisis.

The King's troops still remaining in force at St. Cloud, the barricades are continued.

Everybody seems to think the military force was as ill-managed as everything else. Marmont acted molle-ment.

We have been beaten at Canterbury, and what is worse at Norwich, where a brother of Peel's has been driven out by Eobert Grant, the most decided enemy of the Government. No one declares himself the opponent of Government, and as such asks support; but our candidates do not succeed at popular elections.

334

August 4.

To London early. The King of France is supposed to be gone towards Cherbourg. We fear he will come here. The Duke said the King seemed disposed to receive him, and reminded the King that the Pretender had been three times ordered out of Paris on the representations of this country. I was glad to find a very general feeling that the King of France could not be permitted to remain if intrigues were allowed by him. That he could have no more than a refuge. Peel seemed to feel this most strongly. The Duke seemed to think there had been previous concert on the part of the patriots.

The King is violent against the Duke of Orleans.

Our Duke of Orleans, as I call him, the Duke of Sussex, sticks close to the King whenever he appears.

The Duke of Cumberland has resigned the Blues in a huff because they are placed under the Commander-in-Chief. However, he wore the uniform to-day at the levee.

We have a Cabinet to-morrow at 4, on Civil List and Eegency. Indeed we know not how soon we may meet Parliament. Perhaps on September 15.

The Queen received the address of the London clergy. She had her whole etat major.

August 5.

At four Cabinet. Talk about the Civil List. There are pensions to the amount of about 7, 000*l*. a year which the present King will pay, and he will pay 6,000. a year to Mrs. Fitzherbert, her charge on Brighton. She had 10,000. a year before. Many pensions are struck off, one of 500. to Sir J. Lake, many others, to jockies, c.

335

It seems the late King borrowed 50,000. for himself and as much for the Duke of York, on the revenues of Hanover, which sums have been paid off.

The King of France abdicated, and so did the Dauphin, in favour of the Due de Bordeaux, in a letter addressed by them to the Duke of Orleans, in which his Lieut.-

Generalship was treated as emanating from the King. The Duke of Orleans in his speech to the Chambers announced the abdications, but did not say they were in favour of Henry V. Hence the people of Paris, hearing the King made difficulties, supposed he had receded from his original promise whereas he only said his original promise was conditional, and had not been fairly made known. Be this as it may, 35,000 men set off for Eambouillet to take him, 10,000 were sent afterwards by the Duke of Orleans to protect him, and he has 7,000 at Eambouillet, chiefly cavalry and artillery, for the same purpose. I think there must be a smash.

Stuart and Pozzo went to the Duke of Orleans to represent the personal danger of the King, and to desire that measures might be taken to preserve his life. The Duke is represented as having been tres emu, and as having said that his character depended upon the preservation of the King's life, and the measures I mentiqned were immediately taken.

Chateaubriand and Hyde de Neuville are for the Due de Bordeaux.

Stuart has, I know not why, counselled the Due de Bordeaux's friends to be quiet.

The Duke of Wellington thinks there is Eadicalism in everything that the Lieut.-General will have no power.

The King went in grand state through the City to the Tower. He had six carriages and six. At the Tower the Duke gave him a breakfast. He then went on to Greenwich by water, and returned to London by land. He was very well received.

August 6.

At the dinner we had the Ministers, Household, and Trinity House. Chairman and deputy-Chairman of the East India Company, Governor and deputy-Governor of the Bank, Lord Mayor, and Ward and Thompson, members for the City. The King made speeches and gave toasts as if he was Duke of Clarence at the Trinity House. He alarmed and pained us, but he did less mischief than I should have expected; and as all the people present were real friends, he only let down the dignity of the Crown.

He gave the healths of the Ministers, and afterwards of the Duke of Wellington. Some things he said very well. The Duke answered very well.

There is so much good feeling about the King that his errors of taste are pardoned. He will improve, and wear his robes more gracefully.

August 7.

Cabinet. Determined that the principle of the Eegency Bill should be that the mother of the Sovereign should be Eegent. The Eegent to have unlimited power. If any limitation, it should only be placed upon the creation of Peers, and a Council of Eegency should exist only for that purpose. We separated till the 23rd.

August 9.

In coming down to Sandgate read James's and Cabell's memoranda on the progress of the British Government in India, and our foreign relations.

As I was coming out of Maidstone met the candidates coming in. Sir E. Knatchbull in a cocked hat, attended by thirty or forty gentlemen in black, all covered with dust, preceded by about six blue flags, and followed by some carriages with ugly women. Then came T. Law Hodges (why Law I do not know), with many light blue flags, and some low people few gentlemen. The numbers, however, of the Hodges colours and people were greater than that of the Knatchbull squad. Not a cheer for either. The whole thing flat and ridiculous worthy of Hogarth. There were some people collected in Maidstone, but not so many as on a market day there were none on the roads.

By the ' Times' I see the Chamber has modified the Charter, and has proclaimed the Duke of Orleans King of the French; at least has offered him the Crown on the condition of his acceptance of the modified Charter.

The Chamber of Peers is put by. It is only advised to eliminate the last seventy-six peers.

VOL. II. Z

August 10.

Briscoe comes in for Surrey, to the exclusion of Jolliffe, our friend. Certainly the popular elections have all been unfavourable to us. In fact the Tories have not yet recovered their good-humour, and the Government has some furious enemies, and no warm friends. I do not think we can go on without an accession of speaking strength. Our measures must be modified to meet the circumstances of the times, and so far I have no fear.

August 13.

Cabinet room. Eead Lord Stuart's despatches. There is little in them that is not in the newspapers. He says the Revolution has been brought about by small proprietors acting under the influence of bankers and lawyers. The troops have shown no great popular feeling. Many have taken the opportunity of going home.

The new King's oath-taking was flatly received. As long as he can keep La Fayette with him he is master of Paris.

Lord Stuart seems to have behaved prudently in merely acknowledging the receipt of the communication from Marshal Jourdan of his being appointed foreign secretary. The Neapolitan Ambassador wished to have a note generally agreed upon. All the Ambassadors say they are so sure England will judge rightly, that they will, without instructions, follow in our wake.

La Fayette has originated the idea of a mission of deputies of the National Guard to London to thank the

English people for their sympathy. Lord Stuart hopes the King will induce La Fayette to give up this mischievous and foolish scheme.

August 18.

Lord J. Eussell is not returned for Bedford. He lost it by one vote. He has published a good address, and is evidently very indignant.

Brougham has had questions put to him by Martin Bree, which he has answered satisfactorily to the venereal doctor. It would have been good fun had they fought.

The only merit of the French Eevolution seems to be that it has not been vindictive. If they are wise they will not touch the lives of the Ministers. The new King calls his eldest son Duke of Orleans. All the daughters are to be Princesses of Orleans, distinguished by their Christian names.

This is like Henry IV."s policy in reserving the Duchy of Lancaster. He wishes to be able to make room for Henry V. He has given up his property to his eldest son's little children, and would probably, if he were displaced, emigrate quietly, as he has often done before, and leave his children in possession.

When Brougham accused the Duke of Wellington of advising Polignac, the whole meeting of his own friends expressed dissent. It is incredible that he should be so foolish as to believe such a thing, or as to attempt to make others believe it.

August 19.

I see by the ' Sun' that the ex-King of France is arrived at Portsmouth. I am very sorry for it, although he will not be received by the King, and will probably sail immediately. He may require refitting, for I dare say he brought off little from Eambouillet. His packets are accompanied by two French vessels of war, and all the French vessels at Spithead hoisted the tri-coloured flag when he was known to be there.

August 20. It seems the Eoyal party have landed at Cowes.

August 23.

Went to the Cabinet room to read despatches. Lord Stuart represents the Government as by no means settled; anxious to remain at peace, and to prevent revolution, but not secure. Things which are essential the new King is obliged to ask humbly of La Fayette, who is now really Sovereign.

La Fayette wanted to dissolve the Chamber. The King rightly thought that to do so now would be to make a Convention.[1]

Some persons are gone off to bring Napoleon II., but the Austrians will stop them on the way.

The Prussians on the first intelligence of the events at Paris sent orders to their Minister to come away, but he was directed not to do so without concert with his colleagues. They met, and agreed to recommend him [1 I. e. as in 1792.] to stay. The disposition of Metternich and Nesselrode, who met at Toplitz or Carlsbad, I forget which, was the same and reasonable to leave France to settle her own affairs quietly, and only to interfere if she invaded the peace of other States.

The Duke has left a memorandum on the Cabinet table showing clearly from treaties that this is not a case in which we are bound to interfere. We engaged to support a constitutional monarch against revolutionary movements, but the monarch having violated the constitution has broken the condition. France may still form a part of the Congress of Europe, in ' Union or Pacific Concert with the four great Powers. The treaty of offensive alliance between those Powers is dormant, while France remains under a constitutional King.

The Duke properly thinks that the sooner, after having taken a decent time for deliberation, we can cognise the Duke of Orleans, the better for him and

He expects at no distant period war, as the con-jquence of these events, and I fear he may be right. It will arise by the imitation of the Spaniards and Portuguese, and the ambitious sympathy of the French. It is evident that Eussia means to indulge France dth Algiers.

August 23.

Eeceived a letter from the Duke respecting Eajpootana. He thinks the cession of territory will only lead new demands on our part, and advises that, unless it should be necessary to give some instruction, the letter should not be sent. He thinks, too, that as no brevet has been given to King's officers in Ava, none can be given to those of the Company. I am to see him tomorrow upon these points.

Cabinet at 3. Showed Herries the answer I proposed sending, respecting the Interest Bills, of which he entirely approved.

Peel was not at the Cabinet.

Bead the Duke of Orleans' letter to the King, which is proper. He says he laments and wishes he could have prevented the fall of the eldest branch of his family. He devoted himself to prevent misfortunes which would have endangered the peace of Europe. He avows pacific intentions.

The King is to receive General Baudrand, who brought the letter in the Levee, which will be before the Council on Wednesday.

The King of the French will be acknowledged. A letter will be written to our Ministers with the great powers stating our reasons for doing so. This will be read to the Foreign Ministers here.

I suggested that it might be as well to make the letter substantially the Duke's Memorandum, and particularly to remind France that the Quadruple Alliance still existed. We shall have the drafts of the letter tomorrow.

Parliament to be prorogued to October 26.

To-morrow the Brazilians will acknowledge Miguel as the Eegent, if he will marry Maria da Gloria. Then came some absurd conditions. However, the thing is to be considered to-morrow. Aberdeen's idea is that there is no doing anything with Don Pedro, and that we must acknowledge Don Miguel as soon as he will grant an amnesty.

We were to have a Council on Wednesday for the prorogation. The King will not much like this, as he wanted to go to Ascot, but he may have it as early as he likes, and he ought to receive General Baudrand soon. We may have the Council at 10, and he may be at Ascot in excellent time.

August 24.

The Council is at 1. At 1 I went to the Duke. Told him of my recent letters to the Chairs. He said we must not make bankrupts of the Company, if we would use them hereafter. I said it was my duty to state the case of the public, as the Board were guardians of the territorial revenue.

A letter from Count Moltke, requesting to see me. I have appointed to-morrow at 3.

Cabinet at 3. Aberdeen read the proposed letter from the King to King Louis Philippe. With a few trifling alterations it was adopted.

The Duke called on Marmont to-day, and received him a military account of the affair at Paris. Marmont said he knew nothing of the Ordonnances, and dis-ipproved of them. He was at the King's levee on the uesday, and was told there were quelques inquietudes it Paris, and to take the command of the troops. He found only 7,000 men. Polignac, forgetting any were conge, thought there were 12,000. He occupied the aces de I'Hotel de Ville, de la Bastille, de Victoire, and de Vendome in sufficient force. His troops were not attacked. He withdrew them at night, and reoccu-, pied the Posts in the morning. Then the attack began. The troops maintained themselves, but he found it necessary to withdraw them to the Louvre, the Tuileries, the Pont Neuf, and the Place de Vendome. In the Louvre he had two battalions of Swiss; two battalions of the Line in the Place de Vendome; the Guards in the Tuileries. He kept open his communication with the country by posts at all the avenues leading to the garden of the Tuileries and the Bois de Boulogne, Champs Elysees, c. The battalion at the Place de la Bastille could not retreat by the straight road, and was obliged to march all round Paris, crossing the river at the bridge nearest Charenton, and coming to the Tuileries by the Faubourg.

The two battalions in the Place de Vendome went over to the people. He then sent one battalion from the Louvre to the grille of the Tuileries garden, opposite the Eue de Eivoli, and so protected his flank. On Thursday he had lost 1,800 men, killed and wounded; and 1,200 egares besides the two battalions; but he had received a reinforcement of 3,000 men. The troops were extenues de fatigue. When Lafitte and the others came to him he told him he could not order the fire to cease. He was attacked.

If the fire of the people ceased, his troops would not fire. He fairly told the King it was not une commotion, nor even une insurrection, but une Revolution. There were not above thirty or forty people behind the barriers, but all the windows were occupied by armed men. He counselled concession, but Polignac would not hear of it. He said Polignac was l'homme le plus presomptueux lie had ever seen.

When the Louvre was attacked the Swiss ran out towards the Tuileries and carried with them a battalion he had in the Place de Carrousel, as well as two guns he had with him. The rush was such he could hardly get upon his horse, and the men ran so fast that a person he sent after them on horseback found them almost at the extremity of the Tuileries garden. However, some returned to protect the retreat of about sixty men whom he had got together to defend the grille at the Arc de Triomphe in the Place de Carrousel. They were just enabled to retreat.

Marmont is violent against the Swiss, who were, he says, retained in the French service by higher pay arid privileges for this very thing, and yet they ran away in this shameful manner.

Marmont means to go to Italy for a year. After that he hopes he can return to France. He has no wish to emigrate.

If the account in Lord Stuart's report be correct, France is in a deplorable state. In many parts of the country no taxes are paid, and the Eepublican party has not lost hope.

The conditions of what Don Pedro considers a conciliatory arrangement are entirely inadmissible. They are founded upon the marriage of Donna Maria da Gloria, and England, France, and Austria are to guarantee her against any injure she may receive from her husband. Certainly we may safely say these terms are inadmis-/sible, and so break off all negotiations with Don Pedro, who, since these terms were proposed by him, has recognised the independent Eegency of Terceira. By-the-bye, one of his terms is the payment, by Portugal, of all the expenses incurred by himself for Donna Maria.

It seems the draft of a decree of amnesty has been sent to Lisbon, and if Miguel will pass that decree we are to recognise him.

The Chancellor and others seemed to think this was an awkward time, and we had better wait a little. I think so too. However, undoubtedly our early recognition of Miguel might lead to the prevention of a Portuguese Eevolution.

There was much conversation respecting the Bank Charter. It seemed to be the general opinion that Government should take it upon itself to arrange terms with the Bank, which terms will be prohibition to any other Bank to issue notes within twenty-five miles of London. This being granted, the Bank will do the public business for 100,000. a year less. The whole question of country banking, whether it is to be with limited or unlimited responsibility, a limited or an unlimited number of partners, is to be left open to Parliament.

I suggested that the most important question was the revision of taxation. My view now is that we must take off some of the taxes which press most on the poorer classes, and have an income tax. I dislike an income tax as much as any one. To me it is a very oppressive tax, but I believe it may become necessary.

Walked to the corner of Hyde Park with Lord

347

Eosslyn. Had some conversation with him respecting the changes necessary in the Government before we meet Parliament. He says Lord Althorpe will not come in without Lord Grey, and he is not sure Lord Grey would not stipulate for Lord Durham. The latter is out of the question on account of his temper. I do not think the Government could go on with the Duke and Lord Grey. Of the Huskissonians, Palmerston is the only one. To E. Stanley there is no objection.

August 26.

At 3 Count Moltke came to the office. He had two Danish claims to speak about.

Dinner at the Albion for Clare. There were present of the Ministers, Peel, Eosslyn, Goulburn, Herries; then Lord F. Leveson, Calcraft, the Solicitor-General, W. Peel, Lord G. Somerset, Planta, Gen. Macdonald, Col. Fitz-Clarence, Lord Tenterden. Of Clare's friends Glengall, Agar Ellis, Sneyd, Lord Templeton, besides H. Vyner, and Upton, who go with him.

I spoke feebly, not being well; besides, I did not think it in good taste to make a great speech; but to leave Clare's the first speech of the day. Peel made a very good speech; but too much of it. Clare really spoke very feelingly and well. He spoke a little too much of his gratitude to the Court.

I had some conversation with Loch. I was as well received as I expected, and better, considering the run that has been made at me. The Duke went off to Walmer Castle, very wisely, for lie wants sea air; but Clare would have been more pleased had he been pre-/sent, and the Directors too. The Ministers' healths were well received.

348

August 28.

Eeceived from Elphinstone his remarks upon the proposed letter to Bombay, respecting native education, of which he generally approves. He strongly urges the sending out of European professors, young men, acquainted with English literature, to learn the language there, and teach the natives. I have sent the extract from his letter to Astell, suggesting that the Universities of Oxford, Cambridge, Dublin, and Edinburgh should each name those from whom should be selected the necessary number. I have observed that the object of native education is of such importance that the state of the finances must not prevent its accomplishment.

August 30.

Wrote a very long letter to Hardinge on the present position of the Government and our policy. I gave my opinion that any accession of men which destroyed the unity of the Duke's Government would do harm. That we must meet our difficulties by measures. That the first was a revision of taxation, that no men we could get would add moral strength to the Government, and the Whigs would not support unless they had half the Government. That the question of Reform could not be made an open question. It was best for the country that parties should be decidedly separated. It might then choose which it preferred, and men would be obliged to take a side. We had better be out with character than in with a detachment of the enemy, in pos-/session of a gate. Still TALK we must have, and we want a financier. I said of myself that I cared little about office. I should without reluctance acquiesce in retirement if the Duke could fill my office more advantageously, and I believe Eosslyn would do. I thought Rosslyn would like Ireland or Paris.

I do not think it improbable Hardinge may send this letter to the Duke.

August 31.

An insurrection at Brussels, the houses of the Ministers burnt. The troops fired and killed many. They, not being 1,500, retired to the park, and formed before the palace. An evening paper I got at Ashford says the nobility had joined the people, and the troops had acceded on condition of keeping their arms, and guarding the palace. If this Revolution takes the line of union with France, war is almost inevitable. It may be only for a more popular form of Government, but what the people of the Netherlands desire is annexation to a great State. They are ashamed of being Dutch.

Most fortunately all our manufacturers are in full employment, and the harvest is abundant. The peace and constitution of England have depended upon fine weather.

Clare, from whom I heard to-day, tells me Lord Wel-lesley assures him there is to be a Eevolution in Spain, and named the day. The nobles are supposed to be at the head of it. This may all be true, for our Ministers never find anything out; but my apprehension is that there will be a low, ill-supported revolutionary movement.

Eeceived a letter from Lady Londonderry. She first wishes me to obtain, if I can, Ward's exchange to a better climate. This I have told her I have already endeavoured to do; but that I have no expectation of Aberdeen's doing it.

Lady L. says her brother was two hours with the Duke, and as long with Lord Grey. The latter would have acted a second part, but the Duke would not admit him. I have told her I think she must have misunderstood Lord Camden's account, and that she may be assured it is not the Duke's character to fear an equal.

I sent her letter to Hardinge, and asked him if he knew anything of the affair. I cannot imagine when it can have taken place. Lord Camden was an odd person to employ. He knows so little of Lord Grey. Eosslyn would have been the natural envoy if it preceded from the Duke; but I think it must have been a volunteer of Lord Camden's.

September 2.

Bead the papers relative to the Danish claims. Canning seems to have decided one case, that of the Danish East India Company, hastily. However, we cannot undo a decision of a Secretary of State.

The other case, that of the private individuals at Tranquebar, has been determined in their favour.

September 3.

Had a long conversation with Herries, with whom I rode for a long time, respecting
affairs, both here and abroad. He is rather downcast. However, he thinks this Belgian
insurrection will be put down. Kothschild has exported 800,000. in silver and 400,000.
in gold to meet his bills when they become due diffident of having anything paid to
himself.

September 5.

Cabinet room. Found Lord Eosslyn there. He told me the substance of a report
I did not see of Col. Jones, who was sent by the Duke to the Netherlands, and is
returned. He says the Prince of Orange is with 1,600 men in the park and palace at
Brussels; 5,000 men are close at hand under Prince Frederick of Orange, at Vilvorde,
and two bodies of 10,000 each are marching upon the same point. The troops at the
palace have twelve guns. All the troops show a good disposition.

The first deputation from Brussels was rather insolent. They were treated accordingly, and told to return without cockades, c. They did so, and the Prince agreed
to go into Brussels without troops. There was a great crowd, and for a moment he
was separated from the staff and the Garde Bourgeoise, and alone in the midst of the
people. He leapt his horse over a barrier and so got back. A Commission of very
respectable men has been appointed to investigate grievances. So the thing will rest
till the meeting of the States on September 13.

There is a letter from Lord Heytesbury giving an account of his conversations
with the Emperor of Eussia. The Emperor is violent against the Bourbons; says very
correctly that his treaties only oblige him to maintain a constitutional King. Still lie
may recognise, but shall always consider the Duke of Orleans as a usurper.

Prussia seems very prudent; disposed to recognise, but to state the condition of
peace that the territorial possessions of 1815 shall be maintained. Austria seems to
be less prudent. Metternich sent to Bernstorff the answer he intended to give, which
required a declaration of not having any intention to interfere in the affairs of France,
but required a pledge as to the observance of the Treaty of 1815 before recognition.
Bern-storff very prudently advised Austria to recognise unconditionally.

The Spaniards seem to have been in great consternation at first.

The Minister (Addington) thinks the King and Queen are so popular, and the
public interest is so much directed to the Queen's approaching accouchement, that no
revolutionary movement of importance is likely to take place. He deprecates, however,
the commencement of any such movement, because he thinks it would enable the
Apostolical Party l to induce the King to dismiss his present quiet Ministers, and have
recourse to measures of rigour, which would infallibly ruin the dynasty. Spain, and
indeed all the Powers, seem to look for instruction to England, and there can be no
doubt that all will recognise and all be quiet. Salmon, when he communicated to the
King the events in France, said, ' Your Majesty sees how dangerous l The name given
in Spain and Portugal to the Absolutist and Clerical Party.)

over-zeal is in a Minister. No one could be more devoted to the Eoyal Family than
Prince Polignac."

The King said, ' I see it."

However, notwithstanding this, they say he is so weak that he may adopt a violent
course.

Nothing can be more correct than the conduct of M. Mole, the French Secretary of State for Foreign Affairs. He is most anxious to preserve peace in Europe, the new King's Government in France, and himself in office. He is much alarmed by the events in Belgium, and wished our Minister to join the French Minister at Brussels in recommending some concession to the King of the Netherlands. The Duke has, as Eosslyn told me, written a memorandum to serve as the basis of Aberdeen's dispatch, very civil indeed to Mole, very much satisfied with the disposition evinced by the French Government, but, in our ignorance of the real state of things, declining to advise the King of the Netherlands.

It is very amusing to see the French Government most liberally permitting the Bonaparte family to return to France, and most prudently sending circulars to all the Ministers of the Powers which signed the protocols of 1815, urging them in the name of that treaty not to allow the members of the Bonaparte family to leave their present residences.

It seems this is very necessary; for although their partisans can do little without their presence, they might do much with it.

Martignac has got together sixty members of the Chamber of Deputies who will act en masse for royalty. VOL. II. A A

There is no military force to keep people in order, and the National Guard does not like doing so. In fact the Eevolution is not over. Things may go on as they are, but we have as yet no security. The French seem heartily sick of Algiers. It costs a great deal of money. Tropical products will not grow there. The climate does not suit the French troops, who have besides a most extraordinary maladie de pays. They must send 15,000 men more there to maintain it, as now they have no more than the town. They are willing to give it up to the Sultan if he will renounce tribute, c.

I never considered the acquisition of importance to France. I always felt we might vex the French to death by the use of a little money which would at any time have brought forward all the Arabs from the desert. The port will only hold a few vessels.

The Emperor of Eussia proposes to cut the Greek question short by proposing the crown at once, without the intervention of France, to Prince Frederick of Orange, and if he should refuse, then to Prince Charles of Bavaria, who we know will accept.

I should say from all I have read to-day that if France should make an aggressive movement all Europe would be united against her as in 1813; but if she remain quiet within her own frontier no Power will wish to molest her.

It is satisfactory to observe the increased prudence and reasonableness of the great States; their general union, and the deference which in the hour of danger they all show to the opinion of England.

There are some apprehensions, I hear, of riots at
THE PERSIANS. 355

Manchester. There is no cause for them. All men can get work. I would put them down with a strong hand.

September 6.

Saw at the office Colonel Monteith.

The King of Persia has about six millions sterling left in his treasury in gold and silver, besides jewels unsaleable on account of their high price, but which might be estimated at four millions more.

There will be a civil war on the death of the Shah.

Abbas Mirza might succeed if he had energy, but he is the weakest man on earth. Probably all the Eajahs will be put down and some new dyftasty established.

The chiefs are not likely to serve the Eussians at any time. The Persians are fine men and make excellent soldiers, bearing heat and cold, but not wet and damp. Officers there are none.

The Eussians lose 10,000 men a year in Georgia and Caucasus, and it costs them about 500,000. a year. They have never conquered the country.

The cession lately obtained from Turkey has enabled the Eussians to put down the robbers who lived in Abkasia; [1] but it is of no value for purposes of offensive war of some for defence.

It is cheaper in the proportion of 100 to 220 to send goods to Tabriz by Trebizond than by the Persian Gulf.

The Imaum of Muscat carries on a large trade in opium between the Eed Sea and China. He carries [1 The country at the western end of the Caucasus.] A-A

British manufactures to the Indus, and trades extensively with Cochin China, where sugar is half the price it i in India.

The officers of the Crown Prince's army all speak Turkish. It is more important to have at the head of it a man of energy than one conversant with Persian.

His rank should be increased, as now he is made to rank below the last member of the Mission.

The disturbed state of Persia has driven much trade to the Indus which was carried on by the Euphrates.

Persia may now be considered not as a monarchy, but a Federative State, all the King's sons being independent Princes.

Colonel Monteith was at Algiers the only Englishman in the army. There may have been twenty foreigners in all. He had letters of introduction and got there in a transport, taking his chance of being sent back. He was with the intendant of the army, and at the siege was attached to a division. Bourmont offered to receive him in his family. Bourmont was hated and despised. He seemed to take very little trouble about the army, and to leave everything to the generals of division. On the 19th, the day of the battle, he lost 600 men by not advancing sooner. The moment he advanced the enemy fled. The loss was 2,200 men in all, yet fifty were never to be seen dead and wounded together. The loss was by skirmishing at long shots along the whole of the line. This sometimes lasted all day, and the troops, being young, were too foolhardy. The Arabs are a miserable race, half naked. Everything beyond Algiers seems a desert.

~~THE FRENCH IN ALGIERS~~. 357

For eight miles round Algiers the cultivation is beautiful, and the villas more numerous than near any town he ever saw. A profusion of water. The town, miserable in the extreme, inhabited by Moors and the descendants of Turks, about 50,000. The port is formed by one pier which hardly protects two or three frigates. There is no safety in the bay.

There were 3,000 Turkish soldiers in Algiers, and about 7,000 in the country. These kept order. Now they are sent away the French may colonise extensively, but they cannot keep the country with the present inhabitants.

The Dey had ten millions sterling in gold and silver, a treasure which had been accumulating since the time of Barbarossa. [1] He claimed 400,000. as his own, and was allowed to carry it away. The French enquired about the jewels of the Eegency. The Dey said there were no jewels but those which belonged to his wives, and la galanterie Franchise would respect them as private property. So they did.

There was a magazine containing 250,000. of things in the trinket line. There were 150 ornamental daggers, all the presents of European princes, c. Colonel Monteith saw one officer coolly put into his pocket a watch set in diamonds, which had evidently been given by a King of England, worth, he supposed, 2,000.

General Lavardo pillaged more openly than any one. He had thirty soldiers employed in carrying off his pillage.

The affair at Belida was accidental. Bourmont went out with 1.600 men and invited the chiefs to meet him. [1. A famous colsair of the sixteenth century.]

They were coming peaceably; but some Arabs saw the Erench artillerymen taking their horses down to water without their guns, and they could not help attempting to steal. The artillerymen beat them off; but the firing having begun was soon converted into a battle. Bourinont beat them off, but thought it expedient to retreat.

The beach was particularly favourable for landing. The weather fine, and there was plenty of time to prepare.

The thing best done was by General Yalagi, who in eighteen hours raised a continued work of a mile and a half. He had 1,600 sappers and miners. Colonel Monteith is in admiration of this entrenchment, which was beautifully finished, and was capable of resisting 30,000 regular troops.

The Arabs are miserably mounted. The Dey's two best horses were not worth 30?. each.

Duperre he thought a man willing to do all, but quite overpowered by the management of 100 ships of war and 500 transports. His reports are all lies. Bourmont's are nearest the truth. The ships, with the exception of those which were in the Levant, were not in good order. There seemed to be no discipline.

The army never wanted either water or provisions. Water was within three feet of the surface everywhere. In the gardens on the side of the hills towards Algiers the water was found at the depth of twenty feejt.

Nothing could be more perfect than the equipment of the army. They calculated the cost of the expedition at four millions.

I see by the newspapers that the Prince of Orange yielded the point of the colours to the deputation from Brussels. He seems to have conceded a great deal, but to have acted with great personal courage and decision. It is expected that the Commission he appointed have asked for the separation of Holland from Belgium, and the establishment of a Federal union only; two countries under one King with distinct legislatures, armies, c. The great towns are quiet. Holland ready to march upon Brussels.

I shall not be satisfied unless some of the Bruxellois are hanged for pillage.

The answers of the King seem to have been firm and judicious.

It is impossible not to admire the constancy of the troops, who bivouacked for eight days in the park.

The French Government seems too weak or too timid to prevent outrage in Paris. The printers' devils will have no machinery for printing! It is entertaining to see those who make all revolutions suffer by them.

September 7.

Saw Greville at the Treasury. He told me he had got from Lord Chesterfield that Palmerston had no objection to come in. Lord Melbourne had; but they required the sacrifice of Aberdeen, Bathurst, and Ar-buthnot. There must be some mistake about this condition. I told Greville if he could get a fact to nnmunicate it to the Duke.

It is feared the Prince of Orange is gone away to the Hague. He promised Colonel Jones he would be firm.

September 8.

The Prince of Orange certainly went to the Hague. He was received there enthusiastically. The proposition he takes is for Federal union. I fear he must submit to some modification of that, or encounter real opposition and civil war.

September 9.

Hardinge gives me rather an indifferent account of Ireland. Great animosity still existing between the Catholics and Protestants in the lower ranks; in the higher, peace. A revolutionary disposition raised in the middle classes by the example of France. Great dissatisfaction in consequence of the proposed taxation of last session.

He told the Duke, and so did Arbuthnot, that he might dispose of their offices if he wanted them. He seems to think Peel is tired and anxious to withdraw annoyed at the idea of being unpopular, an idea the defeat of his brothers has given him. This makes him less energetic than he should be with respect to the measures necessary to strengthen himself in the House of Commons.

September 10.

It seems the desire of separation is general in the Netherlands. It is the result of national prejudice and vanity. The Dutch seem just as violent the other way, and the deputies were rather in danger at Rotterdam. The separation will probably defeat the objects of the great Powers in 1814, for it is idle to expect such terms of Federal union as will enable the two States to act cordially together.

September 11.

By withdrawing his troops from the palace, and going to the Hague, the Prince of Orange has ruined his cause. He has appeared to give it up.

September 13.

Eead on my way to London the intelligence obtained by Lord Heytesbury relative to the Eussian trade with Tartary and on the Caspian. It is very full and satisfactory.

The ' Times' has a sensible article on the state of France; the want of materials to form a constitutional monarchy, the growing dissatisfaction that more is not done in a revolutionary sense, and the irresponsible power of a deliberative army of 800,000 men.

Ghent and Antwerp seem to cling to the connection between Holland and Belgium, and I begin to hope that if France is tranquil the Bruxellois and Liegeois may grow tired and become reasonable. Men cannot play at barricades long when no one attacks them.

September 14.

House of Lords. I had to wait half an hour for the seals, which were carelessly carried off by Lady Lyndhurst in her carriage.

Talked to Eosslyn. He told me Aberdeen was led to expect another revolution in France. The paper they were going to prosecute was an qffiche calling upon the French people to overthrow l'aristocratic bour-geoise, which was as bad as the other, and to divide the lands.

362   In the Netherlands the people and their leaders are divided, and if Antwerp and Ghent, c., remain firm, it signifies little what Brussels does. Brussels will be brought into terms by distress.

Eosslyn thinks some of the Whigs as well as of the Tories will be alarmed by events on the Continent and support Government.

He hears of no negotiations for accessions.

The people of Brunswick, very justly provoked, have turned the Duke[1] out of the town and burnt his palace. He escaped with ten Hussars. He deserves his fate. I believe he is mad. He is a complete vaurien.

When Parliament is prorogued, as to-day, the peers are without their robes. The Chancellor was in his legal dress. The Commons appear without a summons by their clerks, and the Chancellor merely desires the proclamation to be read. However, as it is held, improperly, to be the first day of the sitting of Parliament, the return of the Scotch peers is laid on the table. All this is sanctioned by precedent, but contrary to reason.

September 20, 1830.

Wrote a long letter to Hardinge upon the political consequences of Huskisson's death,[2] urging the introduction of Palmerston and Stanley. The latter to pre-[1 This was the eccentric Duke who died a few years ago at Geneva, bequeathing his whole property to the city, who have erected a monument to him.

[2 He was killed, as is well known, at the opening of the Liverpool and Manchester Railway.]

363   vent the junction of the Whig aristocracy with the Radicals.

I am sure, if measures are not taken immediately, we shall have all the Huskissonians, Whigs and Ultra-Tories (the last are insane), united against us.

Eeceived from Sir J. Malcolm a letter with some enclosures about suttees. He has reluctantly and fearfully abolished suttee, making it culpable homicide to assist, and murder to force the victim. He has done it, I think, wisely by a repeal of a clause in one regulation and an amendment. Thus not putting it vainly forward as Lord William did in a pompous document.

He has abolished the Military Board, I believe, very wisely; but there may be a difficulty with the Duke, if I cannot do it without talking to him about it. I believe Sir J. Malcolm is quite right, and that there would have been no hope of preserving a system of real economy had the Military Board been permitted to remain.

I am curious to see his measure of checks on expenditure, that if it be good it may be adopted at the other Presidencies.

Received some letters from Lord W. Bentinck. Lord Dalhousie has been very ill, and the command of the army would fall, Lord William says, into the weakest hands, if anything happened to him.

The spirit of the army was becoming better, I gather from Lord William's letter, but it required much attention. I have been thinking all day of what measures may be adopted for improving it.

September 21.

Office. Eead to Cabell my memorandum on the alterations which might be introduced into the army, which I wrote hurriedly this morning. He was long in the military department, and can be of much use.

Cabinet room. I think the result of Lord Stuart's dispatches is that the moderate party are gaining strength. I should say the facts we see in the newspapers lead to a different conclusion.

The Ministers and the old leading members of the Chamber of Deputies act manfully against the crowd. Their declarations of intention are satisfactory. I really believe they mean to act honestly if they can.

Austria seems to have hesitated about the acknowledgment of the King of the French after the receipt of a dispatch from Petersburg, and Metternich, who seems to be growing weak, wavered after he had received General Belliard very cordially.

Prussia, that is the King, hesitated about signing the letter to Louis Philippe when he heard of the doubts of Austria. The result, however, is that all en-traines by us will acknowledge; the Emperor of Eussia, who was the most reluctant, having determined to do so if the others did. I should say there is this satisfactory conclusion to be drawn from what we have seen, that if France showed a disposition to aggrandise herself all Europe would be against her.

The object of the French Government is to place France exactly in the position in which she stood a fortnight before the ordonnances that is, Talleyrand's wish, and he has redige his own instructions.

Eead Aberdeen's letter, dated the 17th, stating the necessity of maintaining cordial intercourse with and between Spain and Portugal, and intimating that on the promulgation of an amnesty according to the terms recently communicated England will resume diplomatic relations with Miguel, but not otherwise.

Spain seems to be sensible. There was a movement of folly about Eoyalist volunteers which was put down, and the Government seems by no means disposed to give way to Absolutists. If the Queen should have a son Spain will probably be tranquil.

Talleyrand pretends the French will be reasonable about Algiers. I do not wish them to be so. I believe they could not have made a worse purchase. They will find the possession very expensive. Their troops will hate it, they will have nothing beyond their outposts, and it is no port.

My first opinion is strengthened, that they could not be worse than if they were left as they are.

September 24.

The populace and the burghers at Brussels have quarrelled, and fought a little. It seems the Liberals and the Catholics, [1] as the others are called, have been long diverging. The deputies and men of property, excepting M. de. Stassart, have become alarmed. The Prince de Ligne and D'Aremberg and others have left Brussels. On the 21st, probably the 20th, in the [1 They have formed the two opposing parties in the Belgian Chambers since the country became an independent State. They had temporarily united against Protestant Holland.]

366   evening a proclamation was published at Antwerp by Prince Frederick of Orange, noticing the excesses of the populace, and announcing that the troops would relieve the burgher guard. This must have been done in concert with the influential persons of the town who are alarmed for their property. The Liegeois are very violent. They will be expelled from Brussels. No more can get there, as the road is interrupted.

The Dutch have but 20,000 men, of whom the Belgians are as three to five. The Belgians had begun to desert, but they did not join the Bruxellois in any numbers. The hanging of some of the Brussels mob would have an excellent effect.

The Government of France seems to become weaker, and to permit things which discredit it.

A night or two ago some ouvriers insisted on going into the King's bedroom, after he was gone to sleep, woke him, and made him make a speech sitting up in his bed. Twelve departments have united against indirect taxes, and few pay those which are direct. Meanwhile, the Algerine treasure has been pillaged by the officers of the army, and ships clearing for Toulon go elsewhere to land it. They want a loan, while the fallen Government would have had a surplus. They will find the raising of a loan difficult. The French are displeased by the coldness of Austria and Prussia, and by the marching of Austrian and Prussian troops.

The King of Saxony has resigned, or rather he has associated his nephew with himself as Co-Eegent; the brother waiving his claim to the throne.

367   The Landgrave of Hesse Cassel was met by a depu-tation requiring him to do a number of public acts, and amongst the rest the dismissal of all mistresses. It seems the Electoral Prince has one to whom he is going to be married.

The Duke of Brunswick lately galloped off lui troisieme while his palace was burning!

These are odd times!

However, here people seem to be inclined to be quiet. Even the Common Council have by a large majority decided against congratulating or noticing the

French people.

September 26.

Brandreth told me there was a report of the Belgian troops having entered Brussels, and of a great massacre. There will be news to-morrow as the wind is down.

September 27.

No direct news from Brussels yet. There has been fighting for two days, and it was known at Antwerp that the first regiment that entered was nearly destroyed. It seems the invitation of one section was a ruse.

There are to be no Cabinets for eight or ten days, the Civil List not being prepared. When we do meet we are not to separate.

There seems to be every expectation of a new Ministry in Paris, and in the revolutionary sense.

I saw Aberdeen. He rather expects it.

Eead the report of the Commission appointed to form the articles of accusation against the Ministers. It is a party speech, with little points and prettinesses, affecting moderation, and full of rancour. It is a nation which has no idea of justice.

September 28.

Cabinet room. Dispatches of the 24th and 25th from Sir Ch. Bagot; but none from Mr. Cartwright. When Sir Ch. Bagot wrote last thirty hours had elapsed without official intelligence, although the distance is only thirteen hours. It was known there had been hard fighting, that it was necessary to take in succession every house in the Eue Neuve Eoyale, that the troops were in possession of the upper part of the town, and a proposition had been made by the lower town for a cessation of hostilities, after which they had recommenced.

It is evident the resistance has been most serious. 20,000 French are in the town, and these probably direct the defence. All clubs, and councils of all sorts, had ceased to have power two days before the attack. There has been perfect anarchy. The troops behaved admirably. They were much exasperated. No assistance had been sent by the country.

Aberdeen is confident the King's troops have been driven out, because no official accounts were sent. The Duke, and all the military men, say the non-arrival of dispatches proves nothing but that the affair was not over. During an engagement a general can think of nothing but victory. The importance of the result is incalculable.

At Paris the National Guard have dispersed a meeting of lookers on, who were led by curiosity to crowd about a riding school in which the Society of Les Amis du Peuple met the day after they were denounced by Guizot in the Chamber as agitating France. Two officers of the National Guard entered the riding school, and warned the meeting of the danger they were bringing upon public tranquillity. On the representation of the second they adjourned.

At dinner at Lord Eosslyn's the Duke said the French Government could not go on as it was. The chief of the National Guard necessarily commanded everything. The National Guard might become janissaries. I think the Government may go on as it is in form, but it will vary in substance from day to day. Management, a little good fortune, and a few examples of determination may make it a fair Government; a single error may produce anarchy.

The Duke gave an excellent account of the feeling at Liverpool, Manchester, and Birmingham. At Manchester it was better than at Birmingham, but there they received very coldly Tennyson's speech about giving them members, and at last put an end to it by striking their glasses with their knives, which made such a ringing that Tennyson was obliged to sit down. He deserved this for his bad taste.

The Duke was astonished by the machinery. Those who have witnessed the improvements of late years expect progressive improvements so great that they say a man who laid out 100, 000*l*. now in the best machinery would, if he refused to adopt the new improvements they anticipate, be without profit in five years and be ruined in ten.

VOL. n. B B

370

The rapidity of motion is so great in the steam carriages that even the Duke with his quick eyes could not see the figures on the posts which mark the distance at every quarter of a mile, and when two steam carriages crossed no face could be seen. [1] It was like the whizzing of a cannon ball. The cold is great, and they must have some defence against the wind, through which they pass so rapidly.

A new canal without locks, which brings coals to Birmingham in two hours, which by the old canal required nine, is more magnificent even than the railroad, splendid as that is. The railroad cost a million. For several days after it was opened the proprietors made 250Z. a day.

The King has the gout. The Duke goes to Brighton to-morrow. We dine with him on Thursday. Cabinets will not begin till next week.

September 29.

No news in the newspaper from Brussels. No dispatches from Sir Ch. Bagot or Mr. Cartwright arrived at the office; but a gentleman who left Brussels at five on Sunday reports that they were then fighting in the town, but the troops had the worst of it.

The Consul at Ostend reports that the King's troops evacuated Brussels on Sunday night; that reinforcements from the country were pouring into Brussels; that there had been an attempt at insurrection at [1 This was on the Manchester and Liverpool Railway, then just opened, and describes the first impression made by railway travelling]

~~THE BELGIAN REVOLUTION~~. 371

Ostend, which was put down for the time by the Governor, who killed two and wounded six; that eleven or twelve men had marched in from Bruges, which was in possession of the Bourgeois; that Ghent was expected to rise, and in a few days all Belgium would be separated from the King.

A son of Holmes of the Treasury arrived at the Foreign Office at four, and said he had left Ostend at three yesterday, when there was a report that the Dutch had made another attack and had recaptured the park.

It seems they never had more than the park. They had to take, and did take, the Eue Eoyale. They were more thoroughly masters of the Place Koyale. They planted guns against the town, which were answered by guns from the rebels. At five on Sunday the latter were gradually advancing, and picking off the troops in the park.

The first day some rockets were fired and eighteen houses burnt; but Prince Frederick ordered the discontinuance of this, the only efficacious mode of attack.

Lord Blantyre was killed. He was lame and on a sofa, but curiosity led him to crawl to the window and peep out, when a ball struck him in the forehead. Lady Blantyre and his children were with him. He was much esteemed. He was in the Peninsula, and a gallant officer.

I think the employment of European officers in civil situations under native princes may be very useful to their subjects; and while we do not ourselves employ natives

372

in high situations, to force all native princes to employ them is to make a striking contrast between their Government and ours, very injurious to ours.

Jones seemed to hesitate and to think I committed myself. However, I feel sure of my ground.

A letter from Lord Cleveland, expressing a wish to have the Vicarage of Ilchester, and offering an equivalent living in Shropshire, or Cheshire.

I sent his letter to the Bishop of Bath and Wells, saying I should be much obliged to him if he could make the arrangement, Lord Cleveland being a faithful and powerful supporter of Government.

Told Lord Cleveland I had transmitted his letter with a strong recommendation.

I made my letter as agreeable to the Bishop as I could, but I dare say he will refuse. Very likely he has given away the vicarage. I told Lord Cleveland I thought it probable.

September 30.

The Consul at Antwerp writes a long foolish letter in much alarm.

Mr. Cartwright's reports are come. He describes a horrible carnage. The events much as we know them. Sir A. Bagot says his Eussian colleague has, with the consent of the King and the Dutch Ministers, written home to say Belgium can only be preserved by foreign aid.

At dinner at the Duke of Wellington's met Talleyrand and Vaudreuil. The others there were Aberdeen, Goulburn, Herries, Murray, Beresford, Lord F. Somerset, and Eosslyn.

Talleyrand is not altered since 1815, except that lie speaks thick. He has not even changed his hairdresser or his tailor.

Lord Eosslyn showed me a letter from Lady Janet, who was in Brussels during the fight. She walked about frequently, and was treated with civility by the armed burghers. A few grape-shot fell into the courtyard, and she picked up one. She was at the Hotel de Brabant in the Eue Neuve. There was no pillage, nor any riot. The loss of the people was great. She left the town on Sunday (I think) with a passport from Count Hoogwoorst, and got round to Antwerp.

The troops are said to have lost only 600 men. Prince Frederick is about two leagues from Brussels, on the road to Lou vain, waiting for heavy guns. This is the report. I suspect he will retreat altogether.

October 1.

On consideration thought it would be better to have a secret letter on the press, authorising the Government to allow their servants to be connected with the press. To this letter I thought it advisable to add an exhortation to redoubled zeal on the part of the Company's servants on account of the unsettled state in which the minds of men must be until it was decided under what form the future Government of India should be administered, and I directed the Government to make all thoroughly understand that no possible change could effect the public debt, or the rights of the natives or the just expectations of the European servants. My reason for thinking the officers of Government should be permitted to be concerned in the press is this, that if none but those who are unconnected with the Government, and who, according to the existing system, cannot be connected with it, manage the press, the probability is that everything will be said against the Government and nothing for it.

I showed the proposed letter to the Duke. He thought it would be better to pay people for writing than to employ the Company's servants, and that the concluding paragraphs would lead the Government to suppose it was quite decided that the Company should be put an end, to. It is wonderful the sort of prejudice he has in favour of the Company. He thinks that unless Directors selected writers and cadets we should have an inferior sort of people in India. I have no objection to the patronage being in a corporate body, but I am satisfied the present system leads to a degree of delay which is more mischievous than misdirection. He acknowledges, however, that the service is much changed. The exhibition made by Courtenay Smith has produced a strong impression upon his mind. He has done more injury to the Company in his mind than all the evidence. He still seems unwilling to make his opinion up against the continuance of the monopoly. It must fall, however.

The King wishes to have Sir E. Barnes appointed provisional successor to Lord Dalhousie. The Duke thinks him a better man than Sir E. O'Callaghan, who was suggested by Lord F. Somerset. I suggested that it would be expedient to unite the influence of Governor-General with that of Commander-in-Chief, and make

375

Lord William Bentinck provisional successor. The Duke seemed to think Lord William could not execute both duties, and that it was better to adhere to the general usage of separating the two offices. It seems that after Lord Hastings' return the Court intimated a disposition to separate the offices in future. I can do nothing against the King, the Duke, and the Horse Guards; but I am satisfied it would have been better to send Sir E. Barnes as second in command to the Governor-General.

The King (Lord F. Somerset told me) was desirous of doing away witli the Company's European regiments. He could not do a better thing. He has likewise some notion of bringing the army under himself. The Duke thinks it must be a local army, and certainly it must. [1]I believe it is better to make it an army of three Presidencies, not one army. My doubt is whether it would not be advisable to allow exchanges from the King's army to the Company's. Everything would be beneficial that raised the tone of the Indian army.

The Duke showed me a draft letter he had written for Aberdeen to Lord Stuart, informing the French Government that the King of the Netherlands had required the assistance of his allies to re-establish his authority in Belgium. That it was as much the interest of France as of other Powers to put down a revolution not carried on by the higher or the middle, but by the lowest classes of the people. That we were desirous[1 In accordance with this view Lord Ellenborough opposed the eventual amalgamation of the Queen's and the Indian army.]

376   of concerting with France, as one of the contracting parties to the Treaty of Vienna, what course should be now adopted. It could not be supposed the Allies would forego the advantage of the union of Belgium and Holland for which they had sacrificed so much.

This was the substance of the letter. It will not be sent without the concurrence of the Cabinet, which will be summoned the moment Peel comes to town, and he is hourly expected.

I think this letter prudent, inasmuch as whatever may happen it will place us in the right; but I do not expect that France will do anything against the rebels, or sanction the doing of anything.

The Duke considers, as indeed is clear enough, that it is idle to expect the future submission of Belgium to the King of the Netherlands. It may be possible to place it under a Prince of the House of Nassau. I do not think the Duke sees his way; but he expects war.

October 2.

Cabinet. Aberdeen's letter to Lord Stuart. It is founded upon the Duke's memorandum, but much extended a VIndienne. I think none approved of it but Lord Bathurst. I objected to the statement that the treaty of 3815 imposed upon us obligations. It may give us rights, but it imposes no obligation. Then the principle of non-interference is advanced as just and wise, but there are peculiar circumstances attending the position of the Netherlands which make a difference.

[3T7   There is an assertion that the troubles in Belgium have been fomented by French agency, although not assisted by the Government, and a direct reference is made to the Barrier Treaties. France is requested to concert with us and the Allies to suppress the anarchy which exists in the Low Countries. She is at the same time reminded that in no case can the Allies consent to renounce the security given to them by the Treaty of Paris in consequence of an insurrection amongst the lower orders at Brussels. Of this a great deal will be left out. Peel seemed to be rather averse to the whole tenor of the letter, which looks like an invitation to put down the insurrection by force. He sketched in a few words a letter which would be innocuous.

The Duke's object is to make an effort to induce Prance to act with us to settle the Belgian affairs amicably. They cannot be settled without France, without a war. But is there any hope that the French Government will venture to give us her appui? If they be self-denying enough to renounce the hopes of annexing Belgium to France, their fears of the Jacobins will not allow them to do so. My expectation is that they will say they neither have interfered nor will interfere to dissolve the union between Holland and Belgium. That they will not interfere in the internal concerns of other States.

Some think they will go farther and declare they will not allow other Powers to do so. I do not expect this.

Every word of this letter must be well weighed, for every discontented man in England and in France will criticise its words and its spirit. There is no writer more unsafe than Aberdeen.

378   Eosslyn did not seem to like the letter at all, but he said little. I whispered to Peel that I wished he would bring a letter to-morrow. Short. It was at last agreed alterations should be made, and we are to meet at one to-morrow.

Peel takes the letter home, and will, I trust, cut it down.

The King Charles X. is in danger of being arrested, of which he naturally has a great horror, and he desires to be allowed to go to Holyrood House, where he would be safe. At Lulworth they are afraid of the Due de Bordeaux being kidnapped. The pretence is the getting masters from Edinburgh for the children.

It may be feared that the placing him in a royal residence may look or be represented as looking like recognition. On the other hand his removal from the southern coast to Scotland is a renunciation of intrigues with France.

It would be inconvenient if the King should wish to go to Edinburgh next year. Charles X. is to be told he cannot stay there after the spring. However, he will probably live there all his life.

It would be a revolting sight to see a King imprisoned for debt, and all gentlemen, all men of feeling, would have cried out shame!

We are right in feeling, but in policy I am not sure.

Meuport has fallen as well as Ostend. The Bruxellois are drilling, and threaten to attack Prince Frederick. Probably Van Holen drills them to keep them quiet.

Many people have applied to Falck[1] for passports[1 Dutch Minister.]
for Brussels, going in reality to join the rebels. Today two Irish labourers asked for passports! Brussels will become the sink of Europe, and every unquiet spirit will go there.

The Duke thinks our attempt to make France act in concert with us the only chance of preserving peace.

I fear its preservation is almost desperate. One thing is in favour of it, that all the European States desire it yet more than we do.

I cautioned them to-day not to take any advanced position from which it would be difficult and discreditable to retreat. The people would not go in with us in a war to avert a distant danger, nor indeed for any object not commercially interesting.

It came out accidentally in the course of conversation respecting the loan to the Netherlands that we had lent 20,000. to the Greeks; the sum to be repaid by bills to be drawn by our Commissioner whenever the loan we are to guarantee may be made that is, we are to be paid out of our own money.

Of this loan I knew nothing, and my impression is that when it was earnestly pressed by Aberdeen such objections were stated on the ground of illegality that the decision was against it. Certainly nothing was decided in favour of it. I recollect having said I would rather advance a portion of the money myself than be a party to the transaction.

October 3.

Cabinet. The Consul at Ostend announces that nothing remains to the King of the Netherlands but

Antwerp. The troops have everywhere laid down their arms. On the 1st the Brussels papers announce that orders had been issued by the provisional Government for arresting all the Dutch officers.

Peel read first the dispatch written by Aberdeen with the omissions agreed upon, and then his own substitutions. His is much the best. It speaks of' composing troubles' instead of ' suppressing anarchy," avoids all mention of interference, and altogether is a more prudent paper, touching the Barrier very slightly. It was understood that Peel's was adopted.

It is determined to allow the King, Charles X., to go to Holyrood House, but he will be told there is no furniture, or very little, and that he can only stay six months, and that no expense can be incurred on his account. He has admitted no one to an audience, but many have been to Lulworth to ask for places.

Talleyrand says they have found an ebauche of Polignac's, telling Bourmont that his proposal that the money taken at Algiers should be given to the Legion of Honour could not be complied with, as the King intended to distribute it amongst his most faithful friends. They pretend they do not intend to make use of this because there is no proof of its having been sent; in fact they do not use it because it reflects credit on Bourmont.

Lord Eosslyn, with whom I walked as far as Pimlico Palace, showed me the Treasury list of the House of Commons. 311 decided friends and 189 enemies that is 500; the remainder, consisting of moderate Tories, violent Tories,, good and bad

⌊381 doubt-/fuls, as well as Huskissonians (the latter 13), are more likely to be against us than for us.

Bosslyn still hankers after a coalition, but reform has made it impossible. We might have had this time last year Sir J. Graham. We might even now have Palmerston, [I] but the Duke seems determined to go on as he is, Peel and all, even Bathurst, seem to have a correct view of the danger; but I see no flinching.

October 4.

Saw the Duke. Suggested that we must soon consider what should be done with respect to the China trade. If we were to give up the monopoly we had better do so at once, on the first day of the Session, wth a good grace, and not make ourselves appear to do it with reluctance. The Duke said we must certainly consider it. Had I talked with the Chairs about it? I said no. I had thought it best to wait till the Cabinet had come to a decision as to what should be done. I had privately advised them to turn over in their minds the plan of the Company going on with the Government slightly varied, but without monopoly.

The Duke said he could not make up his mind without hearing first what the Chairs had to say. I observed that if they, that is Astell, thought the Government hesitated, they would certainly say they could not go on without monopoly. However, the Duke seemed to think it was impossible for the question to [1 It appears from Lord Palmerston's published papers that this was an error. He had already determined to act with the Whigs, and not to take office without Lord Grey and Lord Lansdowne. See Ashley's Life of Lord Palmerston, vol. i. p. 211.]

382   come before the Cabinet before we had talked with the Chairs. So I have asked him and Loch to meet at the Treasury at twelve on Monday.

I should like to see Tucker and Stuart, but I must do it privately, as I have no principle to go upon in consulting with individual Directors.

The Duke seems very reluctant to give up the monopoly, and to have very exaggerated ideas of the value of the Company's intervention.

He showed me a letter he had received from Mole, in which he takes a very moderate view of the Belgian question. Expresses the most earnest desire for peace, as war would place everywhere the two extreme principles in conflict. France will not interfere, neither can she suffer others to interfere, in the internal affairs of the Netherlands. He hopes to be able to arrange everything amicably.

A letter the Duke showed me from Rothschild's brother is still more satisfactory if the view taken in it be correct. He says France will, with England and the Allies, amicably settle the question; but she will not have to be excluded.

He mentions Leopold as a probable King of Belgium.

The Court of Turin [l] seems to be in a great fright because the French Government took huff at their not recognizing at once. They were afraid to do so till they heard what the great Powers did.

M. de la Tour says they can bring 60,000 or 90,000 men into the field, if Genoa is guarded for them by a [l The first French Republic had made a similar non-recognition a plea for seizing Savoy.]

383   fleet; but Genoa would require 14,000 men. On that place they must retreat.

The Spaniards seem to be going on well. They mean not to be empresses with their recognition, but are advised not to be the last.

There have been insurrections at Hanau, Swerin, and I know not where else. The Diet intend to vary the law of the Empire and to allow any neighbour, whose assistance may be asked, to give it at once.

The Emperor of Eussia received General Athalia very graciously, but he keeps him waiting for his answer. Lieven professes himself well satisfied with our reasons for immediate recognition. So does Metter-nich. In fact they cannot do without us, and if we lead they must follow.

October 5.

Cabinet. Goulburn's Civil List. He transfers to the Consolidated Fund all the salaries heretofore partly paid by the Civil List, and in diplomacy there is a reduction of 28£,OOO£. a year.

It is supposed there can be no reduction in the great departments in the article of tradesmen's bills, or in the Board of Works.

The King gives up the Droits [1] without any compensation. This is all a loss to the privy purse.

It seems possible to reduce perspectively many officers in England and in Ireland who do not really contribute to the state of the crown. This, however, did not occur to Goulburn but to Peel.

[1 'Droits of Admiralty."]

384 The account of Liege is very bad indeed. Things there seem going on in the style of the French Revolution.

Nothing can be better than the account from France. They will be pleased by the letter read to them. All they feared was the attempt to exclude them from all concert in the settlement of Belgium. They think neither the King nor Prince Frederick can return to Brussels; but the Prince of Orange may, and this will, I think, be finally settled.

October 6.

Council at 2. Talleyrand was presented. He backed to the window and read a speech in which there were several erasures. He declared the determination of France to pursue the course so wisely followed by England of non-interference. He spoke of himself as ' Ministre d'une Eoyaute votee a I'unanimitev

The King did not much like receiving him, and was a little nervous. To what Talleyrand said about noninterference the King answered it was a very good thing, especially when exercised de bonne foi. This he said by Aberdeen's advice.

I read the King of the Netherlands' letter. He asks distinctly for military assistance.

Cabinet dinner at the Duke's. The Prince of Orange is gone to Antwerp. This the Duke thinks the very worst step that could have been taken; the only mistake the King has made. In fact the King was unwilling, and ever since the affair of Brussels there has been a coolness between the King and the Prince. The

385 Duke fears the consequences of the Prince's going, because he is a man devoted to popularity vain. The Duke and Talleyrand were talking about popularity. The Duke said those who loved it never loved it with moderation. Talleyrand said," Il n'y a jamais de moderation, oil il n'y a pas de gout et il n'y a pas de gout dans l'amour de

la popularite!" The Duke asked Talleyrand what sort of a man the Duke of Orleans was. 'Un Prince de l'Ecole normale." Of the Queen he said, ' Elle est bonne femme, et surtout grande dame c'est ce qu'il nous faut."

Talleyrand said he had given the King a piece of advice, ' to go to Neuilly ' that is, to rescue himself from the vagabond cortege.

Talleyrand is very well pleased with the letter sent to Paris, and the foreign Ministers are satisfied.

The King (our King) seemed to me to be very weary to-day. Aberdeen said he was a good deal distressed at the state of Europe, and rather anxious.

Lord and Lady Holland and Eothschild appear to be the only people besides the Ministers who have called on Talleyrand. Lord Holland is very much with him. Lord Holland is doing all he can to save the lives of the French Ministers for the interest of the French Government, not of the Ministers themselves. He has written to La Fayette and to the King.

October 7.

I forgot on what authority it was mentioned yester-lay, but it was mentioned as a fact that the Liberaux would not have done anything unless they had been ~~VOL. II. C C~~ certain of the Duke of Orleans. So afraid were they of a revolution that they would have submitted to the Ordonnances rather than run the risk of it.

October 9.

At Canterbury heard more particulars of the machine-breaking now going on in the neighbourhood. Notice is given, and the frames are broken. One gentleman boasted at market they should not break his, as he had armed men to protect them. They on the same night set fire to his rickyard. Sir Henry Oxenden's sons went out to meet them, when they came according to notice to break Sir Henry's machines. One man spoke for the rest. He acknowledged Sir Henry seldom or ever used his machine, and that he was the landlord in Kent who gave most to the poor; but they must do as they were ordered; they would, however, do as little as they could, and they only sawed off a shaft.

The farmers now leave their thrashing machines out in the fields to be broken.

The rickyard of one gentleman was set on fire because he committed a man for machine-breaking. He lost 6, OOOₗ,, nothing being insured.

It seems suspicions are entertained that the machine-breakers are not all of the station they assume. They all wear smock frocks, but their language is better than their dress. When money was offered them, if they wanted it, by the Oxendens, they said they did not want money, they obeyed orders.

It is reported, but this must be an exaggeration, ~~BELGIAN INDEPENDENCE~~. 387 that 500 assembled lately on a Down near Mr. Brock-man's.

The magistrates have no good evidence against any. Some Bow Street officers are here. Lord Winchelsea and Sir Edward Knatchbull have been here at every meeting of the magistrates, although they live eighteen miles off.

The Provisional Government of Belgium have declared the independence of the country and the defeaz-ance of the House of Orange. In the meantime the Prince of Orange is arrived at Antwerp, as Viceroy, with a Belgian Etat Major Civil.

It seems probable the Chamber of Deputies will abolish the punishment of death for political offences, and so save Polignac.

The levy of 108,000 men will hardly make the French army 240,000 effective, for it was not full before the Eevolution, and numbers have deserted; besides the disbandment of the Guards, which was 25,000 men.

October 11.

Cabinet. Aberdeen read Lord Stuart's account of his interview with Mole. Mole suggests an immediate conference, and thinks the Prince of Orange may be made Sovereign of La Belgique. No communication will be held by the French Government with the Provisional Government of Belgium. They will communicate through the King.

It is proposed to have the Conference here. The Mimsters of Austria, Prussia, and Eussia have expressed their readiness to acquiesce in anything proposed by this country. They may inveigh against the diplomacy of England, but in moments of danger all rally under our wing.

Mole distinctly admitted that the existence of the present Government of France depended on its remaining on good terms with England and Prussia, and the affairs of Belgium gave them an opportunity of showing Id droiture de leurs prindpes, c. in short, of gaining a good character.

It was decided against guaranteeing the sum of 500,000. the Dutch wish to raise here. There would be no end to such loans if we once began to assist the credit of foreign States. Parliament would not approve of the measure. To the Dutch Government it is important that this Administration should remain, and likewise that their own credit should not be injured in all Europe by the confession of weakness which their recourse to us implies.

To guarantee a loan is to give money, and to do that is to assist one of the parties to lose the mediatory character, and, in fact, put ourselves out of the Congress.

Hardinge can reduce 57,000. a year in net and on the Civil List, 30,000. on the Pension List, and 27,000. on officers of State.

We had some talk about details, but Goulburn does not reduce as much as Hardinge.

Had some talk with the Duke and Peel respecting the fires in Kent, and the breaking of frames. Five are in prison. The Duke thinks smugglers are at the bottom of it.

There has been alarm at Carlisle. The officers in command of the castle apprehended an attempt to surprise it and seize the arms. Men had been seen measuring the wall. Sir J. Graham was alarmed about it. Orders will be given to provision for thirty days all the places where arms are kept, the town included, where there are 600,000 stand of arms. In the meantime all classes are more comfortable in this country than they ever were, and this alone keeps down insurrection. There are leaders but no troops.

Hardinge reports that the spirit in Ireland is dis-improved since the events in Belgium.

There is to be an Anti-Union Society, which, as soon as it meets, will be put down under the Act.

October 12.

At nine went to Apsley House. Met the Chairs. We went in to the Duke. Our conversation lasted two hours. As they are to send in a proces verbal, it is unnecessary for me to state it. The substance was that, supposing the monopoly to be taken away, they would administer the Government of India as heretofore on one of two conditions; either closing their account with the public and receiving payment in full, or an equivalent annuity for all their property in India, in which case they would require no guarantee of the present dividend; or making over all their property, and taking a perpetual guarantee of the dividend.

The public to make good in either case all deficiency of Indian revenue, and in either case the Company to be the agents for the territory, providing all necessary sums here and receiving repayment at a rate of exchange to be paid from time to time fairly.

The Chairs were given to understand that the public being liable to the making good of Indian deficiency, we should require a strict control over the whole expenditure here, as well as in India.

They show, especially Campbell, a disposition to leave off trading and become gentlemen. They were told by the Duke that if they did so we must be at liberty to revise our arrangement with them. We might as well go to the Bank as to them, if we were to treat with a body not commercial.

The Duke seems much pleased with his foreign prospects.

M. de Choiseul was waiting to see him. I suppose on the affair of Holyrood House.

It seems probable that the French will abolish the punishment of death, and so save Polignac.

October 14.

Found at the office several papers giving accounts of Eadical meetings in Lancashire. All the old Eadicals are reappearing on the scene. They do not as yet seem to be attended by any numerous assemblies, never above 200 or 300.

A letter from a clergyman at Wrotham speaks of burnings near that place, and of the bad conduct of the people who interfere with the working of the engines, and seem to rejoice in the destruction.

Eead all the papers relating to the education of the Princess Victoria, who seems to have been admirably brought up.

At the Cabinet room read a long and excellent letter of Hardinge's respecting the state of Ireland.

The 87th Eegiment at Newry, when paraded for church, refused to march without music, to which it had been accustomed in the south. It had been discontinued in the north to avoid displeasing the Orangemen.

The captain sent for the Lieutenant-Colonel Blair, who was at first disobeyed, but he placed a drum to have a drum-head court martial, and then they marched. The Duke says it is, and always has been, the worst regiment in the service. It ran away at Salamanca and exposed him to being taken prisoner. It has alway been unmilitary, and from the same cause, a disposition to seek popularity on the part of its officers. Hardinge proposes embarking it at once for the West Indies. The Duke prefers bringing it to Dublin, where there are other regiments to keep it in order, and soon sending it to England, and by detachments at no distant period to Botany Bay. They do not expect there will be any further exhibition of mutinous spirit. The only mischief of this is the effect at this time.

There have been apprehensions of an attempt to scale the Pigeon House, and a full garrison has been ordered into it, with directions to add to its defences on the seaside so as to protect it from escalade.

Hardinge can bring twenty guns together in a very short time, at any point in Dublin. He talks of arming the students in Trinity College in the event of an explosion.

They rather expect an explosion about the 18th or. 19th, when probably there will be the first meeting of the new Association.

This it will be the first object to put down by the Act of 1829. The meeting to petition for the repeal of the Union will be permitted.

Hardinge is quite himself on horseback. The only fear is that he should be too lively. Peel seems to think he is; but it is a great comfort to have him there instead of Lord Francis Leveson, who was always wrong.

The King of the Netherlands has called his States at the Hague, the Constitution requiring them to meet this year in Belgium. He takes advantage of the provision in the Constitution which permits him to call the States in Holland in case of war. They fear the loss of Antwerp. The Prince of Orange thinks things look better.

The Netherland Ambassador is much annoyed at the refusal of pecuniary assistance; but, as was expected, the Dutch have got their money, only paying a little more for it.

Our depots are only 160 strong. We have hardly a battalion. One or two at least of those which were going abroad will be retained for a time.

The Duke of Brunswick does not much like abdicating. The Duke of Wellington thought he had brought him to make his brother Governor-General for his life, retaining the succession for his children. However, Aberdeen seems to have blundered him back again. He is to go to see the King on Saturday. The King desired he might come early, that he might not be obliged to have him to dinner, and he desired Aberdeen would remain in the room.

Pozzo thinks the French Government is gaining strength; but they are very inefficient in preventing armed men from assembling on the frontiers of Spain.

The French have exercised such coldness towards the Belgians that they are become unpopular. De Potter was French while he had hopes of becoming so. Now he is a Eepublican.

The Austrians will send troops into the Sardinian dominions if there is any insurrection. [1] This by invitation.

The Queen of Spain has, it is said, a son. [2] This event would, it is thought, secure Spain against any revolutionary movement.

October 15.

Called on the Duke. Settled with him the alterations necessary in the Chairs' memorandum of the conversation on the 12th. He thought we had gone too far in leading them to expect they should be repaid the money they had sunk in the territory while they held the Government.

1 They had similarly interfered to put down the Constitutional movement in Piedmont which followed on the Neapolitan revolution of 1821.

2 It was a daughter, afterwards Queen Isabella II., born October 10, 1830. The alteration of the succession in favour of the female line led to a civil war on Ferdinand VII."s death. A son might have secured peace, but probably without a Constitution.

394   Eeceived from him the opium letter. He thinks the principle good, but considers it is not fair to make the Scindians prevent the transit of opium. We cannot prevent them, for they are independent; but unless we endeavour to persuade them, and succeed in doing so, we shall lose our opium revenue.

October 16.

Chairs at 11. Bead over with them my alterations of their protocol. Astell did not seem to see the greatness of the variations. Campbell did, and particularly observed upon the words, ' value of the fixed property in India which might be adjudged to appertain to the Company in their commercial capacity." He wanted an admission of the justice of the claims, leaving nothing for adjustment but their amount. I said we could not admit claims without examination, the nature of which we did not yet know. All we could admit was that the claims were such as should be submitted to examination, and their validity decided upon just principles.

Astell wished to go back again and recommence the discussion. I said he knew I could decide nothing without the Cabinet, and he nothing without the Court; all he had to do now was to bring the subject before them.

He asked whether they were distinctly to understand that the Cabinet had decided upon the termination of the monopoly? I said that the question not having yet been before the Cabinet I could not give an answer officially; but when the First Lord of the Treasury and

THE PRINCE OF ORANGE. 395 the President of the Board of Control desired to know what the course of the Court would be in the event of its being proposed that the Court should administer the Government without monopoly, I thought it was not difficult to draw an inference.

October 19.

Sent to the Duke a memorandum on his letter. Eead at the Cabinet room. The King of the Netherlands is much annoyed at the desertion, as he thinks it, of his allies. He now proposes a Congress of the Four Powers and France at Breda or Cleves. He admits France very unwillingly, and by no means acquiesces in the reasoning in favour of the advance we made.

Sir Ch. Bagot seems to think the Prince of Orange will be losing the affection of the Dutch without gaining the Belgians.

The German Confederation is arming in the neighbourhood of Hanau for the preservation of the peace. They have put 6,000 or 7,000 men in motion, and have a reserve of 15,000 or 18,000.

The excitement against Polignac and Peyronnet increases, and the Ministers run the hazard of their places by attempting to save them. I fear that is hopeless. The Spanish Eadicals seem to find it would be dangerous to pass the frontier.

October 20.

Office. Cabinet room. The Prince of Orange has written a most offensive letter to the King of the French, almost insinuating that the troubles in Belgium are fomented by France, and saying that by a declaration against the Belgians France would show her good faith, and secure the recognition of Eussia. The French Cabinet is much offended at the silence of the King of the Netherlands, and Count Mole is going to write to the Dutch Minister upon the subject.

Nesselrode seems to see great difficulties in the intervention of France in the settlement of Belgium the union of Belgium and Holland having been made against France. The Eussian Minister at the Hague has general directions to follow the course of England upon all points not provided for by his instructions.

There is a great fall in the Funds to-day; partly, it is said, in consequence of those who desired to keep up the Funds being no longer able to do so; partly from the general aspect of affairs. My surprise is that the Funds have not fallen before, and much more.

Cabinet dinner at the Duke's. Showed the protocol of our Conference with the Chairs. The heads of the speech were read. Aberdeen's will not do at all. To my surprise he intended to announce the recognition of Miguel, he having engaged to do a great act of justice; that is, to publish the amnesty. He will not do it till a British Minister arrives at Lisbon; that is, he makes us, whom he has once deceived, dependent upon his word. This would be a very incautious step on our part. We meet on Friday to consider the speech in detail.

We had a good deal of conversation about the Duchess of Kent's allowance, which is to be much increased. It is proposed to give her 20,000. a year.

She has now 12,000. for herself and the Princess, out of which she pays interest and insurance upon 12,000. she borrowed on the Duke of Kent's death for her outfit.

The King has about thirty people at dinner every day, belonging to the Household. His expense must be enormous in living.

October 21.

Bead in the newspaper the King of the Netherlands' speech. It is querulous and angry. I really thought the Proclamation extraordinary of the Prince of Orange a forgery; but it is genuine, and he throws off all connection with Holland, declaring the independence of Belgium, and placing himself practically at the head of the Kebellion!

On Monday night at a dance at the Lodge, Har-dinge saw accidentally in an evening newspaper, shown to him for another purpose, the advertisement of the Anti-Union Association, and by seven o'clock the next morning the Lord Lieutenant's Proclamation prohibiting it was placarded in the streets. This is decision. There was no riot. Persons in general were satisfied the act was right. O'Connell is alarmed. The Duke of Lein-ster is ready to sign a declaration in favour of the Union. All is safe in Ireland with Hardinge's promptitude. I wish he could remain and not come over to Parliament.

October 22.

Saw Campbell, who was very nervous and anxious, and I at night wrote a letter to Lord Hill in favour of his son more, I admit, from a father's feelings than from a conviction of being right.

It seems the Lord Lieutenant not having been near Dublin when the Proclamation was issued by Hardinge, he must have had a blank Proclamation in his pocket, and have issued it without the opinion of the law officers. He has good debatable Parliamentary grounds of defence; but he has trodden upon the margin of the law. Not the worse for that in these times, when it is most important that every one should see the Government are vigilant and determined.

Valdez, who entered Spain with a few hundred men, has been smashed at once.

At the Cabinet we had a long discussion respecting the Eegency question. Aberdeen started the objection that the proposed measure was destructive of the principle that the King could not die. On the other hand it was contended that we maintained that principle. We made a Eegent for a King. We acknowledged a King; but we deferred taking the oath of allegiance till we knew who he was. The difficulties attending the unkinging of a Sovereign on the birth of a Prince nearer to the present King seem greater than any attending the measure proposed. It was ultimately determined that the Chancellor should consult the judges and the law officers.

October 23.

Cabinet. Twenty-six magistrates at Canterbury sentenced to three days' imprisonment threshing machine breakers, who pleaded guilty! Such has been the terror struck into them! Sir E. Knatchbull was in the chair.

399

We went through the speech not deciding absolutely upon the words; but generally upon the substance.

Then arose a conversation as to the Kegency which, in this last hour, is thought a point of importance. The Chancellor seems alarmed and unwilling to move the suspension of the rights of the presumptive heir until the non-existence of an heir apparent be ascertained, without the opinion of the judges. It is admitted there is no written opinion to guide us. The analogy of property is in favour of the heir presumptive; that of peerage in favour of the heir apparent in utero.

October 24.

Cabinet at 4. Eead two letters from Hardinge. By his account all the men of property will support the Government and the Union.

The press is coming round bought. A Mr. Conway, an able writer, is furious against O'Connell, and, upon the whole, the Press is on our side. Hardinge dilates with delight upon his military preparations and plans of defence, and seemingly will be disappointed if he cannot put them into execution.

The Belgian Ministers resigned after the Prince of Orange's Proclamation. He is left without advisers. He has endeavoured to get Sir Charles Bagot to join him, and Grasioff. He sends for Cartwright. He seems much embarrassed. In fact he is in heart a Belgian, and would sacrifice everything to be King of Belgium. He never knew the Dutch, and not unnaturally likes'the Belgians better. They are indignant at his conduct in

400

Holland, and with reason. He seems to intend to rule the Dutch by means of the Belgians. This he cannot do.

The Duke of Wellington always thought him a silly fellow.

The Provisional Government is going to send some mission here.

We had a long talk about the Eegency. Eeally it does us little credit to begin now, within ten days of the meeting of Parliament, to consider that question seriously.

The Chief Justices will be asked whether, supposing the Queen to be pregnant at the death of the King, the next living heir would succeed? How in the event of the birth of a child the de facto Sovereign is to be put aside? And what should be done if the Queen only may be with child? The difficulty consists in the oath of allegiance, which must be altered and made conditional. But what a curious position the Queen Victoria would be placed in, if a baby were to oust her after eight months of reign!

I think the course adopted will be this to make an oath of allegiance conditional, saving the rights of a child to be born; to appoint the Eegent who would be named for the Princess Victoria, with the provision that on the birth of a child the child's mother shall be

Kegent.

October 25.

Cabinet at 4. Peel read letters he had received from Mr. Foster, the magistrate of Manchester, Mr. Hulton, of Hulton, and a manufacturer whose name I forget. They all give an alarming account of the state of Manchester. The colliers have turned out in some districts, and where they have turned out the mills are necessarily stopped. This has thrown numbers out of employment. These colliers can earn 10s. a day; that is, as much as many clergymen. The spinners can earn 56'. a day. Yet they turn out.

This seems to be a manoeuvre like that of Lafitte when he refused to discount bills. To stop the supply of coal is to throw all mills out of work, and every one out of employment. The question is, Shall the masters resist? If they do, there will be an early collision. If they do not, they may defer it, but not long. Concession was counselled six weeks ago, on the ground that, after the events in Belgium and in France, collision was dangerous; and this even by bold men. It seems there are 3,000 infantry, 3 guns, and about 600 or 800 cavalry near Manchester. Perhaps some howitzers may be sent, but more force there is not. Peel at the Cabinet wrote a letter to Mr. Taylor, saying that under ordinary circumstances he should have counselled resistance or rather non-concession; but now it was a doubtful question whether a collision at Manchester would not lead to collision in many other places, and was our force sufficient? He was desired to see Mr. Hulton, Sir E. Bouverie, and others, and to consider what could be done, particularly whether Volunteer Corps could be formed. The delegates who went to Mr. Chappell seem to be amenable to the law and get-at-able. This will be done.

The law officers came in and were asked as to the power of the Crown to permit the formation of Volun-VOL. ii. DD teer Corps. They were desired to consider the point. By the Act of 1794 there seems to be no doubt about it. Hardinge is arrived. He has been calling out O'Connell. I am sorry for it, for O'Connell had declared he would not fight. O'Connell had called him the Duke's aide-de-camp. So far it does good, that it lowers O'Connell still more, and destroys the value of anything he might say against Hardinge.

October 26.

Called on Hardinge. He says the accounts from Manchester to-day are worse. In the House Lord Hill showed me a letter (from Sir E. Bouverie, I think), giving a very alarming account 30,000 out of work, and apprehension of early collision.

Parliament opened. Took the oaths. Office. Lord Dalhousie was so ill on June 4 that I have no idea of his being now Commander-in-Chief in India.

Received a summons to a Cabinet at four precisely, and went to the Foreign Office; but nobody came. I think it must have been summoned to meet at Peel's house. The times are so critical that I should be sorry to lose a Cabinet. I could not find out that any summonses had been sent from the Foreign Office. There was a crowd of people in Downing Street, who had, I dare say, followed the Duke from the House of Lords. There were a good many about the House. All quite quiet.

October 27.

Levee at two. Addresses from the Church of Scotland, and the Lord Mayor and Corporation of Dublin.

Dr. Chalmers was with the Church of Scotland. The Eecorder of Dublin, Mr. Shaw, who is member for Dublin, made a speech before he read the address a thing quite unprecedented, and which might be very inconvenient. The speech itself was innocent. The levee by no means full.

Peel had an audience of the King, and in half an hour the King slept twenty minutes. He says he never knew any man so much altered in three months. His somnolency increases. He slept during an interview with Aberdeen yesterday. When the Duke saw him he was alive enough.

Cabinet. Prince at the Chancellor's. Some conversation respecting the burnings in Kent. Peel thinks they were effected by a chemical process, by some substance deposited hours before, and igniting when the perpetrators are far off. The persons who met Lord Winchilsea expressed detestation of the burnings, and went away to break threshing machines, but a man who committed persons for breaking threshing machines had his ricks burnt; another suffered the same thing who defended his threshing machines. I believe the two offences to be committed by the same persons. The magistrates are supine and terror-struck; but they have no police, no military. Sir E. Knatchbull doubts whether they would arm as yeomen. Peel does not seem to me to view with sufficient alarm the effect these burnings will produce upon men's minds, and the example of impunity. Nothing was said about Manchester. All seemed to think less seriously of our dangers than they did some days back.

The law officers mean to give in their report on the case put to them to-morrow. They will say it is not provided for. The Chancellor has the judges at dinner on Friday, and he will then obtain theirs.

October 28.

Captain Harvey of the 4th Dragoons called by the King's desire to say the King of Persia told him when he was at Teheran that he was hurt at not receiving a letter from the King. I told Captain Harvey the King had announced his accession to the Shah of Persia as he had to other sovereigns. Captain Harvey was interpreter to his regiment. It seemed to me that he rather wished to command the Persian troops. He is brother to the tutor to Prince George of Cambridge. He is a very gentlemanlike man.

The French insist on having the conferences respecting the settlement of Belgium at Paris, if there are to be any regular conferences. They cannot permit Talleyrand to act for them. The French would be jealous of him, c. We had wished to have the conferences here for the very reason that we thought Talleyrand would do his utmost to have the credit of preserving peace. I see there will be no Congress. The French think that r if they stand still, the fruit will fall into their mouths. The folly of the Prince of Orange will ruin his party in Belgium. The ambition of the Belgians will induce them to attempt to form a separate State, which after much disorder will be found impracticable; and as they will not become Dutch, they will become French. Then we shall have a war, and present forbearance only post-pones it. All the Volunteers who are acting in Belgium are French. All the forces in the field are commanded by Frenchmen. French money is employed. The French are really now carrying on the war covertly.

Eussia is paralysed by the devastating progress of the cholera morbus which has reached Moscow. The Emperor is gone to Moscow to establish order and obedience, for the civil and military authorities are quarrelling, and the troops are unwilling to form the cordon. All cordons I believe to be fruitless. It would be as wise to form a cordon against the wind. The disease advances, however, along the high roads and navigable rivers. It is the most extraordinary plague we have had.

Prussia cannot act for fear of disorders at home, and Austria is literally the only power to which war is possible. The French dare not go to war for fear of a Eepublic.

It seems the French Ministry will be partially changed, the Due de Broglie and Guizot going out. The Due de Broglie seems to be a pedantic coxcomb.

I pity the King of the Netherlands, who is a good man. To be hated by two-thirds of his subjects, betrayed by his foolish son, and abandoned as he thinks by his allies, must be great trials to him; while, although the Dutch adore him and really love him, they will not give him money, and I have a little doubt whether they will fight much. Probably, however, the fear of pillage will make them do that for themselves.

Eead a very well-written pamphlet in reply to Brougham's two. I suspect the writer is Philpotts. It is too powerful for an ordinary man, and far beyond Croker. Neither is it in his style. Brougham has made Ridgway put forth a letter stating that he never communicated upon the subject of the pamphlet with Brougham which is no denial that it is Brougham's.

It is a good and useful pamphlet, and will teach the Whigs good manners by showing them they cannot commit aggression with impunity. There is no part much better done than that in which the falsehood and absurdity are shown of what was said in the Brougham pamphlets respecting me. To be sure my champion had a good case. What was said about me rather leads me to think Lord Durham or T. Moore had a hand in it.

October 29.

The letters from Manchester recommend resistance on the part of the masters that is, non-concession. This will put the colliers to the necessity of adopting force, and in the defence of property we should cpmmence the contest, which can only be deferred, with great advantage. Mr. Foster thinks the views of the Union have been shaken by the increase of force near Manchester; and that, although there might be much disturbance the event would not be doubtful. One committee of the Union has proposed acquiescence in the masters' terms.

The accounts from Kent are bad. Peel has offered to send down a magistrate and police officers, and to go to any expense.

He was to receive Mr. Hammond, Plump tree, Lord Camden, and others to-day. Poor Lord Camden, in the meantime, has the lumbago.

~~STATE OF MANCHESTER~~. 407

October 30.

Cabinet. A very bad account of Manchester. No means of raising Volunteer corps. Little hope of uniting the masters. The operatives triumphant. No disposition, however, on their part to come to blows, and a confidence on the part of the magistrates that a fight would be in their favour; but then they must have troops, keep all they have, and get. more if possible.

Mr. Taylor recommends that constables should have the power of arresting picketers without warrant.

Went through the speech. It will do very well now.

Spoke to the Duke about Indian finance, and told him the result. He wished to see all the papers, which were not yet quite ready. In the meantime nothing is to be done, and we are to appoint the Committee.

The Attorney and Solicitor-General deprecate the prosecution of a libel transmitted for their opinion, and say they think it unadvisable to prosecute without the sanction of Parliament! What this means I do not know, unless it means that they are cowed.

There is an infamous article in the Times to-day, against the conduct of the farmers and country gentlemen, and there are worse in the Morning Chronicle.

Had some conversation after dinner at St. James's with Frankland Lewis. He longs for the Grants. I told him it would not do, and what sort of a man Charles Grant was. Frankland Lewis does not seem to like his office, but he says he shall bring it into order if he remains there, and make it a Privy Councillor's office without drudgery. He and, indeed, all seem to wish they were better and more boldly led in the House of Commons. All we want is that.

[408

October 31.

Cabinet. On Monday the 25th the Prince of Orange left Antwerp. He embarked, and intended to go to see his father, and then to come to England! On the 26th General Mellinot marched in and went on to Breda, with 5,000 men. On the 27th (there having been a parley on the 26th), the populace attempted to seize the arsenal. The citadel fired. The town was on fire when Mr. Cartwright came away, and is nearly destroyed.

At Maidstone two or three ringleaders were seized very gallantly by the magistrates, and carried off to the gaol by the cavalry at a canter. However, there are but thirty-four troopers there. So four troops have been sent from Windsor, a depot from some other place, and two guns from Woolwich. All this was rendered necessary by an intended meeting on Penenden Heath to-morrow. March, the Solicitor of the Treasury, is gone down.

There was much conversation about the state of the Press, and a resolution taken to prosecute, notwithstanding the unwillingness of the law officers. Scarlet appears to be quite cowed by opposition and the Press.

This Press may be bought, but we have no money. Five-sixths of the Foreign Secret Service money are preoccupied by permanent old charges the Secret Service money of the Treasury is preoccupied in the same way.

[409

There is a small sum of droits which may be turned over to the Privy Purse, and then by the King to the Government, but it is not more than 3,000. It is thought that perhaps some of the pensions on the Secret Service money of the Treasury may be turned over to the Foreign Office. The Treasury money is the only money applicable to the purchase of newspapers.

We twaddled a great deal over the speech. It was proposed by Peel to insert a paragraph referring to the disturbed state of the country. He will write it, and we shall consider it in a Cabinet at St. James's to-morrow at one, before the Council.

Lord Bathurst is more alarmed than any one; but Peel is a good deal alarmed too.

There is danger, for there are many to attack and few ready to risk anything in defence. It was otherwise in 1793.

The Duke thinks that with every disposition to do mischief there is no conspiracy, or we should have heard of it.

November 1.

Cabinet at St. James's at one. The Lord-Lieutenant has prohibited, by Proclamation, the meeting of the Volunteer Society. Very properly and consistently. It was a much more dangerous society than the other. He is a firm man, not to be turned from the course he thinks right.

O'Connell has not been spoken to in the clubs he has entered. At Brookes's they turned their backs upon him.

There was no meeting at Maidstone. Probably they had intimation of the movements of troops. Lord Beresford told me there were 3,000 artillerymen at Woolwich, enough to serve guns for an army.

Went through the speech again. Aberdeen is the most obstinate man I ever saw, about the mere words of his part of the speech. We lost half an hour at least in talking about words to-day. Peel read his concluding sentence, which is very good. He laments the outrages, and the attempt to disturb the concord between portions of the empire whose union is essential to their mutual strength and happiness, declares the King's determination to exert the powers confided to him by the Law and the Constitution for the punishment of sedition, and ends by expressing a firm reliance on the loyalty of the great body of the people.

As far as I could judge by the King's countenance when the speech was read, he acquiesced, and thought it right, but was pained at being obliged to hold such language.

I had prepared a paragraph to be used in case it had been thought right to say anything about India. For my own part I thought it better not. We could not produce a measure this year, and it would hardly be fair by the Court to declare to Parliament that we thought the monopoly must be put an end to without having previously acquainted them with our determination. The Duke said he had seen nothing yet to satisfy him that the revenues of India could meet the expenditure without the China trade. I think his reluctance increases to put an end to the present system. My. disposition to terminate the existence of the Company increases the more I see of them.

November 2.

House at five. Lord Bute made a very long, heavy speech. Lord Monson a very little one, not bad. The stuff would do; but he has neither stature nor voice.

We then had Lord Winchilsea, Lord Camden, Duke of Leinster, and Lord Farnham. Lord Winchilsea right in tone, but desiring inquiry into agricultural distress. This, too, was the burden of a mouthy speech made by the Duke of Eichmond, whom I had nearly forgotten. Lord Farnham spoke, as he always does, well. He deprecated the dissolution of the Union, but desired relief for Ireland. This, too, was desired by the Duke of Leinster, who spoke very firmly, as all did, against agitators.

Lord Grey said it was a moment of great danger and importance. Fortitude, caution, and wisdom were required. He spoke strongly against the dissolution of the Union, and against the disturbers of the public peace everywhere. He used the words of the speech, grief and indignation. He joined in the determination to put down sedition by law. Eejoiced no new laws were asked for. Approved of the prompt recognition of King Louis Philippe; lamented the necessity of the French Eevolution. Said ' all Eevolutions were ' in themselves evils," although they might produce eventual good. Expressed his hope, for the honour of France and for the interests of Liberty, that they would not sully a Eevolution hitherto unstained by a single act of vengeance. This part of his speech was very well worded and spoken. He objected to the terms in which the passage respecting the Netherlands was worded, as seeming to cast all the blame upon the Belgians, and so to make our mediation less effectual. He likewise objected to the making the Portuguese Amnesty a seeming condition of the recognition of Miguel. Of the recognition itself he did not complain, as he had so long been King de facto. These objections were fair.

Lord Farnham having suggested the necessity of preparing for war, Lord Grey said the preparation should be by gaining the hearts of our own people and he advocated, but very temperately, Reform. He did not, however, allow that there was any abstract right to a particular mode of constituting a Legislature. The right of the people was to a good Government, and to whatever form of Legislative Assembly might seem best to secure that Government.

His speech was good, and temperate, as well as iirm. The Duke of Wellington followed him. He declared his intention to oppose Reform. He said we were not bound to interfere for the maintenance of the Amnesty further than by advice and remonstrance, not by war.

I should mention that Lord Grey seemed pleased by the abandonment of the droits. He was not very well, and at times was almost unable to proceed.

Upon the whole the tone of the debate was very good, and will do good.

November 3.

Office at eleven to see Col. Houston.

Upon the whole the debate in the Commons was satisfactory. Peel was very much cheered. O'Connell spoke well, and was heard in perfect silence. Brougham made an ordinary speech; theme a bad one, violent.

There was much row in the streets yesterday; but all occasioned by attacks upon the police, and attempts to rescue pickpockets. The Guards were called out rather hastily. Colonel Eowan who commands the police has begged they may be left to themselves. They are quite strong enough.

Cabinet dinner at Lord Eosslyn's. No House of Commons people there. The Prince of Orange is come. He has written to the King, and is to see him to-morrow. It seems there are 7,500 men in the citadel of Antwerp, which can only hold 2,000, and has provisions only for two months. The forts of Lillo and Lief ken shoek are ill-garrisoned; so is Breda, and so is Bergen-op-zoom. The Dutch have not 4,000 men in the field near Breda. The question is, whether the evacuation of the citadel of Antwerp would not be advisable for the purpose of getting out the 7,500 men. It seems that if Flushing be held, the Scheld is of no use. The Conference respecting Belgian affairs meets to-morrow, Talleyrand being sole representative of France. The first object will be to establish an armistice.

After dinner we had some conversation respecting the debate in the Commons of last night. Peel is disgusted at not being supported by the three Cabinet Ministers present, who knew the whole subject which had been so often discussed in Cabinet yet not one of them rose to answer Brougham. The Duke is very angry with them, and says he shall take an opportunity of advising Peel in their presence never to rise till Brougham has spoken, let others be abused as they may. If the three mutes will not speak, it is clear they will not remain in very long.

I consider a debate to be a battle, in which the chief should be able to put every man into the fight, as he would every battalion, with a view to the ultimate object; he himself being the reserve.

November 4.

It seems Sir G. Murray did speak last night, but he went further than he intended on Eeform, and so rather damaged our position as a Government.

Office. Saw Mr. Sullivan. He seems a sensible, liberal man. His evidence would be a death-blow to the government of the Company. He says the cotton of Coimbatore is carried to Tinnevelly and thence to Madras by country boats, where it is taken up by the China ships. It might be sent directly to the sea on the Malabar coast, the distance being 300 miles. There is no obstruction to the cultivation. The country is under a Eyotwar settlement. The unequal demand of the Company is very injurious. Their great demand at some periods encourages cultivation and raises prices exorbitantly the next year there is no demand at all. They now purchase by contract. The contracts are too large for the native merchants, and fall, as jobs, into the hands of Europeans. Sufficient notice is not given of the contract. The native merchants have from one lac to one and a half.

Great injury is sustained by the tobacco monopoly.

The Company's officers sell it as retailers. The Government is, as I always thought, practically in the hands of the natives. They require European co-operation, but if they combine against their European superior he can do nothing.

House at five. Lord Winchilsea made a violent tirade against the Administration, without any motion before the House. The Duke made a few observations on the point of order very quietly, and we rose.

November 5.

St. James's at half-past one. The clergy of the Province of Canterbury were there, with their address on the accession. They were not expected, and there were no gentlemen pensioners. However, they delivered their address to the King on the throne, and a very good address it was. Peel had to write the answer in a hurry.

Eecorder's report. One man left for execution for a street robbery accompanied with violence.

The Eecorder gave but a bad account of the disposition of the City. The Chancellor seems a good deal alarmed, and so does Peel. Every precaution is taken, but I cannot help fearing there is a conspiracy of which we know nothing. Aberdeen suspects connection with France.

We are to inquire into the circumstances of the fires in Normandy, which seem very much to resemble ours. We have had one near Godstone, and another at Fair-lawn, in Kent; the sufferers unoffending persons. The object seems to be to spread general terror. It is clear that they are effected by the discharge of some chemical preparation, which ignites after a time. No watching has any effect. Fires take place where no one has approached.

Goulburn told me he thought Sir G. Murray had said much more than he intended, purely from want of habit of speaking; still he had done much injury.

The new French Ministry is formed, and Lafitte is at its head. He pretends to have the same views as the late Ministry; but it is impossible to suppose the French can resist the offer of Belgium. We shall have no war if we can preserve internal peace and the integrity of the Constitution.

November 6.

A letter from Hardinge, who seems to think we stand ill, not for want of numbers, but of speakers. Astell told me the Duke's declaration against Eeform had injured him in the City.

Saw Wortley, and had a long conversation with him respecting the state of the Government. He thinks we cannot go on. The Duke's declaration against Eeform has made it impossible for any to join him, and upon the question of Eeform it is doubtful if we should have numbers enough.

We talked over possible Governments on the supposition that Lord Grey was at the head, and that Peel remained in. In walking away I was overtaken in Downing Street by Lord Graham, who had been waiting to speak to me on the same subject. He seems to think our fall not so immediately necessary as Wortley does. I then called on Hardinge, who had been with the Duke this morning. Hardinge had candidly told the Duke that if he had a minority on Eeform, or a small majority, he would advise him to resign; and previously to tell the King in what a situation he stood. If he had a good majority he might perhaps get some to join; but if not, the position of the Government would be as bad in February, or worse, than it was now. The Duke said he thought things might do still. He had a number of young men who depended upon him. He would take care to give the King timely notice. The King had behaved very well to him. Indeed I know the Duke feels very strongly how admirably and how kindly the King has behaved.

Lord Maryborough had been to Hardinge to express his fears for the Duke's life, and the Duke has received many letters informing him there is a conspiracy to assassinate him on. Tuesday, as he goes to Guildhall.

Hardinge said every precaution should be taken, but he begged Lord Maryborough not to tell the Duke his apprehensions. Hardinge, however, has the same; and fears there may be an attempt that day to make London a scene of barricades like Paris and Brussels. Troops will be disposed at intervals in bodies of half battalions, with provisions, and there will be 1,000 cavalry. Two guns will be ready with the marines at the obelisk, and two in the park. Hardinge observed to the Duke that he knew he had bolts inside to the doors of the carriage, and added, ' I shall take pocket pistols!"

The Duke said, ' Oh! I shall have pistols in the carriage." Hardinge asked the Duke to take him, which he does. Arbuthnot goes with the Duke, too. I wish I could ~~VOL.~~ ~~ii. EE~~ manage to follow him in my carriage. I shall buy a brace of double-barrelled pocket pistols on Monday. Hardinge showed me his.

The Duke has made himself very obnoxious by declaring his resolution to oppose Keform, which in fact, however, he did not do in such terms as has been said.

Hardinge told me there was a proposal to Palmers-ton and others in the summer, and they at once started the difficulty of Eeform, which put an end to the negotiation. If I thought Reform would tranquillise the country I should be quite satisfied with a change of Ministers which would produce internal contentment, but that I do not expect.

I shall take care to have records in the office to show the line I was prepared to take on the East Indian Monopoly, and the steps already taken. I shall likewise leave a memorandum upon the alterations I propose in the army.

November 7, Sunday.

All the morning occupied with a letter on the Salt question. At half-past two rode to the Cabinet room. The Cabinet was to meet at three. We did not, however, all assemble till four, the Duke having been with Peel at the Home Office.

Before the Duke came we had all been talking of the Lord Mayor's Day, and the manner in which we should go into the City and return, and the precautions taken against riot.

The Duke and Peel came together, and it was evi-dent from the first words the Duke spoke that he and Peel had made up their minds to put off the King's visit to the City. The Chancellor seemed almost to ake fire at the idea of this, but the Duke very quietly begged him to hear the letters before he decided. The Duke then read various letters he had received, all warning him against going, as there was a plot to assassinate him, and raise a tumult. One of them was from Pearson, a Eadical attorney. There was one from a 3oachmaker, saying he was satisfied, from what his men told him, there was such a design, and offering to come with eighteen of his people and guard the Duke. There was another offer, in a letter not read, to the same effect. There was an examination of a man who serves a Badi- cal printer, and who formerly lived with Cobbett, which showed the intention to exist of attacking the Duke. The impression seemed to be general that the attempt would be made. There was a letter from the Lord Mayor elect (Alderman Key) to the Duke, telling him there was an intention amongst disaffected persons to excite tumult and confusion, and to attack him; that he could not be in safety without a guard, and a strong one; and that if an attack was made in one quarter the civil force would not be sufficient.

The Duke said he would not go. Peel, who had received many letters informing him of the intention to assassinate him, said if he went he would go privately, come away privately. He observed that if our force, the disposition of which was mentioned, and was admirable, succeeded in putting down a riot along the line of the procession, he could not answer for the secu-rity of life or property in other parts of the town. We had information that the Duke's house would be attacked while he was in the City, and it was to be feared that fires might take place to exercise terror and create a diversion.

The feeling in the Duke's mind was that we should not be justified in giving an occasion for the shedding of blood, by means of a crowd of our own making. The consequences of the collision would be incalculable, and might affect all parts of England.

The consequences of putting off the King's visit were-not lost sight of; the effect it would produce on the Funds, and on public confidence all that would be said against the Government as weighing down the King by its unpopularity,

The letter it was proposed to send was written, and the Duke and Peel went with it to the King at a little before seven.

While they were gone the feeling of the Cabinet underwent a change. Lord Bathurst first observed that it would put an end to the Government, and carry Eeform. The Chancellor was most unwilling to postpone the King's visit. It would be said we did it for our sakes only, and sacrificed him. Lord Bathurst thought the King would take the advice, but be very angry, and get rid of us.

There would be a violent storm in Parliament, and the mobs would come to our houses. All these feelings-rested upon the supposition that the procession could return without a tumult, but the letter had been written on the supposition that it could not; which was the cor-[rect one. The Duke and Peel came back and told us the King had thought the advice quite right, and had behaved as well as possible. The tears were in his eyes while the Lord Mayor's letter was read. He said he had already determined in his own mind to bring the Duke and Peel back in his own carriage. The Duke thought the King had rather expected the advice, and that his mind was relieved by it.

We knew the Queen was much alarmed; but it had been said that the King would not hear of there being iny danger.

The account of the King's manner of receiving the advice seemed to tranquillise those who had before been dissatisfied with the resolution which had been come to. We then went to the Home Office, where we found Alderman Thompson, Mr. Oldham (the Chairman of the Entertainment Committee), Lord Hill, Lord F, Somerset, Sir W. Gordon, General Macdonald, and Mr. Phillips. There were two City men I did not know.

The Duke told them the course we had determined to adopt. Alderman Thompson said he anticipated the decision that it could not be announced in more proper terms. There would be disappointment undoubtedly, but he thought people in general would be satisfied with the reasons. He was almost in tears, and indeed all were much affected the cause of the measure being the apprehended danger to the Duke.

Just as the letter was going off Alderman Thompson observed that although he had no doubt the letter from the Lord Mayor elect was written by his authority, as it was in a handwriting in which a letter had been received/from him by the Entertainment Committee, yet it was not in the Lord Mayor elect's handwriting, nor was it dated or signed by him as the other letter was. It was immediately determined that it must be ascertained whether the Lord Mayor elect had authorised the sending of the letter before Peel's letter to the Lord Mayor was delivered.

Many began to think there was a hoax, and certainly the forgery of one letter would have thrown suspicion upon all the rest.

We were to meet at half-past ten. In going down at half-past ten I called upon Hardinge, who was in his dressing-gown. His servant gone to bed. He did not seem at all surprised.

Went on to the Cabinet room. Found every word of the letter was in the Lord Mayor elect's own handwriting.

Mr. Phillips, Sir E. Binnie, and Col. Eowan came in,, and Lord F. Somerset, and Sir W. Gordon. The artillerymen and marines, of whom there were to have been 500, with two guns, at the Obelisk, are not to be moved up. All the other troops are to remain, and every precaution to be taken, as an attempt to create disturbance may be expected on Tuesday.

After we had disposed of this matter we spoke a little of Civil List and Eegency. Notice is to be given to-morrow of the two bills, as if we were still a Govern-merit, but I now think nothing but general alarm can enable us to weather the question of Eeform.

423 November 8.

The letter to the Lord Mayor is in the Times, and the measure is temperately approved of.

At the same time the result of the Conference on the affairs of Belgium is announced namely, the declaration that there must be an armistice. This will, I trust, give more solid expectations of peace than men have entertained since the King's Speech. The opening of the West India ports to American ships is likewise announced. Both the measures are well-timed.

Eode down to the Horse Guards. Overtaken by the Duke, who said he heard that people were delighted with the measure of postponing the King's visit to the City. However, whether they would say so was another thing. He spoke with much feeling of the King's kindness. He said he had behaved as well as possible.

Some boys hooted, but in general people took off their hats.

Dodd, the coachmaker, told me the people in his neighbourhood were almost all well-disposed. There were very few Kadicals. Colonel Jones had told him he could get very few people to attend his meetings, and none who were respectable.

Met Hardinge. He considers it to be the end of the Government. We met Lord Hill, who lamented the measure, but concluded it was necessary. Went to the office, where I saw Wortley. He thought it a sad business, and fatal to the Government. He said London had been full of reports yesterday. Wynne was talked of for the India Board.

424 Hardinge's idea (as well as the reports) was that Leach would be Chancellor, and Brougham Master of the Eolls.

All the world was much amused by the Chancellor's giving a dinner to Lord Grey, Brougham, Lord Lans-downe, and others. They themselves must have been much amused, and the Chancellor's not getting to dinner till a quarter past eight, and going away at a quarter-past ten, must have satisfied them that something was in the wind.

Desired Jones to make out the appointment of Leach's son to a clerkship immediately, and signed it in the course of the evening.

House at five. It was very full. Every Whig who is above ground and some who are half under it were present. After an hour of talk about everything but the only thing men were thinking of, the Duke of Bich-mond outed with it in an offensive manner, and he is the last man who should have done so. The Duke made his explanation very well. Lord Grey afterwards spoke in a very bad temper, with personal civility, however, to the Duke. The Duke replied, which prevented my speaking at all. Lord Grey had spoken ' of measures tending to bring this country into the situation in which France was the time of the late Eevolution; ' words which should have been taken up, but the Duke's rising after him prevented it.

Upon the whole I think the measure is considered right, and people are very glad; indeed, the danger is no longer hanging over their heads. I hear that in the Commons Peel did admirably, and that he was cheered by the whole House when a Colonel Da_yies sneered at the letter from the Lord Mayor to the Duke. Brougham made as mischievous a speech as he could.

The Chancellor gave notice of the Regency Bill for Friday.

I do not think our friends see our danger, and they will never forgive us if we go out of office without absolute necessity.

November 9.

Looked into the Salt question in the morning. Cabinet at two. There was last night a meeting at the Eotunda; about 2,000 people within, and 3,000 or 4,000 without. About half-past ten they dispersed, and from 200 to 600 ran down to Westminster, first going to the House, which was up, and then to Downing Street. The police licked them well, and sent them off. They came so quick that a man who headed them, and brought information to the Home Office, where Peel and the Duke were, could not, by hard running, get in advance above a minute, and they had passed the Horse Guards before the Duke, who went there by the back way from the Home Office, had got into the courtyard. He was going out at the door when the porter told him the mob was passing. One man was taken, in whose pocket was found his will, leaving his body to form a rampart against the troops, c.

It was determined to endeavour to induce the mob to disperse as soon as the Eotunda was full, and then to read the Eiot Act as soon as the law justified it, and to disperse them by police. There will be common constables there besides. Mr. Chambers will be there; and if he sends for assistance to the Horse Guards, two bodies of fifty each, each headed by a magistrate, will go over Westminster Bridge, one by Stamford Street, the other by the Blackfriars Eoad, to the Kotunda.

There will be about 300 or 400 new police, there, I suggested to Chambers the having a boat ready to take a note to the Horse Guards, as his messenger might be impeded in the streets. Persons are flocking in from Brixton and Deptford, and by the Kentish roads.

Mr. Chambers represents the mob as very cowardly.

There are two shorthand writers at the Kotunda. The speeches are not very seditious.

The Times is turning against us, and I hear the Press is worse than it was none of the newspapers-fighting our measure well.

After the Duke was gone there was a little said about Eeform. Many defections announced the Staf-fords, young Hope, Lord Talbot, the Clives very unwilling to vote against it, thinking the public feeling so strong. I suggested that neither the Duke nor Peel had gone further than to say that no proposition had yet been made which seemed to them to be safe, and that we might perhaps agree to a Committee to inquire into the state of the Representation, and afterwards defeat the specific measures. Peel said he thought the terms of the motion did not signify. It was Reform, or no Eeform!" He never would undertake the question of Eeform. Lord Bathurst, of course, was against me, and generally they were; but they had, before my suggestion, said, ' Had we not better, then, consider what we shall do? Afterwards they said nothing.

Peel and the Duke both think the measure generally approved, and Peel is satisfied with the House of Commons. Goulburn, on the other hand, thinks the general feeling is against us.

House. Nothing said. There was a crowd at the, door, and much hooting. I had to drive my horse through it. While we. were in the House the mob was removed by the police. Not knowing this, Clanwilliam and I came home in the Duke's carriage. There was no mob till we passed Bridge Street, where there were a good many people who recognised the carriage, and followed it hooting. They ran into Downing Street, and we passed on through the Horse Guards. I was glad to find a Grenadier at the Duke's. Clanwilliam said he had ten or twelve there.

Altered the Bill respecting the fees of officers in the Superior Courts, and sent it with a letter to Lawford,, appointing eleven on Thursday for seeing him at the office.

November 10.

Office. Wrote a placard and showed it to Peel, who will have it printed. The tide is turning. Carlisle began to abuse the Duke last night, and found it would not do. Some cried out, ' He gained the Battle of Waterloo!" and Carlisle was obliged to begin to praise him. He then tried to abuse the new police, but that would not do, and he was obliged to praise them too.

There was a good deal of rioting in different parts of the town. The City Police was inefficient, and at Temple Bar rascals were masters for some time. The new police, however, gave them a terrible licking opposite Southampton Street, and not far from Northumberland House. They got licked, too, in Piccadilly and the whole was put down by the Civil Power.

The military were so arranged that, had they been called for, they would have enveloped the rioters. The thing may be considered as nearly put down, and the Government strengthened by it.

The Funds have risen to-day, and are as high as before the postponement of the King's visit indeed higher. So much for Lord Clanricarde's speech.

Cabinet dinner at the Duke's. The King is anxious about the duration of his Government. He would concede on the subject of Eeform, although he is against it. Peel told him he thought that by opposing all Eeform in the first instance the Government would be able to make better terms afterwards. The King said either course had its conveniences and inconveniences. He did not decide between them; but he evidently inclines to concession.

It seems the Queen now declares herself much disappointed at not going to Guild-hall, and the Fitzclar-ence family are turning against the Government, wishing, as the Duke says, to be Dukes and Duchesses, which is impossible.

On Tuesday night 4,000 troops could have been collected in St. James's Park in ten minutes. There were 2,000 police near Whitehall as a grand reserve. The Lord Mayor wrote to Peel acknowledging the total inefficiency of the City Police. The contrast between the City and Westminster was most striking.

429 The Press is turning against us. Like cats, they are leaving the falling house.

In the House of Commons this evening there was ar almost unanimous shout when Peel admitted that the new Bishop of Exeter was to hold the living of Stanhope in commendam. It seems all unite upon that question, which is an unlucky one, although the interference of Parliament is quite irregular.

There was much talk about the Eegency question after dinner, and I left them talking still at half-past eleven.

On Friday the Chancellor should open the question to the House, and we are not prepared, having called Parliament together for this specific purpose!

We have neglected the Press too much. The Duke relies upon the support of 'respectable people and des pises the rabble; but the rabble read newspapers, and gradually carry along with them the ' respectable people" they outnumber.

I do not think the being out of office for a Session would be of any ultimate disadvantage to me. I am sure I should enjoy better health, and I should have much more to do in the House. I should be enabled to regain my proper place.

November 11.

Office. Saw Wortley. He says the spirits of our friends are improved, and those of our foes lowered, the few last days as to Eeform. Cabinet at two. A fire at Melton-Constable. The country round Battle and Hawkhurst almost in insurrection. Troops sent there.

430 The accounts from France good. The French Government acknowledges the right of the Diet to drive the Belgians out of the Duchy of Luxembourg, which is a part of the German Empire. They have instructed Talleyrand to promote the interests of the Prince of Orange.

Eegency Bill. Decided that the Princess Victoria shall be considered Queen, and the oath of allegiance taken to her with the reservation of the rights of any child that might be born. If the child should be born, the Queen Dowager to be Eegent. During the Princess's minority the Duchess of Kent.

The Duke saw the King to-day, and found him very well satisfied with the postponement of the dinner, and tranquil.

House. The Duke of Buckingham told me they had formed their Government, and expected to be in in a week. They think the Duke will resign after Tuesday. Lord Grey to be Foreign Secretary. The Duke of Eichmond to be First Lord of the Treasury. Palmerston and Grant Secretaries of State. Lansdowne President. The Government to be as Tory as possible. The Chancellor to remain.

Lothian told me all the best old friends of the Government were against Philpotts. I told him the reasons why Parliament should not interfere; with which he was satisfied, and was sorry he had not heard them before.

Lord Camden spoke to me on the same subject. I wish we could get rid of Philpotts. He will damage us more than Eeform.

431 The Funds have risen to 84£ that is, 7/ per cent, in three days. I believe this is the consequence, not only of the broken heads, but of the idea that the Duke will be firm and not run away.

We had a two hours' talk about agriculture; the Duke acquiescing in a motion of Salisbury's for a Committee on the Poor Laws.

November 12.

Wrote a note to Hardinge, suggesting to him the expediency of calling upon Dr. Philpotts and placing before him the hopelessness of his keeping Stanhope, the damage to himself of a vote of Parliament, and to the Church from the example of Parliamentary interference, leading him to propose the exchange of Stanhope for a living near Exeter, and I mentioned Dr. Barnes. If this could be. managed we should turn evil into good,: and avoid the division we must lose. The Funds rose to S5, and then fell to 84, being still a rise. In the City they think the Government will stand.

There have been threatening notices as near as Oolnbrook. In Sussex and Kent things are very bad. I did not, however, see Peel to-day. There was nothing in the House.

November 13.

It seems Peel and Scarlet licked Brougham well yesterday. The temper of the House is said to have been rather good. Hardinge told me Goulburn made an indifferent speech. Philpotts has so good a case that he looks confidently to the result of the debate. We agreed that there was no reason why the congé d'élire should not issue. Philpotts himself decides that it should, happen what may as to Stanhope.

We had some talk as to the division on the Civil List. Peel is for refusing a Committee, and the separation of the diplomatic expenditure, and will not yield because he is weak. I think he is right. The better face we put upon it, the more votes we shall have.

Hardinge suggested the placing of Doherty in Ar-buthnot's office. Nothing could be better than that arrangement; but he thought, and I think, the Duko would not displace Arbuthnot. Arbuthnot knows more-about my office than any one else. Where would they put me?

We had some conversation respecting the Eegency. It was determined to legislate as little as we could.

November 14.

Cabinet at four. Peel is of opinion that the fires are in many cases perpetrated for stock-jobbing purposes. They are certainly done by persons from London.

He said he was satisfied that, whatever might be tho division on Eeform, the question was carried. Admiral Sotheron, Lindsay, he thought, and I think he mentioned another, voted for it. If the county members did, and it was thrown out by the representatives of Scotch and English boroughs, it was impossible to stand much longer. He read a paper, circulated for signatures in the parish of St. Ann, in which the subscribers declare their readiness to be sworn in as special constables, and their determination to protect property.

PEEL'S ATTITUDE TOWARDS REFORM. 433

At the same time they declare their opinion that there ought to be a Eeform, first in the House of Commons; but of Church and State. This he considers the commencement of a Burgher Guard. I cannot understand his reasoning; if he thinks Eeform must be carried, surely it is better to vote a general resolution, and to fight the details. By objecting to the general resolution we shall probably be turned out, and have much less power to do good out of office than if we were in.

It seems to me that obstinacy, and the fear of being again accused of ratting, lead to this determination to resist when resistance is, in his own opinion, fruitless.

Clive, whom I saw to-day, is for a modified Eeform; but he will vote for us in order to keep the Duke in.

We had a long conversation about the Eegency, and agreed upon the substance and form of the Bill. Aberdeen wanted again to open the whole question, on which he has no fixed opinion. He has come round entirely. First he thought the right was in the presumptive heir; now he thinks it must be in the child in utero.

It appears certain that at Carlisle the 9th was looked to as the day of signal to them and to all England. It seems the plan was to attack the Guildhall and massacre all in it. There would have been a smash, but a most signal defeat, for there w r ould have been 250 cavalry, and from 700 to 800 Volunteers there (the East India Volunteers and the Artillery Company), besides a battalion within reach.

Sir Claudius Hunter has published in the Sunday Times a denial of the speeches attributed to him, and a statement of the City force. Their ordinary force is fifty-~~VOL.~~ ~~n. PP~~ four men! With Volunteers, Artillery Company, Picket men, Firemen, Lumber Troop, c., they would have had about 2,250.

November 15.

House. A very temperate speech of Lord Durham, and a very good one of Lord Suffield, respecting the new police. Lord Bathurst observed to me they spoke as if they expected to come in. I mentioned Salisbury's motion for a Committee which is to be made on Monday next, and Lord Bathurst said ' Shall we be alive then?" He has a serious apprehension of being out.

The Chancellor made a most excellent speech in moving the first reading of the Eegency Bill, and was cheered on both sides of the House. It seems as if the measure would be unanimously approved. Lord Eldon seemed to say he should advise the Duke of Cumberland to acquiesce in it.

The ultra Tories were to have a meeting to-day thirty-eight of them to decide what they should! do about Reform. Yesterday the report was they joined us; but the Duke of Richmond will do all he can to make them go against us, and, if they do, I suppose we shall be obliged to make our bows.

November 16.

Goulburn opposed the submitting the Civil List accounts to a Committee, and was defeated. We had 204 to 233. Majority against us, 29. Hobhouse asked Peel whether Ministers would resign, to which he got no answer. Brougham rose and said Ministers would have time for consideration.

I suppose this division must be considered to be fatal to us. Henry is going off to take chambers. He means to apply himself to the Law. He is rather in a hurry. For my own part I am by no means sorry to be out of office. I think I shall be better able to regain my proper station in Opposition than I could have done in office, and the emoluments are of no value to me now.

Office. Saw Wortley. He is glad that the division against us has been upon the Civil List, rather than upon Eeform. He thinks we should resign to-day, and thus throw upon the Whigs the burden of bringing forward Eeform as a Government measure. Probably Brougham would postpone his motion if we resigned.

At about half-past three I received a note from Sir Robert Taylor desiring my immediate attendance at St. James's. I dressed and went, and in a few moments was admitted to the King. I met Lord Melville coming away. The King desired me to sit down, and asked me whether I had any expectation of the division of last night? I said no I thought that upon any question connected with the Civil List we should have had a majority; that the question itself was one of little importance; but, as the Committee had not been granted before, Sir E. Peel thought it would be a confession of weakness not to oppose it now, and I thought he was right. The King said it was probably chosen as a question merely to try strength.

The King asked me what had taken place between the Government and the Company. I told his Majesty, and added an outline of the plan I had for the new military arrangements, of which he seemed highly to approve. I then said I supposed I must take leave of his Majesty. He said in one sense his Ministers seemed to think they could not go on.

I said I could not but express my sentiments, which were I was sure those of all my colleagues the sentiments of deep gratitude to his Majesty for the constant kind and honourable confidence he had placed in us.

His Majesty said he thought it his duty to give the full support of the Crown to his Ministers. He had confidence in those he found at his brother's demise; and since July 26, which was the commencement of our troubles, he had regarded with admiration that which was most important in their conduct, their Foreign Policy. He had a feeling of entire satisfaction with them.

I said it must likewise be satisfactory to his Majesty to feel that his late Ministers, fully aware of the real difficulties of the country, would never be led by any personal or party feelings to do anything which could be prejudicial to the country, and that whatever might be their differences in principle from his new Ministers they would ever support his Majesty's interests.

The King was much affected, and had the tears in his eyes all the time I was speaking to him.

I then rose and kissed his hand, and he shook hands with me, and wished me good-bye for the present. I asked for the entree, which he gave me very good-naturedly. As I came away I met Eosslyn going in. The three Fitzclarences were in the lower room, seemingly enjoying our discomfiture.

House at five. The Duke had already declared that the occurrence which had taken place elsewhere had induced him to think it his duty to tender his resignation to the King, and his Majesty had been graciously pleased to accept it.

Lord Grosvenor asked a question as to the appointment of a successor to Mr. Buller, and Lord Bathurst said none had been made.

It is a sad loss to Wm. Bathurst, who would have been Clerk of the Council if the Government had lasted three days longer.

Nothing was said. Lord Grey has been sent for by the King.

I went through all the protocols on the table, and have left hardly anything but two unanswered letters to my successor one respecting the rate of Exchange between territory and commerce; the other respecting Hyderabad affairs.

November 19.

Office. Saw Cabell, Jones, and Leach. They had all the tears in their eyes. Old Jones could hardly help bursting altogether into tears. Left directions with Leach for placing certain papers before my successor, showing the state of the finances and expenditure pros-pectively, and the position in which we were as to the renewal of the Charter.

Cabell will place the Hyderabad papers before my successor, with my letter to Astell, and his reply.

Called on Hardinge, who was not at home.

I can only leave a memorandum in the office showing the nature and extent of the military alterations I projected.

Called on the Duke. He told me Peel came to him in a very nervous state on Monday night. Arbuthnot and Goulburn were with him. It was clear that the majority would have been against us if there had been a House of 500. The Duke sent for the Chancellor, who said as soon as he heard of the division he thought the game was up that we could not go on. The Duke went to the King in the morning, and told him it was better he should resign immediately, and so force the new Government to bring forward their measure of Eeform. It was better for the country. The King asked the Duke's opinion of Lord Grey, and whether he had ever had any communication with him. The Duke said No. The King knew the personal objections the late King had to Lord Grey, and he could not, although often pressed by Lord Grey's friends, have any communication with him without either deceiving him or deceiving the King; and he would not do either. The King asked what sort of a man Lord Grey was? The Duke said he really did not know. He had the reputation of being an ill-tempered, violent man; but he knew very little of him. He had never had any political conversation with him. The King was much agitated and distressed.

I told the Duke what passed at my interview with his Majesty yesterday.

Drummond, Greville, and Sir J. Shelley, whom I saw in the ante-room, congratulated me on being out, but condoled on Lord Durham's being removed out of my way. He goes Minister to Naples vice Lord Burgh-ersh, dismissed. It is understood Brougham will not positively take my office.

Levee. The Duke of Buckingham told me the King was much out of spirits. He expressed himself much pleased with his Ministers.

The King desired Lord Camden to come and see him frequently every three or four days.

The Duke of Newcastle, Lord Falmouth, Sir E. Knatchbull, Sir E. Vyvyan, will not support the new Government. Having had their revenge they mean to put their knees in our backs and do all they can to get out the others. They are sorry for the work they have performed, and regret their vote. They had intended to stay away on the question of Eeform now they mean to vote against it.

Lord Anglesey goes to Ireland; a very bad appointment. The Duke of Devonshire would have been a very unexceptionable one.

Whig

None of the Whigs or ~~Whig!~~ Eadicals were at the levee, but a good many Tories. We were there as usual as Ministers, and those who had business with the King went in to him as usual.

I proposed to Herries, Goulburn, Arbuthnot, and others, that we should in each department prepare a statement of what has been clone since the Duke came into office. This we shall do to-morrow.

I likewise proposed we should have a large sheet of paper with columns for the new Ministers, and in each column their pledges with the dates.

440　Croker has promised to undertake a newspaper, probably the ' Star '.

Arbuthnot told us before dinner that as yet no progress had been made by Lord Grey, except in getting Lord Althcrp after much solicitation. Brougham has a ain in the House of Commons to-night declared he has nothing to do with the new Government, and will positively bring on his motion on the 25th. The new Government wish to postpone the question till March, when they promise to bring in a Bill.

Lord Lansdowne is said to be much dissatisfied, and the Palmerston party think they have not enough offered to them. It is evident that Brougham prefers power to temporary emolument and distinction, and he will be very dangerous acting at the head of the Whig Eadicals.

The Duke said 300 people had called upon him today amongst the rest Lord Cleveland, with whom Lord Grey was early this morning, and whom he in vain endeavoured to induce to go to Ireland.

William Bankes, whose father did us most mischief on Monday, and who did not vote with us, came to ask the Chancellor for a living to-day I

Lord Grey was much agitated when he was with the King, and has expressed himself as very much struck by the strong terms in which the King declared his approbation of his late Ministers.

441　My fear is that the Whigs will not be able to form a Government. It is of much importance to the country that their incompetence should be exhibited, and the fallacy of the grounds upon which they have been attempting to obtain popular favour. We shall never be strong until it is proved they cannot form a Government. Again I say my fear is they will be unable to take the first step. It was considered that we ought to transact all the ordinary business of our several departments.

November 18.

Called on Hardinge. He is out of spirits. Yesterday at the meeting of the employes Lord G. Somerset asked Peel if he would lead them to which Peel gave a damping answer. Hardinge feels that he is capable of business, that his circumstances require he should exert himself and be in office; and, as he would not take office without the Duke's acquiescence, he thinks it rather hard he should be deprived of a Parliamentary leader, and thus of the means of coming in.

.1 told him Peel would be in Opposition in a fortnight, as soon as he recovered his health and his spirits. There has been a report that the Duke had declared he would not take office again which is untrue.

Office. Saw Jones. Eeceived a letter from the Chairs asking whether I had given Sir J. P. Grant authority to appeal to my sanction for his remaining in India, notwithstanding the Order in Council for his return. My answer is No. I add that I

imagine the misapprehension arose out of some private communications from Sir J.
P. Grant's friends, of the purport of a conversation with me which must have been
inaccurately reported to him. I showed my draft reply to Lord Eosslyn, and begged
him to show it to Grant's son.

The report Hardinge gave me was that Lord Welles-ley was to succeed me.

THE END.

Xpolisuoode Co., Printers, A 1 'fir-street Square, London.

The Memoirs of Prince Metternich, 1815-1848.

Containing particulars of the Congresses of Laybach, Aix la Chapelle, and Verona, the Eastern War of 1829, and the Eevolutionary period of 1848, c. Edited by his Son, Prince KICHABD METTERNICH. The papers being classified and arranged by M. A. DE KLINKOWSTROM. Translated by ROBINA NAPIER. lu two volumes, demy 8vo. 36s.

BY LOBD ELLENBOBOTJO-H.

A Political Diary, 1828-1830.

By EDWARD LAW, Earl of Ellenborough. Edited by Lord COLCHESTER. Containing Anecdotes of George the Fourth, William the Fourth, the Dukes of Cumberland, Wellington, and Richmond, Lord Hardinge, Sir Kobert Peel, Lords Brougham, Grey, Bathurst, and Palmerston, Huskisson, Sir Win. Knighton, Marchioness of Conyngham, Sir Henry Halford, Lord Aberdeen, Grant, Lord Melville, c. In two volumes, demy 8vo. 80s.

BY LADY FLOBENCE DIXIE.

Across Patagonia.

By Lady FLORENCE DIXIE. In demy 8vo. with numerous Illustrations from Sketches by JULIUS BEERBOHTVI, and engraved by WHYMPER and PEARSON. 15.

BY DB. THIBLWALIi.

Letters of the Late Dr. Thirlwatl, Bishop of St. David's.

Edited by Dean STANLEY and Dean PEROWNE. In 2 volumes, demy 8vo. BY DB. DUNCKEB.

The History of Antiquity.

From the German of Professor MAX DUNCKER, by EVELYN ABBOTT, Balliol College, Oxford. The Fourth Volume, containing the History of India from the Earliest Times down to the Keign of Azoka. It describes the movements of the Aryas from the Indus to the Ganges, and their Settlements in the South of India, and gives an account of the Conquests of Alexander and the Empire of Chandragupta. The various forms of Indian philosophy and religion are also traced among which the life and teaching of Buddha occupies a prominent place. A short Summary is also given of the Indian Epos and the Institutes of Manu. In demy 8vo. 21s.

This volume should form a valuable assistance to students preparing for Indian Civil Service Examinations.

BY H. STONEHEWEB COO FEB.

The Coral Lands of the Pacific.

Being an Account of nearly all the Inhabited Islands of the Pacific, their Peoples and their Products. By H. STONEHEWER COOPER. In two volumes, demy 8vo. with Illustrations, 28s.

BY CHABLES WOOD.

Round about Norway.

By CHARLES W. WOOD, Author of Through Holland," c. In demy 8vo. with numerous Illustrations, 125.

Richard Bentley 8f Son's New Works.
BY ADELAIDE KEMBLE.
Past Hours.
By the late ADELAIDE SARTOUIS. Edited, with a Preface, by her Daughter, Mr. GORDON. In two volumes, small crown 8vo. 12.
BY THE KEV. R. D. BABHAM.
The Life of the Rev. Richard Harris Barham,
Author of ' The Ingoldsby Legends." A New Edition, revised and re-written by his Son, the Kev. DALTON BARHAM. In one volume, crown 8vo. 6s.
BY THE REV. R. H. BARHAM.
The Ingoldsby Lyrics.
By the Rev. RICHARD HARRIS BARHAM, Author of ' The Ingoldsby Legends. Edited by his Son, the Rev. R. DALTON BARHAM. In one volume, 3s. 6d.
BY FREDERICK WEDMORE.
Studies in English Art.
By FREDERICK WEDMORE, Author of 'Masters of Genre Painting," c. The Second Series, containing Romney, Constable, David Cox, George Cruikshank, Meryon, Burne-Jones, and Albert Moore. In one volume, large crown 8vx. 7. 6d.
BY THE REV. W. R. W. STEPHENS.
Dean Hook: His Life and Letters.
Edited by the Rev. W. R. W. STEPHENS, Vicar of Woolbeding, Author of Life of St. John Chrysostom," c. The Popular Edition, in one volume, crown 8vo. with Portrait, 6s.
BY COL. WARREN.
The Temple or the Tomb.
By CHARLES WARREN, Author of ' Underground Jerusalem," In demy 8vo. with Illustrations, 10s. Qd.
BY LIEUT. CONDER.
Tent Work in Palestine.
By Lieut. CLAUDE R. CONDER, R. E. A Popular Edition, in crown 8vo. with Illustrations, 7s. 6d.
BY M. BTTRDO.
A Trip up the Niger and Benueh.
By ADOLPHE BURDO, one of the leaders of the present Belgian Expedition to Central Africa. Translated by Mrs. GEORGE STURGE. In demy 8vo. with Illustrations, 10s. 6d.
BY MISS G. FORDE.
A Lady's Tour in Corsica.
By GERTRUDE FORDE. In two volumes, crown 8vo. 21s. BY M. TISSOT.
Unknown Hungary.

Lightning Source UK Ltd.
Milton Keynes UK
15 December 2010

164417UK00001B/128/P